D

E N

A

S

ALLISON DRUIN

AND CYNTHIA SOLOMON

New York · Singapore

Designing Multimedia Environments for Children
Publisher: Katherine Schowalter
Senior Editor: Diane D. Cerra
Managing Editor: Frank Grazioli
Graphic Design: Norman Cherubino
Text Design and Composition: Celeste Hime
Illustrations and Diagrams: Eric Mueller
CD-ROM Development: Vineel Shah, Sabrina Liao, Vera Kark, Michael Chanover, Celeste Hime, Allison Druin
Technical Support: Ben Bederson

Library of Congress Cataloging-in-Publication Data:
Druin, Allison
    Designing Multimedia Environments for Children / Allison Druin, Cynthia Solomon.
      p. cm.
    Includes Index.
    ISBN 0-471-11688-2 (alk. paper)
    1. Computer-assisted instruction. 2. Interactive multimedia. 3. Computers and children.
    4. Multimedia systems. 5. Instructional systems—Design. 6. System design. I. Solomon, Cynthia.
II. Title.
    LB1028.5.D78 1996
    371.3U34—dc20   95-37039
                                                                    CIP

Printed in the United States of America

10 9 8 7 6 5 4 3 2 1

ABOUT THE AUTHORS

Allison Druin has been developing educational multimedia environments for children for over 10 years. She began her research in this field as a Master's student at the MIT Media Lab where she developed NOOBIE, a five foot computer/Muppet creature that replaces the mouse and keyboard. She later went on to co-found the New York University Media Research Laboratory, where she was the Director of Educational Programs for Multimedia Professionals. Her research included developing Immersive Environments: experimental room-sized multimedia environments which immerse people in entertaining educational experiences. She has organized and taught courses on designing multimedia environments for children at such conferences as CHI'90, CHI'94, CHI'95, and SIGGRAPH/Multimedia'93. Today she is a researcher and Ph.D. student at the University of New Mexico in the School of Education.

Dr. Cynthia Solomon has been designing and using multimedia and computers with children since the mid-sixties. Through graphics, animation, and text children have told stories and learned mathematics. Solomon began this work in collaboration with Dr. Seymour Papert at MIT using Logo with first graders through college graduates. Solomon has taught university courses to teachers and students of computer science. In the eighties she set up one of the first multimedia laboratories, Atari Cambridge Research. Since then she has written books on children and computer environments. In collaboration with Druin she has taught professional development courses at leading computer conferences including SIGGRAPH/Multimedia 93, CHI '94, and CHI '95. Currently she is a freelance consultant.

ACKNOWLEDGMENTS

The majority of today's multimedia environments benefit from a team of multi-talented professionals. The same can be said of this book and accompanying CD-ROM. There were numerous professionals that offered their expertise from the worlds of editorial design, visual arts, commercial multimedia development, university research, and classroom teaching. There were also countless children in classrooms around the world that added their ideas, experience, and multimedia projects. Without all of you, this book and CD-ROM could not have been created.

The multimedia developers that offered their experience and insights into the world of educational environments for children:
Eadie Adamson—Scholastic Inc., Richard Bolt—MIT Media Lab, Bruce Cameron—UCI, CHI'95 Tutorial Attendees, Bonnie Cushing (and her second grade students)—University of New Mexico, Bob Davis—Rutgers University, David Dockterman—Tom Snyder Productions, Ken Goldstein—Brøderbund, Craig Hickman—University of Oregon, Roger Holzberg—Knowledge Adventure, Paula Hooper—MIT Media Lab, Anita Kopec—CCC, David Macaulay—Dorling Kindersley, Peter Marston (a.k.a. Captain Granville)—the Barn School, Margaret Minsky—the MIT Media Lab, Tom Noser—Vanderbilt University, Page1, Seymour Papert—MIT Media Lab, Mitchel Resnick—the MIT Media Lab, Mark Schlichtig—Living Books Company, Brian Silverman—Logo Computer Systems, Patrick Suppes—Stanford University, Colleen Takahashi—CCC, TERC Researchers, Roger Wagner—Roger Wagner Publishing, Sandy Wagner—CCC, Dan Watt—EDC, Leslie Wilson—Brøderbund, Kristina Hooper Wosley—Apple Computer.

The staff of John Wiley & Sons, Inc. that offered their editorial and production expertise:
Diane Cerra, Tammy Boyd, Frank Grazioli, Michael Green.

The designers and developers that supported the creation of this book and CD-ROM:
Norman Cherubino—Langton Cherubino Group, Celeste Hime—University of New Mexico, Eric Mueller—Eric Mueller Designs, Vineel Shah—R.D.A. International/ New York University Center for Digital Multimedia, Michael Chanover—T/Maker, Vera Kark—Kark Art, Sabrina Liao—New York University Center for Digital Multimedia, Bill Henneman—Pondred Associates, Ben Bederson—University of New Mexico.

The friends and family that intellectually and emotionally supported this book and CD-ROM:
Margaret Minsky, Marvin Minsky, Marianne Henneman, Erric Solomon, Jon Solomon, Gary Drescher, Gloria Rudisch, Oliver Steele, Miles Steele, Alan Kay, Nicholas Negroponte, Priscilla Norton, Jim Hollan, Barbara Copolla Jones, Jack Schwartz, Ken Perlin, Eadie Adamson, Norman Cherubino, Teri Weidner, Susan Ettner, Vera Kark, Jayne Gould, Celeste Hime, The Druin Family, The Bederson Family, Pete, Fred & Tria, and Ben Bederson.

To all of you, we say thanks.

TABLE OF CONTENTS

An Introduction:
The
MULTIMEDIA
Landscape

Allison Druin

A MULTIMEDIA MUSEUM

There are places where children read, enjoy, and respect books *because* of computers. There are places where children are emotionally involved with discussing complex issues (from environmental to personal choices) *because* of computers. There are places where lonely, seriously ill children in hospitals can find someone to talk to *because* of computers.

This is not to say that these places exist in all of our homes, classrooms, or on-line communities, but they do exist and should be acknowledged. In all likelihood, these places are the exception rather than the norm. For every exciting development or use of computers with children, there are numerous examples of stifling, unimaginative, isolating uses of technology. However, without thoughtfully examining the exceptional, it is hard to expect that these places will ever become the norm.

This book and accompanying CD–ROM attempt to examine these exceptional environments, in hopes of understanding what can be done to design for the future. Both the book and the CD–ROM ask you to wander through a multimedia *museum* of examples, to see what's been done and by whom. So often, when we wander through museums, we only see the end results. We don't see the process that it has taken to get to this result, and we don't see the impact that this result has had on people. In this book and CD–ROM, we will focus on all three aspects: the process, the results, and the impact. You will have the opportunity to explore not only the educational approach each multimedia environment takes, but also the impact each has had on children and on the design of environments for children. You will also come to understand the people behind the design of each multimedia environment: what their past experiences have been; what biases they have had; and what goals they have set for themselves. You will come to understand how these factors can profoundly influence the development of any multimedia environment.

- An overview of the past, present, and future trends in multimedia for children
- Compare the process, results, and impact of different multimedia approaches
- A framework to develop your own approaches to multimedia

goals

This book and CD–ROM will attempt to build a museum that not only will inspire you, but will also provoke you to paint your own masterpiece. It is not a *How To… Book*—"Insert floppy disk" here, "double-click" there—and it is not a *laundry list* of the newest, the neatest, and the never-to-be-forgotten. Rather, it is a small museum with a few chosen examples that can build a framework for designing and thinking critically about multimedia environments for children. We will start by looking at three foundational computer environments for children that have strongly influenced much of what we see today. We will then move on to look at a number of outstanding examples of today's multimedia environments. Our tour will continue by considering tomorrow's technologies that may be used in future multimedia environments for children. Finally, as we leave this museum of examples, we will ask you to consider what you know about these models by discussing the process of design.

Keep in mind, this is a museum built by myself and Cynthia Solomon, with our own biases, experiences, and views. Make no mistake about it; we are professed *constructivists*. We believe that children should be constructors of their own realities. We believe that as designers we should strive to harness technologies to be an expressive medium, rich in content and accessible in a wide variety of ways. We believe that the key ingredient to exciting learning environments is that children are not led by the computer, but rather, have an interactive relationship with it. So, while this book and CD–ROM do not limit themselves to presenting only constructivist examples, you should remember that your tour guides through this multimedia past and present are constructivists.

MULTIMEDIA WITH A DASH

Ten years ago, when I was writing my masters thesis at the MIT Media Lab, the word *multimedia* still had a dash in it: *multi-media*. As the hype and press attention increased surrounding the coming of multimedia, the word lost its dash (some would call it a hyphen, but I prefer to call it a dash). To my mind, that dash was critical in defining what it truly is. The word *multi-media* represented visually and literally the act of combining different forms of media.

In the 1960s, this meant artists experimenting with a combination of live performance, sculpture, painting, music, and so forth. In the 1970s through the early 1980s, *multi-media* became synonymous with large, multiscreen slide shows with music and voice-overs. As the 1980s progressed, researchers at universities and corporate labs experimented with the combination of multiple representations of information on one computer (e.g., text, graphics, sound). The exciting part was that these different representations could be *interactive*. The computer user could wander among various combinations of media and see, read, and hear information. As these environments became more powerful, the programming (or authoring) environments became easier to use. In the late 1980s, Apple Computer commercially released *HyperCard*, one of the first multimedia authoring tools that gave the desktop computer user a set of tools to create interactive multimedia.

However, it was not until CD–ROMs became commonplace in the desktop community, that *multimedia* lost its dash for good and became a commercial industry. By creating a compact disc that could store large amounts of digitized information, yet be as portable as a floppy disk, multimedia CD–ROMs were born. It became a commercial possibility to combine text, graphics, sound, video, and animation all on one disk. As the industry grew, so too did the number of children, teachers, and parents using multimedia for teaching, learning, and playing.

In the past few years, the impact of multimedia in our homes and schools has been profound. Pictures, sound, music, and text offer children with different learning styles and strengths multiple paths to the same information. Children can learn to read by hearing a word, by seeing an animation of that word, or by creating their own stories with that word. Children can learn about new cultures by seeing video footage of the people, hearing their music, reading their stories, or communicating with them daily through electronic mail. Children can wander through information at their own pace, in a way most meaningful to them. For children who have strengths in understanding visual or auditory information, multimedia can now open new paths to learning which in the past might have been represented only by text.

To critics who suggest that multimedia is replacing our essential but traditional forms of media, I ask them to look at the second grade class described in Chapter 4. These children spent weeks researching information on southwestern animals in books, magazines, and in their local communities. Then these same children wrote stories, created puppet shows, and finally gave a multimedia presentation of their own. Multimedia did not replace their books or outdoor adventures. Multimedia did not stop their imagination or creativity. Multimedia simply enhanced and supported all of these experiences and offered children one more way to learn.

KIDS TODAY

When developing multimedia environments for children, we as designers must remember that children are not just short adults. We cannot *water down* multimedia environments designed for adults and expect them to be valuable environments for children. Young people have their own likes, dislikes, curiosities, and needs that are not the same as their adult teachers or parents. If you spend some time watching children, you will see that they love to draw, use clay, build with blocks, watch videos, and play games. You will also see that they love to do all of these things over and over again. They love repetition. Kids are the only ones I know who can watch a video of Disney's *The Lion King* 17 times before they've had enough. But, if a teacher or parent told them they *had* to do that, they wouldn't want to. Children love repetition, but only when they are in control.

Another thing you will notice about children if you spend some time with them, is that they are honest. Most of them won't tiptoe around a topic if you ask them for an honest opinion. They'll give it to you straight: "This is great!" "This is dumb!" "This is fun!" "This is boring!" With this honesty, children are also naturally curious (unless of course it's brutally squashed out of them by our educational system). They'll passionately pursue an idea, a person, or an activity, if it's something that's important to them. But again, if they are told by an adult to be curious and to do a certain 10 steps to find an answer, they will almost surely lose interest.

Honesty, curiosity, repetition, and control are all ingredients we need to consider when designing multimedia environments for children. Sadly enough, though, most designers think that bright colors or loud noises are what's important to children. These are the inventions of adults, not the concerns of children. In this book, we will look at multimedia environments that support children's curiosities, their love of repetition, and their need for control. We will look at environments that respect children for their ability to challenge themselves and question the world around them. We will look at environments that are imaginative and exciting for children, because their designers stopped to listen, to observe, and to collaborate with young people.

THE NEW MULTIMEDIA DESIGNERS

The process of designing children's multimedia environments brings together diverse professionals that might normally have little to do with each other, but must now work together: graphic designers, musicians, animators, videographers, teachers, technologists, researchers, and so forth—the list is endless. The intersection of these professional talents is crucial in developing creative and meaningful multimedia environments.

Yet, few books acknowledge this important intersection. There are many words written about multimedia just for technical software developers or only for classroom teachers. But this book is for the *new* multimedia developers. It is for the *Internet surfers* who know little about children, but must now develop on-line communities for them. It is for classroom teachers who want to develop and integrate multimedia environments into their teaching, but know little about the different technologies available. It is for the emerging CD–ROM business community that knows there's money to be made with this stuff, but isn't sure how or why. It is for researchers of our future technologies (Interactive TV, Virtual Reality, etc.) who want to understand what educational approaches have been developed, but know little about them.

There are many people who will become multimedia designers in the future. Discussions must begin today that can be useful to *all* different designers. Without thoughtful analysis and critical searching we cannot hope to create exciting, creative experiences for children in the future.

A FRAMEWORK FOR ANALYSIS

In recent years, thanks to the proliferation of CD–ROMs, people have come to believe that *multimedia* means only a CD–ROM in a desktop computer at our homes or schools. To many people's surprise, *multimedia* does not come in just one flavor. Rather, there are numerous educational and interface approaches, various technological platforms, and a vast variety of places and reasons to use it. Multimedia environments range from systems that guide children piece by piece every step of the way, to systems that encourage children to develop their own paths to learning multiple disciplines. Technologies that drive multimedia today can be everything from CD–ROMs to on-line multimedia environments.

Each factor—whether it is (1) an approach to teaching and learning, (2) what technologies were used, (3) where each environment is used, or (4) where each environment was developed—influences what the final multimedia environment is and what impact each has on children. The visual look, the strategies for interaction, the content design, and the purpose for each product are all strongly influenced by each factor. These layers of factors combine to form a framework that can support informed decisions when developing and using multimedia environments for children. To make sense of the complex multimedia landscape, this book will use this four-factor framework for analyzing each chapter's multimedia examples.

The first and perhaps most important framework factor that will be examined is the varying approaches to teaching and learning. Each multimedia environment will be analyzed to understand where it fits on a continuum of teaching and learning approaches. On one end of the spectrum are multimedia environments that use computers as an *Interactive Textbook*. These environments guide children every step of the way, offering a given path to learning (e.g., *Drill-and-Practice*). On the other end of the spectrum are those multimedia environments that use computers as an *Expressive Medium*. These environments offer children tools to create and explore their own paths to learning (e.g., *Logo* programming, *HyperStudio* authoring). Between these two extremes live *hybrid* approaches to teaching. These environments offer children both the option of guided learning through a given set of information and the option of creating their own representations from this information (e.g., videodisc simulations, *The Living Book Series*). Each approach to teaching and learning strongly affects what content may be offered and how it will be presented to children.

Keep in mind, that no matter how open-ended or guided an environment may be designed to be, that same environment may offer different learning experiences because it is used by different children, teachers, or parents. For example, the children's programming language Logo was designed to be an *Expressive Medium*. Its developers wanted to create a tool that could offer children the opportunity to construct their own ideas about animals, world cultures, or mathematical concepts. This same *Expressive Medium* has been used by teachers who test their students each Friday on the definition of *variables* or *debugging*. With the same tool some children may construct their own paths to learning and some may be told they must learn in a prescribed way. Unfortunately, what children learn and how they learn may have little to do with the way designers envision the use of their environment. All that designers can do is understand this, and support children and teachers with the best possible multimedia tools.

Another factor in this framework for analysis is the driving technology each different multimedia environment uses. Some environments make use of CD–ROMs for desktop computers (e.g., commercial *Edutainment*: game-like educational environments), others make use of videodiscs (e.g., problem-solving simulations), and still others make use of on-line technologies (e.g., *World Wide Web, The National Geographic Kids*

Network). However, people cannot always assume they will find one type of technology being used for the development of one type of multimedia environment. There are no clear-cut answers. When organizing each of the chapters that follow, it was difficult to decide what examples should be grouped together. Commercial CD–ROMs contain *Edutainment* as well as multimedia authoring tools. Simulations can be found on-line or presented by videodisc players. And, for that matter, it is even hard to decide if *on-line* is a type of technology, or a different *place* that multimedia technology can be used. Whatever technology is used to offer different types of multimedia experiences, you can be sure that each technology affects how the content is organized, accessed, and presented. Each technology has strengths and limitations that must be acknowledged when designing multimedia environments for children.

Still another factor that will be examined focuses on where each of these multimedia environments will be used. Some of these multimedia environments can be found in the home (e.g., commercial *Edutainment*, on-line environments), some can be found in the schools (e.g., videodisc simulations, authoring tools, on-line environments), and some can be found in both. Where each of these multimedia environments will be used helps to define the types of documentation, support materials, and educational approaches that may be developed for children.

A final important factor in this framework focuses on where each of these multimedia environments was developed. Some of these environments come directly out of university research labs which have commercialized their research efforts (e.g., Vanderbilt University: *The Adventures of Jasper Woodbury*; MIT: *Logo*); others come out of commercial software development companies (e.g., Brøderbund: The *Carmen Sandiego* Series; Knowledge Adventure: *My First Encyclopedia*); and still others come out of software development companies started by ex-classroom teachers (e.g., Tom Snyder Productions: *The Great Solar System Rescue*; Roger Wagner Publishing: *HyperStudio*). How each multimedia environment has been developed and by whom will strongly impact all aspects of the final product. The designers' expertise, interests, approaches to learning, and the resources available for the project will be important factors in how a multimedia environment will be developed.

We hope this framework for analysis will offer you a way to consider what others have done, how they have done it, and why they have done it. You should understand that there are no *right answers* to what should be done as a developer of multimedia environments for children. There are only excellent examples to use as guidelines for the future.

DIFFERENT FORMS OF MEDIA

Many have asked, "Why not just produce a CD–ROM which includes this information? Why bother with a book?" To that, I counter that multimedia does not just mean the use of text, graphics, video, and so forth, on a computer. It also means all of those things *off* the computer as well. Many forms of media offer many different types of people with varying lifestyles, strengths, and weaknesses an opportunity to interact with different types of information. The most exciting multimedia environments for children suggest interactivity on and off the computer. Therefore, when envisioning how to present this type of information to numerous individuals, we felt it was crucial to offer it in a truly multimedia format.

If you are an information wanderer (a person who reads the last page of a book before you get to the rest), you may want to start by wandering the CD–ROM. Then come back later and fill in the gaps with the book's text. If you are a person who likes a good story printed in words and pictures, keep reading: You will find what you're looking for here. Later on, you may want to flesh out the book's discussion with some interactive examples from the CD–ROM. Whichever your approach to learning, reading, and enjoying, please feel free to become involved in the content of designing multimedia environments for children.

- This book and accompanying CD–ROM attempt to examine exceptional multimedia environments, in hopes of understanding what can be done to design for the future.

- Both the book and the CD–ROM ask you to wander through a multimedia *museum* of examples, to see what's been done and by whom.

- You will have the opportunity to explore not only the educational approach each multimedia environment takes, but also the impact each has had on children and on the design of environments for children.

- We will attempt to build a museum that will not only inspire you, but will also provoke you to paint your own masterpiece.

- In the past few years, the impact of multimedia in our homes and schools has been profound. Pictures, sound, music, and text offer children with different learning styles and strengths multiple paths to the same information.

- When developing multimedia environments for children, we as designers must remember that children are not just short adults. We cannot *water down* multimedia environments designed for adults and expect them to be valuable environments for children.

- The process of designing children's multimedia environments brings together diverse professionalls that might normally have little to do with each other, but must now work together: graphic designers, musicians, animators, videographers, teachers, technologists, researchers, and so forth—the list is endless.

- Each factor—whether it is (1) an approach to teaching and learning, (2) what technologies were used, (3) where each environment is used, or (4) where each environment was developed—influences what the final multimedia environment is and what impact each has on children.

- On one end of the spectrum are multimedia environments that use computers as an *Interactive Textbook*. These environments guide children every step of the way, offering a given path to learning.

- On the other end of the spectrum are those multimedia environments that use computers as an *Expressive Medium*. These environments offer children tools to create and explore their own paths to learning.

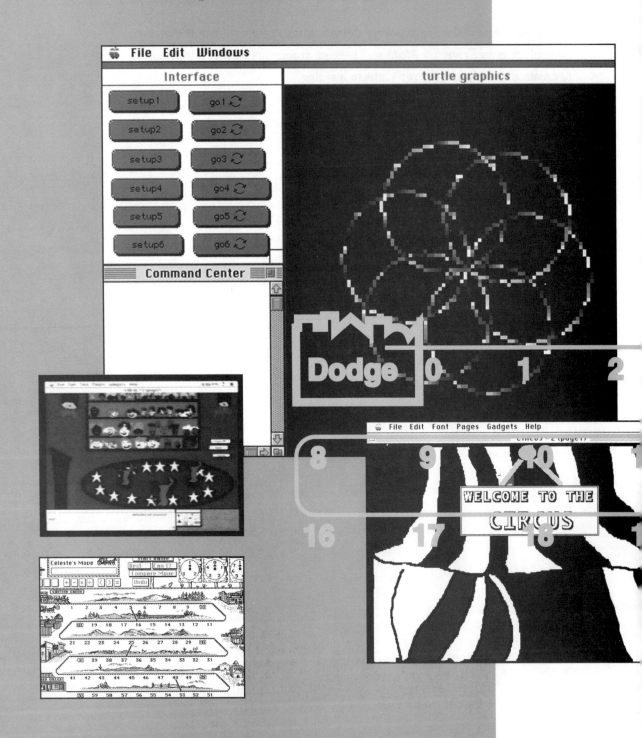

ORIGINS
of Educational Multimedia Environments

BEING A DESIGNER

As a parent or teacher you might see that your child is having trouble doing arithmetic, so you look for some software package to help her. You can't find one that's suitable. Or, your child watches what you do with a computer and wants to do it too. But *SuperPaint* is too complicated for your six-year-old. So, eventually, you design and build something. It's cute. You debug it and expand it. You give it to friends. You make it available to the Internet community as *freeware* or *shareware*. Someone suggests that you get a company to publish it. You can either start your own or make a deal with an existing company. Then the package is polished and supported with documentation, packaging, and marketing acumen. In time it becomes a big hit.

A wonderful example of such a software environment's origins is *Kid Pix*, designed by Craig Hickman as a drawing world for his child. Of course, Craig Hickman is also a teacher of the subject and had prior experience using paint and draw programs on computers. He had a sense of what would appeal to his child and what would extend that child's world. And, he debugged his theories as he implemented *Kid Pix*.

Tom Snyder Productions started in a somewhat similar fashion. Tom Snyder was a middle school social studies teacher who developed role-playing material on the computer. He started designing and debugging his ideas and received lots of feedback from his students. Of course, what started out to be a small project began to eat up all of his time as his ideas multiplied. He had to either turn entrepreneurial or collapse in a heap. In his early hits *Decisions, Decisions* or *Choices, Choices* students assume a specific role, for example, the president of the United States. Students, playing the role of president, are confronted with multiple real-life situations and have to make decisions, describe strategies, devise new plans, and so on. The computer served as a source of stimulating experiences for group discussion and group work within his classroom and enhanced his teaching. Snyder's role-playing games differ from role-playing worlds that connect people through telecommunications or computer games like *Where in the World Is Carmen Sandiego?*. With Snyder's games, a teacher was very necessary to give life and direction to the class discussions—while the computer's presence allowed for a new vitality in the classroom.

Another scenario of how a computer environment might be designed is the following. You are an educator, a professor of mathematics, physics, music, design, English, or some other discipline. You see what might be if only your students had been given a foundation in this or that. Now, computers with sound and animation capabilities offer new possibilities. You build a proof of concept, use it as a basis for a proposal, get funded, build a real system, and try it out with children.

A kind of pattern emerges. I have a kid, I teach kids, I teach adults and see what might have been if only they had this or that experience as kids. I've built a game, and my kids love it. I am a physicist, mathematician, artist, musician, writer… and I see a way to use computers that will help children to learn certain material. I have tried using various computer tools, but I finally have had to design my own. Now I have funding to develop my ideas further. I have a new job at a company that is expanding into the educational computing market for elementary school children. What do I do? What do I read to ground myself a bit more in this area?

Of course, you might be a virtuoso programmer, graphic designer, or subject matter specialist, but you have not built stuff for children. What's involved in designing computer environments for children? What do you have to know? What are the things you need to be aware of?

The intention of this book is to provide an arena for sifting through some of these issues. We want to present you with ways of looking at the issues with samples of a few computer environments to critique and from which to learn.

THINKING ABOUT THINKING ABOUT SOMETHING

In order to talk about models of thinking about computers in education, I take to heart Seymour Papert's slogan that you can't think about thinking without thinking about thinking about something. The something I choose to think about in this chapter is the development of computer cultures to enhance children's learning of elementary school mathematics. Later chapters of this book discuss a variety of applications in a variety of subjects. The intention of this chapter is to lay a foundation for the other chapters. I will do this by discussing the specifics of three multimedia environments developed to enhance children's learning of mathematics. These environments originated in the 1960s and 1970s and have had considerable influence on today's products. Moreover, they are products which themselves have evolved over time and are commercially successful today.

Choosing computer-based mathematics environments as the context for discussion makes sense for several reasons. Historically, the most popular use of computers in education has been in the mathematics classroom. The issues relevant to mathematics education reform are relevant to the teaching of reading and writing as well. The successes and struggles are similar despite the popular belief that some people are mathematically minded and others aren't. In school, this often translates into a feeling that most people just can't learn math—but we have to teach it anyway. This stands in contrast to the popular belief that almost everyone can learn to read and write. But, society needs literate and mathematically minded citizens. Thus, the dilemma arises of how we can meet society's needs. We can learn from studying what happened in the past in terms of ideas, popular understanding and acceptance, and technology. As designers, we are faced with diversity, a diversity of interests and opinions. This chapter seeks to celebrate diversity.

A PROBLEM FOR YOU TO THINK ABOUT

The boss' nine-year-old twins are having trouble with multiplication. So, how about designing an environment to help them. What do you do? A little research (like asking the boss) unveils that the twins are in the fourth grade and are feeling a little down because their classmates don't seem to be having a problem with multiplication.

Three Approaches to Solving the Problem

What are your first thoughts in rushing in to help them? Let's build a tutoring program, a computer-assisted instructional program for them. The computer can look over their shoulders and nudge them appropriately. We can give them lots of multiplication to do until they get better at it. So we could design a system that will state *4 x 5* = and then, if the typed-in response is *20*, it might say yippee! and go on to another problem.

Perhaps, the kids are only having trouble with multiplying by 7. We could tailor a teaching program to provide different exercises using 7 as the multiplier or multiplicand. Now we can concentrate on the presentation of the exercises: Where on the screen do we place the exercise? When do we present an exercise vertically and when do we present it horizontally? Do we keep track of the number of tries for each exercise and do we keep track of the number of correct answers on the first try? How do we report that information? As long as we are doing this for sevens, maybe we can do the same for other numbers, and so on.

What frequently happens is that you get carried away with the design and forget about the educational issues. When does the computer indicate it is looking over the child's shoulder and how does the computer intrude? What are appropriate interactions between child and computer? Is the computer the teacher or a colleague?

One solution might be a system of continual drill-and-practice where a problem is posed and, if the input matches the expected answer, a new problem is posed. If the input does not match, the problem is reposed. Implemented in its purest form, this teaching strategy is based on a rote learning theory. Most of us have been exposed to this style of teaching. For many years, rote learning was the dominant theory of how children learn. Their minds are empty vessels into which knowledge is poured. The key is to break information up into discrete and sequenced facts that children can learn. Learning the multiplication tables is a good example of this.

Many systems have been developed by adopting both this style of teaching through drill-and-practice and this theory of learning where a topic is broken into discrete facts and organized sequentially. One of the most outstanding examples of this theoretical approach is the material developed by Patrick Suppes, now Professor of Philosophy, Emeritus at Stanford University. The environment is available from Computer Curriculum Corporation, a recent subsidiary of Viacom. The section titled "Drill-and-Practice, Suppes, and Behaviorism" later in the chapter details his work.

Here's another approach to help kids. Let's invent a game that requires kids to use multiplication. As a preliminary to the game, we have kids play with Cuisinaire rods or similar concrete materials. We could create a situation in which kids have three containers; they fill each container with balls and find each container holds five balls. They figure out how many balls there are all together. They do this by successive addition (something they know how to do already). So, they find they know what multiplication is and they can derive it from addition. (The children could use Cuisinaire rods in a similar way.) This is a different teaching strategy, but it is also a different emphasis on the subject matter. This situation engages children in a dialog about the problem. They are often guided by their teacher to *discover* the answers by learning to derive them from real-world situations and concrete materials. Discovery learning is well-articulated in the work of Robert B. Davis, Professor of Mathematics Education at Rutgers University. The section titled "Meaningful Math, Davis, and Constructivism" later in the chapter contains a detailed discussion of his work.

Finally another approach involves talking to the kids and asking them to collect information from their friends and others about multiplication. For example, ask what are hard multiplications to remember. Ask for suggestions about teaching strategies. Then ask them to teach the computer how to teach multiplication. In other words, ask the children to be designers, teachers, and psychologists. Then give them an environment which has appropriate building blocks for such investigations.

The work of Seymour Papert, LEGO Professor of Learning Research at the Media Laboratory of the Massachusetts Institute of Technology, is based on this educational approach where children play a multiplicity of roles as teacher, student, designer, and so forth as they explore their environments and acquire knowledge as needed to function well in the environment. Children learn by manipulating objects in their world. The goal of Papert is to create worlds (microworlds) where children can continue in their natural learning styles to acquire new information. I discuss Papert's constructionist theories of learning and his teaching strategies in the section "Logo, Papert, and Constructionism."

THEORIES OF HOW CHILDREN LEARN

In this book we look at computer environments and their cultures within this framework: *Expressive Medium*—where the child is in control of the computer—and *Interactive Textbook*—where the computer is in control of the child [Solomon 1986]. Although this dichotomy is helpful, it is not the whole story. We also explore popular theories of how children learn. To simplify the discussion, we look at three different theoretical positions and their practices: *constructionism/Piagetian learning*, *constructivism/discovery learning*, and *behaviorism/rote learning*.

Constructivists and *constructionists* acknowledge that children know a lot before they get to school and need help in building on what they already know. Children are active participants in their own learning. The big job for education is to help bridge the gap between informal learning and formal learning.

The emphasis for constructivists is on identifying relevant material and employing good teaching strategies to encourage children to learn. Robert Davis' work is an excellent example of a constructivist approach to education.

Constructionists go a step further and seek to create environments for children to play in and objects for children to play with so that they can continue to learn new things as naturally as Piaget showed they learned without instruction. For Seymour Papert, creating Logo culture and its offshoots is motivated by constructionist thinking.

Behaviorism and *rote learning* approaches to education have dominated our American school culture for many years and have supported the image of teacher as the disseminator of information. Certainly, the bulk of educational software can trace its origin to this teaching strategy. Patrick Suppes' work is a clear example of this position.

For Papert, the child is both teacher and learner as are the computer, the teacher, or any other person or objects involved in the investigations. For Davis, the computer offers a new kind of manipulative experience for the student to learn a body of mathematics; the computer remains an experiment in teaching. For Suppes, the computer learns about the child from her or his performance on exercises and the child learns to perform certain skills.

Seymour Papert, LEGO Professor of Learning Research at the MIT Media Lab.

Suppes, Davis, and Papert, have different visions of what elementary mathematics education is, how children learn, the role of the teacher, and how computers can help. Their views were important in the sixties and still are today. They have had considerable influence on today's multimedia environments for children and their computer environments are also commercially successful today. Their environments fall into one of two images: With Seymour Papert the computer is used as an *Expressive Medium* so that the child is in control of the computer. With Patrick Suppes and Robert Davis, the computer is used as an *Interactive Textbook,* so that the computer is in control of the child.

ELEMENTARY SCHOOL MATH DESIGN ISSUES

One of the reasons for discussing the work of these three is that they focus on one subject area, elementary school mathematics. Elementary school mathematics is an area which is constantly under scrutiny and attack. We have never quite gotten it right, but keep on trying. Since at least the beginning of the twentieth century, educators in the United States have tried to fix things in the math classroom. Yet, it seems the majority of elementary teachers and students have remained alienated. Societal needs for people who are comfortable in mathematical thinking escalate while the gap widens. The reality and pervasiveness of computers in our lives creates new needs and new opportunities to look at mathematics education reform.

As educators, designers of educational material, graphic designers, programmers, parents, teachers, or critics, we need to identify our own biases, learning theories, and educational strategies. For example, as designers we need to come to terms with our aesthetics. Do we like little characters? Do we make our own or do we use someone else's? What are their personalities? One of the charms of the Carmen Sandiego series is the characters: Carmen and her gang. One of the annoyances of some packages is the character development. Thus, this design decision impacts the educational experience.

Often when we don't know what to do, we do what was done to us. It is comforting to think that someone can actually lead us to knowledge. (It's as if you can lead a horse to water and you can make him drink!) There is something comforting about knowing that someone has analyzed a whole body of information and knows how to get me to learn it. There is something comforting in the idea that by following this method we will arrive at an agreed upon destination. The reality is not so simple. The path you have laid out may not work for me. For that reason, I need to know what your underlying goals and teaching strategies are. I need to be aware that my assumptions and interpretations might be very different from yours or from what can be obtained from this environment. This kind of awareness is what I take as literacy, whether in computing, reading, or writing: to be aware that each environment or system carries with it many underlying assumptions and to be aware of one's own role and assumptions within the environment.

LOGO, PAPERT, AND CONSTRUCTIONISM

Some readers might wonder why I discuss Papert, constructionism and the development of Logo first. There are a few reasons. I think it is harder to come to grips with what is meant by the computer as *Expressive Medium* and the child controlling the computer in the context of reading, writing or mathematics. By putting this discussion first, you can compare it to the others more easily. You probably already have a sense of the computer as interactive textbook in charge of the student. I immediately want to encourage you to think about truly interactive textbook environments in which the child is in control and the computer serves as a guidepost and personal aide. In a sense, this book is about designing for the future by learning from the past. It is easier to create alternatives after looking at some alternatives. So, looking first at an environment in which student, teacher, and multimedia are all expected to interact with one another in often interchangeable roles is intended to propel you into thinking about the future, now.

In this section, the discussion of Logo, Papert, constructionism, and other ideas guiding Logo's development will be seen through the eyes of one who collaborated closely with Papert during Logo's initial development. The early ideas and their continued interplay in various design decisions to improve Logo, the language, the culture, and the environment will be highlighted.

LOGO AS A COMPUTER CULTURE

Logo has become the name of a programming language, an environment, and a culture—a way of thinking about computers and learning and putting the two together. The culture is made of ideas, things, and people. The things include not only the computer and the language, but computer-controlled devices like turtles, LEGO motors and lights, as well as integrated facilities to express yourself in words, sounds, pictures, and animation.

In the culture, people become researchers and designers; and actions and ideas take on animate qualities. Ideas from computer science like naming, procedurizing, and debugging intermix with anthropomorphic thinking and become lively tools in problem-solving situations.

Problem-solving is a dynamic process of trying ideas out, observing how they work, making changes, rethinking, and reconfiguring. Debugging is a positive experience. In this world bugs are not mistakes, but interesting phenomena that you learn to identify and classify. Sometimes they are removed and other times they are celebrated as they point to new and unexpected results. Sometimes they are just coded around! Children experience debugging as a natural part of learning as they "learn by doing and thinking about what they do." (This is Papert's extension of John Dewey's slogan that children learn by doing.)

A typical Logo Turtle.

Not Just Turtles

While the Logo culture is closely tied to turtles, it is certainly more universal. The turtles were invented as vehicles to convey this culture to beginners. They make certain images more vivid and certain ideas more concrete. But the goal is to convey these ideas and images, to make them real, comfortable, and personal for a beginner of any age. Turtles and turtle geometry represent a first step in creating new mathematics and new problem-solving worlds for children.

Functionally, the Logo culture is made up of several things, including a computer; a programming language and operating system; a collection of computer peripherals, usually including graphics and turtles; a collection of projects; a meta-language, that is a consistent vocabulary with which to talk about the language, the projects, and so forth; a relationship between teacher and learner; and a collection of *bridge activities* like juggling, puzzle-solving, unicycling, and so forth for which learning is enhanced by procedurizing and debugging. All of these components are interdependent and the special virtues of the environment follow from their coherence with one another. Taken individually, they have no great merit or utility. For example, I would expect very limited educational benefits to come from teaching programming, even Logo programming, in an *abstract* environment or from using turtles as toys without a vision derived from the computer culture.

AN EXAMPLE OF LOGO, MULTIMEDIA, AND MULTICULTURES

An outstanding example of Logo being appropriated and encultured by children can be seen at Paige Academy, an "alternative, African-centered school" in Boston [Hooper 1994]. There, children have been working with Paula Hooper, a graduate student of Papert's in the learning and epistemology group at the MIT Media Lab. Some of the children have been working for over three years, albeit with different versions of Logo. Using the newest version of Logo, called *MicroWorlds*, they tell stories either by making up their own or by retelling well-known stories such as fairy tales. Children have been working together on collaborative projects. The authors of this project are Shamikah James, age 8; Kyle Johnson, age 10; Myracle Grigsby, age 11; and Shani James, age 11.

Here is one of their stories called "Welcome to the Circus."

Once upon a time there was a bummy grungie lady named Kalua. She gathered her pennies and went to the circus. They did not except [sic.] pennies and they kicked her to the curb.

So, she gathered all her friends and they made a magical circus. In the magical circus, there were dancing horses, divers, rabbits that turn into horse people, and dancing girls.

After welcoming the user to this circus, the scene changes to inside the tent where there is a ring of dancing horses. The children who worked on this project became

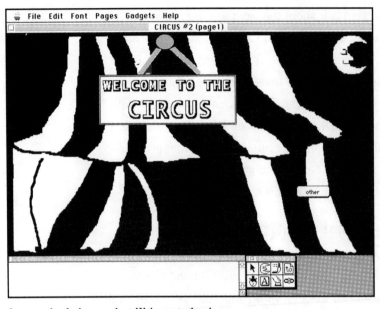

An example of a Logo project: Welcome to the circus.

designers as well as artists, programmers, and writers. This version of Logo gives them painting tools so that they can paint the background. The faces are stamped on the top of the background as are the stars using Logo's computational objects or turtles to place the images on the screen. The horses are turtles that have taken on the shape of horses. When the user clicks on the button marked horses, the horses dance in place. When the user clicks on the button marked music, circus music is played. The programming consists of controlling the turtle animations, changing their shapes, playing music, and changing the scenes.

This is the kind of experience that I want for every child. Logo or other forms of *Expressive Media* ought to encourage these kinds of learning opportunities. The children have appropriated the material at hand. For example, they recast preexisting shapes for their own purposes, changing them to be "African-centered." What comes through in their work is their own unique sense of design, color, shape, and action. They become multimedia storytellers. They paint their own sets, write their own introductions and dialog, create special characters in costume, give their characters special behaviors and animation on the screen, provide voice narration and singing, play music, and so on. Seeing their work, you just know that the days and weeks spent developing their projects were an incredible learning experience.

AN INTELLECTUAL HISTORY OF LOGO

The next sections will focus on the intellectual influences on Papert prior to his inventing Logo, then a discussion of the evolution of Logo and the research leading to the development of new microworlds.

Pre-Logo Influences on Seymour Papert: Minsky and Piaget

In creating Logo, Papert drew on his background as a mathematician and two other important interests of his: artificial intelligence and child development.

Artificial Intelligence

Papert's work with Marvin Minsky, which focused on making machines intelligent, had considerable influence on the creation of Logo. Studying computer intelligence might give children insights into their own learning styles. So, why not give kids an opportunity to teach computers how to do things?

Marvin Minsky and Seymour Papert met at a conference in England in 1962. There was an immediate kinship as they delivered papers on similar topics. Minsky was already at MIT leading the Artificial Intelligence (AI) Group. His colleague, John McCarthy, had just moved to Stanford University to start an AI group there. Papert was in France, Switzerland, and England. But in 1963 he visited MIT at the behest of Warren McCulloch, one of Minsky's mentors. McCulloch's work with Walter Pitts in the 1940s "began to show how machines might be made to see, reason, and remember" [Minsky 1986a]. By 1964, Minsky and Papert were a working team at MIT. They were kindred spirits and their collaboration over the next 20 years had a profound influence on current thinking about thinking about how people and machines learn.

Child Development and Constructionism

Papert had spent several years working with Jean Piaget, the Swiss psychologist and epistemologist, whose studies of children's learning have had a profound impact on current educational practice. Piaget showed that children know a lot before they get to school. If you want to know what children think, ask them. He created situations in which children have opinions and elicited them. A researcher would interview the child and use concrete materials to talk about. The same interviewing situation would be conducted with many children of different ages.

One such experiment used to investigate children's development of conservation of volume is the following. There are three containers and a pitcher of water. One is tall and thin; two are short and wide. The short and wide ones are identical. The same amount of water is poured into the two short, wide containers. This is done in front of the child. The question is: Is there more water in A or is there more water in B? The children all agree they are the same. Now the water from A is poured into the tall, thin container. The question is asked whether there is more water in B or C. Lo and behold, children before the age of six would declare there is more water in C, the tall container. An older child would say that B and C have the same amount and thus conservation of water.

What accounts for this transformation in thinking? Papert would argue that children develop new knowledge from using what they know in different situations and being confronted by conflicting views, which the children eventually resolve. In Minsky's words, a key insight of Papert's is that "a mind cannot really grow very much merely by accumulating knowledge. It must also develop better ways to use what it already knows" [Minsky 1986a, 102].

Piaget's experiments show that children acquire knowledge without being taught by a teacher. The conclusion from this fact is not that teachers are unnecessary, but that children are good learners. The role of a teacher is to capitalize on what children already know and on their learning strategies and to help them develop more strategies for acquiring more knowledge. This includes giving them good models of how to do things.

Another area in which Papert reinterprets Piaget is in his stages of development from sensori-motor to concrete to formal, where "at last thought is driven and disciplined, by principles of logic, by deduction, by induction, and by the principle of developing theories by the test of empirical verification and refutation" [Papert 1993, 153].

Papert believes that debates over Piaget's "neat picture of successive stages" has obscured the really important contribution. Piaget's "description of different ways of knowing is far more important than quibbling about whether they neatly follow one another chronologically" [Papert 1993, 153]. Papert feels that the middle stage, the stage of concrete operations, is extremely important. "This is the task to which he [Piaget] devoted the greater part of his mature life and all but a handful of the more than 100 books he wrote about how children think in a staggering range of domains including logic, number, space, time, motion, life, causality, machines, games, dreams" [Papert 1993, 153].

Papert sees himself as a constructionist, with his "personal reconstruction of constructivism." It relates back to Piaget where children are constructors of their own knowledge. Papert believes that

... the construction that takes place "in the head" often happens especially felicitously when it is supported by construction of a more public sort "in the world"—a sand castle or a cake, a LEGO house or a corporation, a computer program, a poem, or a theory of the universe. Part of what I mean by "in the world" is that the product can be shown, discussed, examined, probed, and admired. It is out there. [Papert 1993, 142]

Logo Gets Launched

Although Logo as a language and culture drew upon Papert's previous interests, knowledge, and research, the actualization of Logo is due to lots of different people—children, adults, students, professors, mathematicians, computer scientists, physicists, music educators, and a bevy of virtuoso hackers. I can attest to this diversity since I collaborated with Papert for Logo's first 15 years.

A catalyst for Logo came out of Papert's consulting with Wally Feurzeig, who in 1965 was head of the Educational Technology Group at Bolt, Beranek and Newman (BBN). One of the first computers-in-the-mathematics-classroom projects had started up using a language called TELCOMP, which was similar to BASIC. (BASIC was on the horizon, but not yet out!) Papert observed that students having trouble in algebra with ideas like variables were not given any new insights by learning an algebraic programming language like BASIC. A language designed for engineers and scientists was not the best language for children to learn to speak and think in mathematics.

Logo was first used with children in 1967. Discussion and implementation began in the summer of 1966 when Papert presented a rough design plan to a group of us at BBN, including Wally Feurzeig, Dick Grant, Danny Bobrow, and me. Grant and I worked in Feurzeig's group. Bobrow was head of the Artificial Intelligence Group at BBN and a former student of Minsky's and Papert's. The group shared a common background in programming environments. Lisp was the language of choice, but not for children. Nonetheless, some powerful ideas imbedded in Lisp influenced Logo's development: having procedures, giving procedures names and not putting funny restrictions on them, being able to extend the language by writing procedures in the language itself, and having debugging tools by which to trace or step through the program's behavior.

A Pattern of Debugging the Language

In principle, we could have developed our ideas and teaching materials without actually teaching a class. In practice, we could not have generated material of the same quality without the help of children. Subjectively, contact with them seemed to produce a deeper sensitivity to their needs and reactions. Thus, a pattern to Logo development was established from the outset. It was to develop a working prototype, try it out with children and teachers, and then revise the language based on the bugs encountered in actual teaching situations.

We worked with kids in the summer of 1967 for three weeks. Papert was the lead teacher with Feurzeig and me as observers and teaching assistants. That first version of Logo was quite different from the Logos that are in popular use today. It also had much in common.

The initial context was a place where children could play with things—these things were words and sentences. So the primitives in Logo were designed with this kind of playground in mind. In fact, in the first version of Logo *multiply* and *divide* were not built-in procedures. They had to be written in Logo. The important idea was that they could be written in Logo and by children.

This initial experience strengthened our belief that young children could learn to program. We also developed some ideas on how to talk about Logo programming and the kinds of engagements children would find interesting. We learned that they could assimilate numerous new mathematical functions, but we needed our next teaching experiment to evolve our ideas further and to gather more specific information on what were interesting projects.

After the first experience with children and Logo in 1967, a new version of Logo was implemented on a time-shared computer entirely dedicated to Logo. This version was used by children for the entire school year starting in the fall of 1968 in place of their regular mathematics class. The summer of 1968 was spent conducting workshops for teachers. One of these teachers was to be the lead teacher in the fall. The others were to work with other classes in the school, depending on schedules and interest.

A group of 12 seventh graders attending the Muzzey Junior High School in Lexington, Massachusetts were selected to be in the special computer math class. The children were picked to represent the middle stream, children who for the most part had poor self-images of themselves as learners.

An important idea that was realized with this group of children was that they would work on projects, not exercises (or problems in the mathematical sense). A project is not confined to one concept or one class period. A project might extend across several domains and require research and development over a period of days or weeks. Moreover, because there is usually more than one way to design and develop a project, each child can make something that is uniquely hers or his.

The Emergent Computer Culture

Before the Muzzey experiment, we had some experience in teaching children to program in Logo and other languages. The operational status of the Muzzey class, however, forced us rather brutally to recognize misleading facets of this previous experience. The most important was that our personal teaching methods depended heavily on what we call our computer culture. The meaning we attach to the term includes the effects of long experience in seeing the world in terms of programs, so that we have at our fingertips many examples, analogies, ways of looking at pro-gramming, jokes, turns of phrase, and other useful aids for developing a lively, stim-ulating, and supple interaction with the children. The Muzzey experience brought out this facet first by making us face the problems encountered by a teacher with a very limited *computer culture* and then by putting a strain even on our own accumu-lated resources by the need to confront a class every day.

Our reaction to the problem was to recognize the need for an extensive formulation of teaching ideas, and an even more extensive formulation of relevant elements of a *computer culture*. The ideas we developed had very little to do with physical comput-ers. They were more concerned with the description and manipulation of concepts like *process, project, procedure*, and, of course, *description, manipulation*, and *concept*.

In 1968 the distinction between project versus problem was not fully understood out-side of the art room. That was one of the reasons that about a month or so into the fall term, I took over as the lead teacher and collaborated with Papert on both teach-ing and developing material.

Learning Logo, moving toward constructivist practice, and especially being able to differentiate between project and discrete problem were not possible to absorb in a short workshop. All of these ideas were too new. Remember, this was 1968! If we already had experience with children in a Logo world, then we could have focused on what teachers needed. We ourselves had not developed a bag of tricks or a col-lection of possible projects. We really didn't know what was possible with children, so we needed to have a teacher with more expertise.

For example, the initial part of the Muzzey course concentrated on teaching the meaning and syntax of Logo commands and operations. It was a mistake. It is possi-ble to write exciting active programs with a small subset of Logo words without any idea that they can be composed or chained. We know today that early teaching should ignore syntax and variety of Logo words and should concentrate on concepts that have an immediate pay-off in programming and excitement for children. In fact, I have learned that it is extremely important to show children in their very first expe-

rience that they can do something with the computer that they could not have done without the computer.

Our first major project was to write a program to play a simple game (*one-pile Nim* or *21*) Our intention was to give the children a model of how to go about working on a project. The children learned a lot about playing games and figuring out strategies. In this version of Nim, for example, two people can play; they remove one, two, or three sticks until there are no more left in the pile. The player who took the last stick won. The children learned that they could predict the winner if they knew the number of sticks in the pile at the start and which player went first. This was both disappointing and exciting. These children liked the outcome to be a mystery. Their debugging strategies involved making plans, simplifying, testing, revising, and discussing what they were thinking and doing.

Our task was to identify more projects that children would find challenging and engaging. This first year of a year-long course certainly challenged us and led Papert to think about the need for a more concrete object to play with than words and sentences. And so, came turtles.

Turtles Arrive and Logo Goes to MIT

Besides consulting at BBN, Papert was a professor in the applied mathematics department at MIT and co-directed with Marvin Minsky the Artificial Intelligence Group. At the time that Logo was happening, Papert was working with Minsky on their book, *Perceptrons* [Minsky and Papert 1969]. They were analyzing the behavior of a simple machine. Thinking about the need for a more concrete object for children to play with, Papert invented a kind of automaton-like creature and called it a turtle. It behaved on a local level without global knowledge of its environment. It could move forward and back and pivot to the right or the left. It had a pen and so could leave a trace of its path. Thus, in conversations with Minsky and other MIT faculty, Papert began to create a new computational object and a new mathematics for children. This was not a trivial mathematics, but one rich enough for adults as well [Abelson and diSessa 1981].

Papert had students, staff, and faculty at MIT develop two kinds of turtles. One was a mechanical thing that crawled around the floor on its wheels. It was referred to as a *floor* turtle.

The first floor turtle was a yellow canister with a thick cable connecting it to a special portable terminal. Then, there was also a *graphics* turtle that resided on a cathode ray tube (CRT) screen. The graphics turtle was in a usable form in a laboratory setting a few months before the floor turtle. However, to use it, you needed to be in the computer room where a DEC PDP-6 was used to drive the CRT and was controlled by Logo programs running on a time-shared PDP-10. Although the lab setting was not accessible to children, it allowed turtle geometry to begin.

In 1970 I had joined Papert at MIT and the Logo group started as part of the Artificial Intelligence Laboratory. In April of that year, Papert put on an all-day public event at MIT called Teaching Children Thinking. The closing panelists included Robert Davis, Patrick Suppes, and Marvin Minsky. There were 700 attendees. Logo became public knowledge, but not yet publicly available.

A Philosophy of Learning and Teaching

To the extent that children are really able to see themselves as creative researchers and designers, they are learning something much more important than using computers. When used in this way, the computer becomes an ideal carrier for the image of learner-as-researcher and learner-as-designer. In fact, the learner acts and feels like a researcher and designer.

The approach applies to teachers as well as students. When I have taught Logo, I honestly see myself and the child as engaged in a genuine joint research and design project. The exact situation has never really occurred before. It poses problems I have never seen before as well as some I have. I do not know in advance what the answers are or what path the child will follow. One of the most exciting discoveries made by the children is just that: "You mean you really don't know how to do it?" exclaimed one child in amazement and reaction to a hundred remembered situations in which teachers put on the stance of "let's do it together" while really knowing the answer in advance. For some children, the prospect of an honest relationship with the teacher is something new and inspiring. This culture is especially good for developing such relations because the environment is so *discovery rich*. The collaboration between teacher and student as researchers and designers, together, is one way in which the effect of the computer presence goes beyond using computers. Its real impact is on the total culture of which teacher and child are part.

Out of experiences in this culture a new breed of teachers emerges: These teachers are thoroughly imbued with a coherent computer cuture and its language. They know how to use this language to talk interestingly about things people from outside the culture know and care about. The teachers have a fluent mastery of certain powerful ideas. They are thoroughly familiar with project terrains through which they will guide those who come for instruction (but will be given something better!). They have been there often! They know how to observe people engaged in thinking, learning, puzzling, agonizing, rejoicing— they know through experience when to intervene and when to let the learner struggle. They believe that the key goal for any learner is to improve her or his self-image as a learner and as an active intellectual agent.

COMMERCIAL LOGOS: A NEW GENERATION

For most of us, it was an exciting time. Logo was finally getting out of the laboratory and would be accessible to anyone with an Apple or IBM home computer. It seemed incredible that Logo fit on these computers. There were compromises. The most noticeable was the lack of animation capabilities. Making moving pictures had been a real motivating factor and it was disappointing that children couldn't segue from turtle geometry studies to animated storytellers.

In 1983, Atari Logo for the Atari 800 home computer was released. This was a lovely version because it combined sprites and music. You could have four turtles which could each assume different shapes and different speeds. Rules could be set up so that if a turtle bumped into another turtle or crossed over a line, a specific action could be taken, such as turn 180 degrees. (For an interesting collection of projects see *LogoWorks*, edited by Solomon, Minsky, and Harvey 1986.)

Another issue arose around getting Logo out of the lab and into children's lives. Logo is not just a programming language, but a carrier of a culture. How was this culture to be transmitted? Papert's book, *Mindstorms,* had recently been published and it generated a lot of interest and excitement all over the world. Many people wanted to get involved, use it themselves, and share it with kids. Adults, like children, learn by doing and thinking about what they do. But who do they share their experiences with and how? Today on-line communities (discussion groups) through which people can ask for help and offer help have become popular. More and more people have access to on-line bulletin boards, chat groups, and so on. If schools don't have facilities then teachers and parents have accounts on *Prodigy, America On Line,* or a *Freenet* from their homes.

But in 1982, the on-line communities were mostly made up of computerists at universities or in industry. So, the Logo endeavors tended to be insular. Success rested in the hands of a few dedicated devotees, who for the most part wanted to reform their classroom activities or were already reforming their classrooms. The Logo philosophy as represented in *Mindstorms* resonated with many people. As with other good ideas there were many stumbling blocks along the way. The struggle to learn enough to feel comfortable often magnified the differences in teachers' deep-seated teaching strategies. The point is that in its initial explosion onto the scene, there were too few experts and not enough support material to help newcomers soak up the culture.

MicroWorlds

Briefly, a *microworld* is a limited, defined world in which you can explore and construct. Turtle geometry is one such world. It is defined by the turtle and its capabilities. You as an explorer, constructor, and designer can get to know that world and add to it, and perhaps, make other microworlds in it. Thus, construction tools, such as a programming language, underlie the world. This feature of a microworld—that it can be expanded by the user, who is most often not a professional programmer—is a distinguishing characteristic.

Recently, Logo Computer Systems, Inc. (LCSI), the Logo company Papert is associated with, came out with a new version of Logo, which is called *MicroWorlds*, in an attempt to reappropriate the word *microworlds*. In a sense Logo, itself, is a microworld in which it is possible to construct other microworlds.

In the accompanying picture, there are three turtles in a large black circle. The turtles are continually moving forward a step. They do not escape their play area because the child-designer has made a rule. Whenever a turtle encounters a black line, it turns 135 degrees. This kind of control structure was first possible in TI-Logo. At that time, the children were told there was a demon or creature in the computer that was constantly on the alert. Thus, the child talks not only to a turtle and to Logo, but also to a creature in the machine.

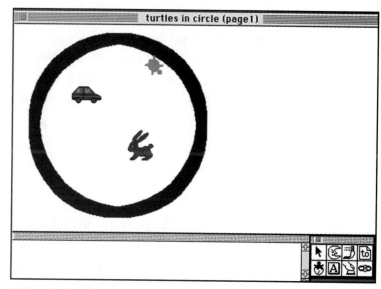

Three turtles in a circle.

In Logo *MicroWorlds,* children can command the turtle to write or draw on the screen or they can draw on the screen themselves using MicroWorlds' painting kit. Other multimedia authoring tools have been added to MicroWorlds. At the same time ideas that were first developed in the 1970s such as multiple turtles, animation, and sprites have been re-engineered. MicroWorlds is a commercial attempt to encourage teachers to use Logo as an authoring tool and create their own teaching environments that might be considered microworlds.

RESEARCH ON NEW WORLDS

With the microcomputer revolution, a lot of the emphasis in Logo studies shifted from research to development and productizing. This was very necessary. If those who understood the issues were not willing to devote their energies and share their expertise, how would Logo and its culture have a chance of surviving outside of the lab. So, until Apple Logo was completed in 1982, most of the MIT Logo staff were immersed in the process of getting Logo out in the world. But an opportunity opened to start a new research phase. This work predated the existence of the MIT Media Lab which many of the researchers were later to join as students, staff, or faculty.

Research at Atari Cambridge Research, 1982 to 1984

In 1982, I set up a new research laboratory through the auspices of Dr. Alan Kay, then chief scientist of Atari, formerly at Xerox Parc where his Learning Research Group developed Smalltalk and a computer system on which the Macintosh is derived. Atari Cambridge Research existed for not quite two years. In that time other Logo researchers and I had an opportunity to rethink what an environment for kids might be.

The overall goal was to create an environment where children could make their own video games and storytelling environments based on intelligent animation capabilities. So we had to have a programming language (authoring system) in which knowledge about objects could be expressed. We had to be able to construct different kinds of computational objects, turtles being one example. We (Margaret Minsky especially) had talked for a long time about making a system in which children could have intelligent animal parts as building blocks. That is, rabbit legs would know about being rabbit legs and have particular jumping behaviors. Bird wings would know about flapping, soaring, gliding, and so forth. Using these intelligent parts children could construct new creatures and make new parts. We wanted to be able to construct creatures that displayed emotions as well. We also wanted an interactive musical companion with which to compose or play in different musical styles.

From our experiences we knew we needed a powerful programming language. It had to be like Logo, but not Logo. It had to be like Smalltalk, but not Smalltalk. Our playstation for the future had to provide lots of media inputs and outputs—music, sound, video (tape and disc), graphics, animation, and text. We also knew that keyboards were not good input devices; we wanted to communicate more expressively through gesture. Therefore, a big focus of our activity was on gestural communication. We built force-feedback joysticks and a force-feedback steering wheel. We also had a force-feedback touch screen. (With this force-feedback touch screen we developed a fingerpainting system.) We also studied the possibility of understanding bodily communication through video cameras and other special hardware input devices.

With the demise of Atari Research came the founding of the MIT Media Lab, Papert's new home as head of the Epistemology and Learning Group. Some of the projects found homes in different parts of the Media Lab, others became commercial products, and still others just drifted into a hazy history. But the energy for creating totally new microworlds that had a very different look and feel from the "classical view of Logo" was put out, absorbed, and certainly continued at the Media Lab. In a sense, the Atari Lab served as a model for the possibility of doing this work outside of a university laboratory.

StarLogo: Exploring Massively Parallel Microworlds

In Logo *MicroWorlds* you can have more than one turtle on the screen and can talk to them all or to each one. The problem is that the system was not designed for parallel processes to work efficiently. You want each turtle to have its own set of behaviors and you can do that to some extent. However, as you try to explore actions among large numbers of turtles, the system almost comes to a halt or can't check on whether a particular event has occurred in time to take action. In the past there have been other attempts to design and build a Logo where you can have any number of turtles and each one can be given unique characteristics. None of them has done what Mitchel Resnick's *StarLogo* does.

In *StarLogo* you can have thousands of turtles, all engaged in different actions at the same time. This realization has occurred because of the changes in technology and the thinking about the technology—*StarLogo* was initially implemented on a *Connection Machine*, a massively parallel machine which had a minimum of 64 processors connected with one another. StarLogo, redesigned to run on a Macintosh, a one-processor computer, is available from the Learning and Epistemology Group at the MIT Media Lab.

Resnick wanted a microworld in which he could simulate the behavior of a flock of birds or a colony of ants and so study decentralized systems:

A flock of birds sweeps across the sky. Like a well-choreographed dance troupe, the birds veer to the left in unison.... How do birds keep their movements so orderly, so synchronized? Most people assume that birds play a game of follow-the-leader... But that's not so.... The bird in front is not a leader in any meaningful sense—it just happens to end up there. The flock is organized without an organizer, coordinated without a coordinator. [Resnick 1994, 3]

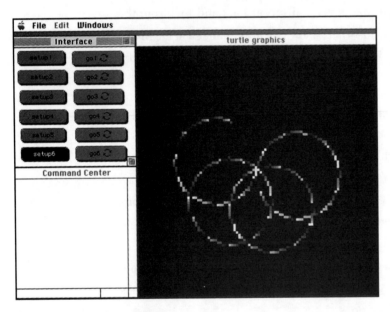

Fireworks circles under construction.

The jaggy line segments making up six intertwining circles are turtles, and not lines drawn by turtles. Each circle is a 36-sided polygon made by creating three turtles one turtle step apart and then rotating the turtles 10 degrees to be ready for the next set of turtles.

What do you expect to happen when you give the command *forward 10*? You can tell by the accompanying picture that all the turtles are going forward at their particular headings and they maintain a formation.

StarLogo is not a commercial project and may not be. What it points to is a direction of research in which children can not only be the subjects, but also substantial contributors.

Some Remarks on Math, Computers, and Computer Cultures

The original goals Papert set out upon in 1966 are still guiding Logo's development. Foremost is to create a *Mathland*, a place where children can talk about what they are doing, think about what they have done, and debug their plans and procedures. This artificial place is still in its early stages. Pieces are there for kids to invent and learn. What computers might bring to children's lives is still full of wonderful and intriguing possibilities.

I have gone into more detail about the hardware and software development and less detail on the rash of new projects kids, teachers, and researchers have evolved. I made this decision because I wanted to illustrate the evolution of designing products for children. There are several good resources on projects but very few giving an historical development of the culture which has always included people, ideas, and things.

I also want to emphasize the culture in a different way: That teaching children about computers or how to program can be as disengaging as learning arithmetic. "No one ever learns a language from being told its grammar rules. We always start with stories about things that interest us" [Minsky 1986b, vii].

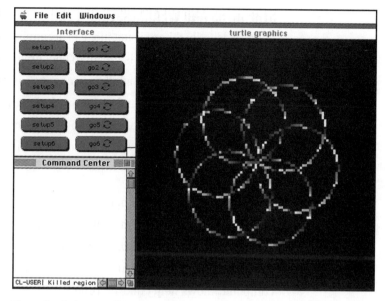

Fireworks circles complete.

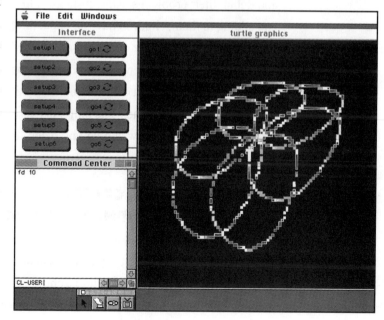

Fireworks turtles advance 10 steps.

STRENGTHS AND WEAKNESSES OF LOGO

Logo as described here is not just a programming language. It is an environment for exploring microworlds. It is meant to encourage a kind of computer culture in which children, computers, and adults are engaged in a process of teaching and learning. In this culture reflection and action work together as children issue commands and debug their effects. Teachers find their personal experiences with Logo as exciting and creative as children do. A big question is where does this plug into current school curricula?

The intention of Logo has been to create new ways of thinking about thinking. Programming in the sense of making procedures that describe to a computer how to do a particular task is one step. Another step is testing out and debugging the description. Learning from bugs and discussing teaching strategies to enhance what the computer knows help children reflect on their own learning. Turtle geometry is an area of mathematics. Unlike arithmetic, it is a domain in which children can explore and debug their problem-solving strategies. In identifying with the turtle's attributes and adding to them, children have an opportunity to explore their own thinking. The Logo culture (as do other rich multimedia environments) extends to other school subjects in more tangible ways than school math does. Turtles, graphics, writing, animation, and sound lead children to use multimedia for self-expression and to integrate what they know. Their learning falls across traditional school subject boundaries. They write and draw and compute and draw on literature and science as well as mathematics.

DRILL-AND-PRACTICE, SUPPES, AND BEHAVIORISM

Patrick Suppes is the grand master of using the computer as an *Interactive Textbook*. He is closely identified with a style of instruction called drill-and-practice. For Suppes, this means that a student is taught school subjects through a series of carefully moderated exercises. They are not randomly generated or randomly repeated. The subject matter has been analyzed and broken into strands, which in turn have been divided into *concept blocks* or *skill objectives*. Each concept block contains exercises at different levels of difficulty that address the same skill objective. Portioning out the mix of topics and exercises is managed by the computer system. This management system is at the core of the success of Suppes' work and an extremely important element of his research studies.

The computer work began as a research project in 1963 at Stanford University's Institute for Mathematical Studies in the Social Sciences (IMSSS). In 1967, Suppes and colleagues from IMSSS established Computer Curriculum Corporation (CCC) to market and distribute the material. As well as being a professor of philosophy, Suppes was president of CCC. He held that position until 1990 when he sold the company. It was bought by Simon and Schuster Publishing, which is now a part of Viacom . CCC has 600 employees and, for the moment, ranks second to Jostens in delivering Interactive Textbook systems to schools. These are often called *Integrated Learning Systems* (ILS) because they provide material for entire courses typically in math, reading, and language arts—the *basics*.

Suppes focused on developing courses for both disadvantaged children and gifted children as well as for Stanford college students. The research "dealing with basic skills for disadvantaged students" led to "a fairly widespread use in the United States of computer-based supplementary courses in elementary mathematical skills and concepts, basic reading skills and language skills" [Suppes 1975, 237]. Thus, from its early period, Suppes' research at Stanford extended to schools all over the country. The material was easily transportable because it did not require on-site expertise or the participation of a teacher.

In the laboratory, courses were developed requiring a combination of text, graphics, and audio with a graphical pointing device and/or keyboard for communicating with the system. In the first 10 or 15 years following its commercial availability, material that required multiple forms of media was excluded from distribution due in large part to the cost and clumsiness of the technology. The latest version of CCC material uses multimedia—text, graphics, audio, and animation—with mouse as well as keyboard input.

SAMPLE INTERACTIONS

An interaction without multimedia consists of an exercise presented on the computer screen. For example,

7 x 6 = _____.

If the student types in the correct answer, then a new exercise is presented. If the student types in an incorrect answer such as 43, some feedback is supplied. Typically, it is:

TRY AGAIN

Then the exercise is represented.

7 x 6 = _____.

If the student now types in an incorrect answer on this second attempt, she or he will be presented with the correct answer:

7 x 6 = 42

followed by TRY AGAIN and a restatement of the exercise. If the student delays too long or again types an incorrect response on the third attempt, the correct answer is presented and the student goes on to another exercise. Meanwhile, the management system takes note of the difficulty, remembers the exercise type for later presentation, and determines what the next exercise will be. The management system decides what remediation to take. Either new types of exercises or exercises of the same type but easier (from a lower level) will be presented.

In CCC's new release, which uses multimedia, the style of interaction and the underlying structure are the same. There are surface differences that behaviorists would probably find important. For example, the rewards for a correct answer are different. If a child inputs the correct answer on the first try, a yellow ribbon appears on the lower right of the screen. If the child answers correctly on the second try, a hollow ribbon appears on the lower right of the screen. If the child needs to be given the correct answer, it appears in red ink on the screen.

ELEMENTARY SCHOOL MATH AND BEHAVIORISM

Suppes, a philosopher by training and a philosopher of psychology by interest as well as a college professor, had a commitment to improving education. His direct involvement in elementary education began in the mid-1950s, when he co-authored first and second math textbooks which introduced young children to school math through set theory. Suppes is a logician, so there was a natural appeal for him to teach set theory and logic as part of a children's elementary mathematics curriculum.

Suppes comes out of the behaviorist tradition, of psychology. In this tradition studies of people or animals were based on their behaviors, not on hypotheses about their mental processes. That is you really cannot know what is going on in the mind; all you can know is what the stimulus is (that is the outside world event) and what response is elicited. Behaviorism with its different groups became a dominant influence on psychological and

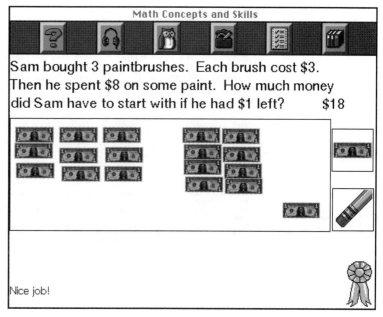

Drill-and-Practice example: Adding correctly on the first try. (CCC)

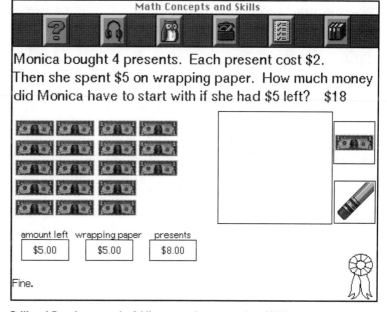

Drill-and-Practice example: Adding correctly on second try. (CCC)

educational thinking in the United States. The powerful message to education was that there were principles and laws which can be transferred to teaching. Already the effect was felt in the development of standardized written tests. Moreover, the research in the lab was easily reproduced. A content area or skill could be analyzed hierarchically and then taught in that fashion. By 1960, the work of Skinner in behavior modification was well-known. His development of *teaching machines* or *programmed instruction* was also well-known and imitated in labs as well as textbooks. Negative reinforcement was becoming a teaching strategy as well as a psychological tool.

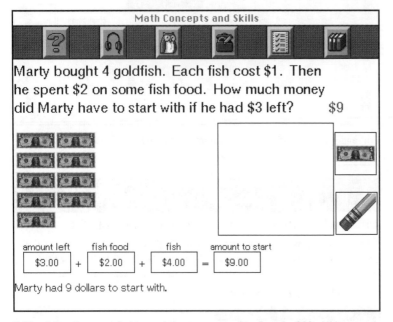

Drill-and-Practice example: Incorrect answer on second try. From the CCC addition strand.

Suppes deplored negative reinforcement. In his work using the computer as an Interactive Textbook, students were never told that they were wrong. In response to an incorrect answer the computer gave positive reinforcement by encouraging the student to try again and by telling the student the answer, then asking her or him to try again.

Suppes, well aware of the jokes and jibes showered on rote learning, can give logical coherent rebuttals. For example, in response to "the much heard remark that the newer revisions of the mathematics curriculum are particularly significant because of the emphasis they are placing on *understanding* concepts as opposed to the perfection of *rote* skills," Suppes suggests that the remark "is essentially banal." It's obvious to him that understanding is a good thing, and that the possession of "mere rote skill" is a bad thing. The problem is

...not knowing what we mean by understanding. This failure is not due to disagreement over whether the test of understanding should be a behavioral one. I am inclined to think that most people concerned with this matter would admit the central relevance of overt behavior as a measure of understanding. The difficulty is rather that no one seems to be very clear about the exact specification of the behavior required to exhibit understanding. Moreover, apart even from any behavioral questions the very notion of understanding seems fundamentally vague and ill-defined. [Suppes 1964, 2]

In keeping with a behaviorist view of school math, Suppes' work embodies an analysis of the essential skills and concepts needed to fulfill society's needs as indicated by national standardized tests. The form of these tests is similar to the form of the CCC material. Questions and exercises are posed that can be answered either by a number, a word, or a multiple choice selection.

SIMILARITIES BETWEEN SUPPES AND PAPERT

What do Pat Suppes and Seymour Papert have in common? They share a vision that computers can create learning environments that would not be possible without a computer. The computer is not merely a tool, tutor, or tutee [Taylor 1980]. It is the essence. Computational ideas permeate how Suppes and Papert look at the world.

Suppes sees the computer as a very individualized teacher who has a complete agenda in mind and will patiently lead a child through a series of planned exercises. From this sequence of exercises the child will be able to progress through a particular school subject at his or her own rate. The computer will keep accurate records of the student's progress, so the classroom teacher can review each child's performance. The teacher will also be free to do other kinds of teaching and preparation.

Personally, Suppes sees computational ideas as support for his theories of learning. The computer becomes a laboratory for testing out his theories. He also welcomes new technologies to enhance the computer environment. His research on learning by computer has involved visual and auditory input and output. In practice, the environments leaving the laboratory were constrained by the cost of graphics and speech output and the difficulty of speech recognition.

Suppes' base of operation is Stanford University where he is professor emeritus of philosophy. (At one time, if a person was interested in computers and education and lived in California, he or she was bound to have been a student or employee of Suppes.) The intellectual community was very different from Papert's. Nonetheless, they share an ability to attract and interact with some of the best minds in the world, either at world conferences and symposia or in classes at their own universities. Thus, Suppes on the West Coast at Stanford University and Papert on the East Coast at MIT not only had a ready pool of bright and interested students, but also a pool of leading scholars and scientists to give additional substance to their work. This is an extremely important element. These computer worlds could not have been built without the collaboration of a talented team of people.

In looking at computers in education through the dichotomy of computer as an *Interactive Textbook* or as an *Expressive Medium*, it is easy to see Suppes and Papert standing in opposite extremes. With Suppes, the Interactive Textbook is in control of the student. With Papert the Expressive Medium is controlled by the student. Neither Suppes nor Papert see the computer as a tool in and of itself. The computer for both of them carries a culture and a way for them to create learning environments for children. The computer is crucial to their work and integrates their previous research. It offers them possibilities for creating their visions of positive learning experiences.

MATH CONCEPTS AT STANFORD AND COMPUTER CURRICULUM CORPORATION (CCC)

In 1963, the computer-assisted instructional work began at Stanford University's Institute for Mathematical Studies in the Social Sciences (IMSSS), a laboratory under the direction of Patrick Suppes and two other professors: Richard Atkinson and William Estes. Suppes focused on mathematics education while Atkinson worked on teaching reading.

Suppes had been involved in the elementary mathematics reform movement of the early 1960s, commonly referred to as *new math*. Of course, mathematics educators had different images of what *new math* might be. The call for reform was catalyzed by the Soviet Union's lauching of Sputnik, thereby beating out the United States to be first in space. Concern for mathematics and science education gave rise to new funding and new impetus to reform school mathematics. Suppes was active in elementary mathematics education in the mid 1950s, before he used computers. Suppes' background and interest lie in logic, probability, and statistics. For him, set theory and logic are foundational to doing mathematics. So, introducing children to these ideas at an early age would enhance their mathematics training. In fact, the first computer-as-teacher course developed at IMSSS in 1963 was for elementary logic used by a few sixth graders. But the bread-and-butter parts of the arithmetic teaching programs were developed beginning in 1964.

Cost played a role in the curriculum. What made the enterprise at all practicable was the invention of time-sharing. Many people could use the computer at the same time with immediate feedback. People could talk to computers from a typewriter terminal and no longer had to submit decks of punched cards to the computer room. A new intimacy was allowed. Suppes seized the opportunity opened up by time-sharing to begin his work on developing high quality courseware which eventually spanned elementary as well as advanced university courses.

In 1963, time-shared computers were physically large but, especially by today's standards, they had relatively small workspaces—permanent storage was expensive. In the 1964 and 1965 academic year, arithmetic courses for first and fourth graders were used experimentally. The elementary logic program was a space hog and therefore not practical for use with large numbers of children. The first grade math relied heavily on graphics and was also too costly for use with large numbers of children. For the same reason geometry was also omitted as it, too, needed graphics. The arithmetic project of the 1964 and 1965 academic year, nonetheless, was a successful experiment and encouraged Suppes to expand the curriculum materials and the numbers of children involved.

School Setup

For many years, a typical setup consisted of a separate room, sometimes a portable classroom, where there were 30 stations. The stations in the 1960s and 1970s were typewriter terminals. After the microcomputer revolution, the stations became computers. In either case, a host computer was needed to manage the system and record the students' progress. Usually, there were trained attendants to proctor the room. Teachers would ship their students to the lab and remain removed from the activity.

The 1990s elementary school computers are found more and more in classrooms rather than in laboratories. A typical classroom setup today is to have four computer stations connected to a host computer in another part of the school. For the newest release, the machines might be Apple Macintoshes or IBM computers with *Windows*. Children in the fourth grade or below will use headsets for many of the lessons, especially children at grade levels K through 2. In other words, some instruction is given verbally. A typical session is about 15 minutes long with a few extra minutes to log in and out.

The Curriculum

The math curriculum was divided into a number of strands. Each strand was made up of an ordered sequence of exercises grouped into concept blocks or skills objectives. Concept blocks consisted of a fixed number of levels of the same type of exercises. The level of difficulty was determined by the student's performance; that is, if a certain percent of exercises were answered correctly then she or he would go up a level, go down a level, or stay at the same level.

The formation of a company to market this material fit in very well with Suppes' research interests in collecting and analyzing large amounts of data as to children's performance within the curriculum and on standardized math tests. Study after study showed that there was a statistically significant improvement in many children's math skills, especially in schools with a large population of poor minority children.

CCC

Computer Curriculum Corporation (CCC) was founded in 1967 by Patrick Suppes and Richard Atkinson. Suppes was already an established professor and reseacher. He then added successful entrepreneur to his list of credits. He was president of CCC for over 20 years. At the time of CCC's founding, Atkinson was a codirector of the Institute for Mathematical Studies in the Social Sciences (IMSSS). A Stanford professor of psychology, a former head of the National Science Foundation, and currently provost of the University of California at San Diego, Atkinson was responsible for the initial elementary school reading material developed at IMSSS and later marketed and expanded by CCC.

CCC became a successful enterprise. There are several reasons for that. Drill-and-Practice on a computer transferred with relative ease from laboratory to actual daily classroom use. It supported traditional thinking about what teaching and education are. That is there were clear objectives and the success of meeting them was measurable by quantitative methods. The public interest in evaluating children's learning through easily quantifiable tests was at an all-time high. The style of teaching as well as the emphasis on developing *basic skills* fed into long-time popular beliefs as to what schooling is. The research in the laboratory enriched and supported the popularization of this teaching aid. Furthermore, CCC was continually enriched by the influx of IMSSS members. These were people who were already enculturated. They were familiar with the issues surrounding improving education. They knew about statistical models of learning. They were acquainted with behaviorist learning theories. They shared a common view of what mathematics is and of what the computer as teacher could do in schools. This discussion is focused on mathematics, but the same could hold true for reading and language arts, the other two curriculum materials offered by CCC.

By 1977 the math curriculum consisted of 14 strands. In 1984 a new revision of this curriculum was released. It was made up of 12 strands: addition, number concepts, U.S. measurement, subtraction, equations, applications, metric measurement, multiplication, problem solving, division, fractions, and decimals. The laws of arithmetic strand and the negative numbers strand were integrated into other strands. The horizontal and vertical layout of exercises in addition, subtraction, and multiplication were combined. A geometry strand was available as an extra. In later releases, measurement again becomes a single strand including both U.S. and metric measurement.

A major revision took place in the 1990s and was released in 1994 and 1995. The new CCC, Viacom Company, incorporated multimedia into these strands. The curriculum was revised and expanded. CCC took note of the new standards of the National

Council of Teachers of Mathematics (NCTM). These standards, published in 1988 and 1989, have caused mathematics curricula to be revamped throughout the education publishing industry. New strands became part of the curriculum. They included probability and statistics, science applications, and word problems. This drill-and-practice material is now the *Math Concepts and Skills* package. A whole new set of curriculum materials released in 1995 as the *Math Investigations* package is built around a set of on-line tools and manipulatives called the *Math Processor*.

With color graphics, a mouse, buttons, and other changes in the user interface, the material has a different look and feel to it. Not only do children type numbers in, but also for some exercises they use the mouse to select items.

EXTENDING THE CURRICULUM: MATH INVESTIGATIONS

The CCC math material first developed at Stanford in the mid-1960s is now part of the *SuccessMaker* system; it "is a technology-based learning system that helps teachers and administrators meet educational goals. State-of-the-art multimedia—including digitized sound, full-motion video, and animation—provide interactive learning experiences for students at all grade levels" [CCC 1993, 2].

Math Concepts and Skills is now only one component of the *SuccessMaker* math courses. Release 16 introduced in 1994 with its multimedia version of *Math Concepts and Skills* included in 1995 an all new multimedia component called *Math Investigations* which initially has material for grades 5 through 8. *Math Investigations* is a response to the recommendations of the NTCM standards to teach problem-solving in elementary school mathematics. So, CCC obtained the *Math Processor*, a set of tools, published by LearningWays. It contains "online math tools and manipulatives" such as dynamically linkable graph, spreadsheet, and chart generators, a geometric construction set with linear and angular measurement tools, and other such tools. Thus, a version of the modern math teacher's collection of computational tools is part of the *Math Investigations* package. Children are given problem-solving situations which require calculations of various sorts.

With all of the tools at hand, problem-solving situations that we are told are real and authentic, are presented to the children to find solutions. The problems are more interesting than the traditional word problems. However, the answers are the answers. Nontheless, this interpretation of open-ended problems that relate to children's living skills is implemented as behaviorists do. We will see multimedia and mathematics education meet along these lines in forthcoming products. This approach contrasts sharply with the constructivist approach discussed in the section "Meaningful Math, Davis, and Constructivism" that follows.

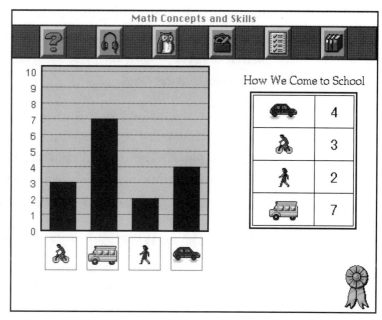

Graphing activity. (CCC)

DIFFERENCES BETWEEN SUPPES AND PAPERT

Suppes and Papert are poles apart in how they see children learn and in the kind of mathematics they do. Suppes is a behaviorist while Papert is a constructionist (a variant on constructivism). "Behaviorists are fond of using the designation *learning theory* for the foundations of their thinking, but what they are talking about is not *learning* in the sense of something a learner does but *instruction*, in the sense of something the instructor does to the learner" [Papert 1993, 164].

For Papert, "It is not enough to be able to use many kinds of reasoning; one also must know which to use in different circumstances! Learning is more than the mere accumulation of skills. Whatever we learn, there is always more to learn—about how to use what was already learned" [Minsky 1985, 100].

For a Piagetian, "to know is to invent"; this means personalizing knowledge, using what one already knows to acquire new knowledge, and that this kind of learning takes place by constructing new internal representations. Piagetians theorize that children construct knowledge by building on what they know and experience as they interact with the world.

For Suppes, the logician and behaviorist, the focus is not on theorizing about internal constructions, but rather on encouraging learning through step-by-step presentation of regulated stimuli. "The logician in him supported a view of knowledge as made up of precise particles; the statistician in him liked to see knowledge as particulate and therefore countable; the neobehaviorist required it to be so" [Papert 1993, 164].

STRENGTHS AND WEAKNESSES OF DRILL-AND-PRACTICE

Detractors of drill-and-practice are now calling it "drill and kill." Suppes' work remains outside of the *Math Blaster* or *Reader Rabbit* imitators for several reasons. It is a complete supplementary curriculum that has been through many revisions. It is used for a limited amount of time. It has been tested and tested and shown to do what it claims. It raises children's test scores. Teachers are kept informed but do not have to actively participate in the drill. It is available in Spanish. The material, especially with audio, is very helpful in English as a second language classes.

One weakness of the system is that the delivery is relentless; therefore, after a while it becomes boring. Deeper issues arise as to what is being learned through these materials. Are the concepts and skills emphasized here important to master and are they necessary to increase the numbers of mathematically minded women and men for tomorrow's society?

A major weakness is in its model of learning and in the content to be taught. "It is very bad to insist that the child keep his knowledge in a simple ordered hierarchy. In order to retrieve what he needs, he must have a multiply connected network, so that he can try several ways to do each thing." In the old *New Math* of which Suppes' approach is a part, emphasis was placed on "the use of formalism and symbolic manipulation instead of the heuristic and intuitive content of the subject matter. The child is expected to learn how to solve problems but we do not teach him what we know, either about the subject or about problem-solving" [Minsky 1987, 238].

MEANINGFUL MATH, DAVIS, AND CONSTRUCTIVISM

This section explores a view of mathematics that stands in contrast to the one represented by Suppes. Mathematics cannot be reduced to a collection of facts and algorithms. Learning mathematics is about the process of doing mathematics and so goes beyond mastering *the facts*. Teaching is also a process and involves developing strategies to enhance children's learning.

Unlike Papert, Davis believes that elementary school math (such as arithmetic and algebra) is a rich area of mathematics. What needs fixing are the topics chosen, the materials used, and the teaching strategies. Davis' reform effort for school mathematics is known as the Madison Project and began in 1956 in Syracuse, New York, at the Madison School. At that time, Davis was a professor of mathematics education at Syracuse University. The Madison Project's vision of elementary school mathematics underlies the elementary school mathematics material implemented on the University of Illinois' Plato computer system in the 1970s.

Between 1973 and 1976 over 100 hours of mathematics lessons for grades 4, 5, and 6 were prepared by members of the Computer-based Education Research Laboratory (CERL) at the University of Illinois. Professor Robert B. Davis directed the group that produced these elementary school materials. *Plato*, CERL's computer system, was designed to be an interactive textbook and was intended to support hundreds of users at the same time, both authors and students. Plato was a time-sharing system where terminals could be connected remotely over phone lines to the central computer in Urbana. The Plato terminal was a plasma panel on which text, graphics, and limited animation could share the screen; it also had audio capabilities. With this ability to intertwine text, graphics, audio, and animation coupled with the promise of accessible and affordable technology, the computer as an textbook was establishing the need for multimedia. Like the Macintosh with *HyperCard*, Plato made its authoring tools both powerful and accessible to a wide variety of people.

The following is an example of Plato math using the features of the Plato terminal. Tom is learning about fractions. In this lesson he is asked to share jumping beans among three children on the screen. He does so by touching the screen at key places. (Plato's graphics, animation, and touch input provide an engaging context for him. The problem itself reflects the Madison Project's philosophy of introducing children to new ideas through experiences they have already had. Most children have had to share a pile of things with others.

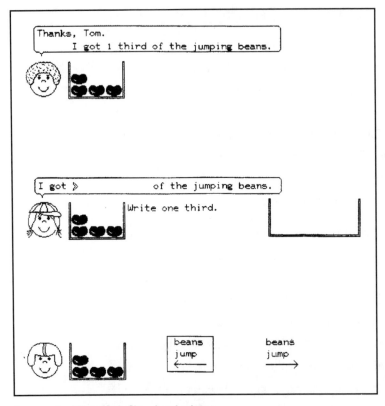

An example of Plato Math: Share jumping beans.

DISCOVERY LEARNING

Davis is identified with a pedagogical approach called *discovery learning* or *discovery teaching* by which he means "that a teacher might call attention to a problem, but the task of inventing a method for dealing with the problem was left as the responsibility of the student" [Davis 1992, 339].

The Madison Project encouraged children's mathematical development through *discovery*, by building up a set of activites around specific topics and by having a repertoire of teaching strategies. Davis' constructivist foundations support this approach. In doing mathematics, which is creative and complex, what you think as you do it is very important. After all, only you can build up your internal structures. Discovery learning is one approach that teachers can use to help you build your internal structure and also help you correct this structure when it is wrong.

One of Davis' favorite examples of children's discovery in the mathematics class-room is of Kye, a third grader, who invented his own algorithm for subtraction. The story points to a relationship between the creativity of children and the sensitivity of teachers. Because his teacher was open to children's originality, Kye felt confident enough to stand by his method.

Kye's Story

Kye Hedlund, a third grader in Weston, Connecticut was being shown how to subtract by borrowing or regrouping if necessary.

...in Weston, Connecticut, a third grade teacher was discussing the subtraction problem

$$\begin{array}{r} 64 \\ \underline{-28} \end{array}$$

and was saying something of the familiar sort "I can't take 8 from 4, so I regroup the 64 as 50 plus 14" (or whatever), when a third grade boy named Kye interrupted.

"Oh, yes, you can! Four minus eight is negative four...

$$\begin{array}{r} 64 \\ \underline{-28} \\ -4 \end{array}$$

...and twenty from sixty is forty

$$\begin{array}{r} 64 \\ \underline{-28} \\ -4 \\ 40 \end{array}$$

...and forty and negative four is thirty-six."

$$\begin{array}{r} 64 \\ \underline{-28} \\ -4 \end{array}$$

40

36

[Davis 1965, 3-4]

What was so exciting about this story is that the teacher did not know this algorithm, nor did others in her town. This was really Kye's discovery and he was a third grader. This story is one among many that Davis has collected over the years to demonstrate that mathematics classes can be creative rather than routine. By routine, he means that you do what you're taught to do, the way you are taught to do it. Kye's story shows a creative use of mathematics where Kye used techniques that had not been taught to him.

Two Teaching Strategies

Two teaching strategies guided the development and use of the mathematics materials. The Madison Project teachers adopted a strategy of teaching children new ideas by relating them to things children already know, so children use rods, sticks, cubes and blocks, scales, and other tactile materials or manipulatives, as well as a variety of games in the process of doing mathematics. Madison Project teachers avoided telling children facts. Instead they introduced new ideas to children by asking them questions. Not only did this Socratic method give children an active role, but also their answers gave teachers feedback from which they could tailor the lesson to better meet the children's needs.

So, in introducing children to the new ideas of variable and equation, a Madison Project teacher

might write on the blackboard

$$3 + [] = 5$$

and ask something like this:

What can I write in the box that will make a true statement?

This kind of interaction gives the teacher a better idea of… how the student is thinking about the task… than could be gained from telling the student… about what 'variables' are, what 'equations' are, or how either is used. [Davis 1992, 345-6]

Paradigm Teaching Strategy

The Madison Project makes extensive use of the *paradigm teaching strategy*, in which new ideas are introduced through carefully chosen examples. The teacher builds on what the child already knows. For example, one way to introduce fractions is to ask children to share a candy bar or a box of jumping beans with two friends. Children know how to share these things; they have done it often. Then they are told that each child has one third of the candy bar. Thus, the teacher relates mathematics to what the child already does and the image remains sharp for the child.

For Davis, learning mathematics is learning a creative process, so teachers need to devise strategies that draw on what children already know and help them reassemble what they know into a new *frame* as they acquire new knowledge. In the Plato math lessons Sharing Jumping Beans is a good example of this teaching strategy.

Teaching by Challenging the Learner

Another teaching strategy of the Madison Project is to *challenge* the children. In a sense this is the opposite of the paradigm teaching strategy because children are asked to do something they have never done before, then they are given help in the form of examples, hints, and so on. A well-known example of a Madison Project challenge is the "Guess my rule" game. It can be played in different ways; here is one way. A child suggests a number to which the teacher responds with another number computed from a rule, such as $x + 2 = y$, where the child's number is x and the teacher's number is y. The game continues (other children can suggest other numbers) with the class trying to formulate the relationship or *rule* formally as an equation.

This strategy builds on the belief that children are challenged by their environments everyday; thus, they should be challenged in the math classroom, where a rational explanation will eventually come forth. The process exemplifies how it is possible to meet challenges and sometimes solve a problem without help. Often, as the problem is resolved, children see that this new knowledge was developed out of what they already knew. An important aspect of this strategy is that the challenges interest the children and are based on Davis' accumulated knowledge of children and mathematics.

THE MADISON PROJECT AND TEACHERS

The Madison Project material was developed in collaboration with some very gifted teachers. It has been a collaborative effort of a team of people with Davis as the catalyzing and organizing agent. The group in the 1960s consisted of leading mathematics educators from the United States and England. Over the years he has collected ideas from colleagues around the world. He has allied himself with those thinkers who believe that it is possible to talk about what goes on in children's heads. By the mid-1960s workshops had been given to over 18,000 teachers.

For the Madison Project teachers, mathematics is a creative activity and they want to share that experience with children, so they encourage children to invent their own ways of solving problems. They personalize classroom activities by using the child inventor's name as the name of the newly found method. They celebrate children's novel ways of solving problems. At the same time they guide children in their learning by giving them manipulatives to play around with and to use as learning tools. Teachers have been active participants in shaping the Madison Project.

For Davis, teachers can be compared to actors who function in two different capacities: by "presenting well-rehearsed lines scripted by someone else" and by improvising or "responding in a new and unique way to a new and unique challenge" [Davis 1979, 58]. The Madison Project activities were "carefully crafted and carefully tested" and "intended to be taught with careful fidelity to the *script*." Teachers were given extensive training toward this end. At the same time they were given experiences to encourage their own spontaneous behavior.

These materials were created through direct observation of classrooms, descriptions of actual interactions with children, and analysis of content being taught. Thus,

Davis developed his math materials from his own classroom teaching and from the work of others reporting on their teaching experiences.

Given all of this, there is a lot for a teacher to know; this vision of mathematics education can be realized only if teachers can own it. As Davis, himself, is aware it is easy to misunderstand this new way of thinking about mathematics. Teachers inadequately prepared and with a rote learning mindset will find that their students "discover it wrong." The Madison Project teacher knows a lot of mathematics and a lot about children's thinking. The problem is that we "cannot tell teachers all they need to know about teaching" [Davis 1967, 60].

The computer represents a possible way out of the problem. If characteristics of the best teachers can be implemented into well-constructed programs, some aspects of a good teacher's strategies can be captured and reproduced. The intention would not be to replace teachers, but to give them some concrete examples of math topics and strategies and allow them to step back and observe the children's interactions, understandings, and misconceptions. As a tool in teacher education this kind of environment would be invaluable.

DAVIS AND PLATO

In 1972 Davis was enticed to the University of Illinois (after the death of Max Beberman, another mathematics education reformer). Davis took on the responsibilities of running University High School and also directing the development of a computer-based elementary math curriculum. He brought many of his Madison Project colleagues with him to Illinois. He also acquired people who were already on board at the University of Illinois' Computer-based Education Research Laboratory (CERL). The university's Plato system was under the evaluative eyes of the Educational Testing Service. A demonstration of Plato was carried on from 1972 to 1976.

Over 100 hours of instructional material were developed for the Plato elementary math curriculum. This was necessary so that children could have half-hour lessons on the computer five days a week. The computer as an Interactive Textbook took on a new dimension that was clearly distinguishable from print material and from the original CCC material. It is a startling predecessor to many of today's multimedia applications for education.

A slight detour is necessary now so as to better understand the significance of this demonstration. In the next few sections I will discuss the computer system itself.

Plato: The System

When the demonstration started in 1972, the time-shared computer could support a maximum of 10 terminals in operation at the same time. By the close of the demonstration 500 terminals could be in operation at the same time.

The Plato system was designed to be a large time-shared or multiple-user environment for teaching courses, whether they be chemistry or computer or reading or mathematics. It was expected to handle different teaching styles as well. It was meant to accommodate the needs of university, community college, high school, and elementary school teachers. It was to allow a flexibility of expression so as to handle rote learning teachers as well as discovery learning teachers.

Graphics and the Plasma Panel

By 1972, Professor Don Bitzer built and debugged the plasma panel terminal for use over phone lines to the main computer in Urbana. The plasma panel was a major breakthrough at the time because of the cost factor. Text and graphics appeared on the same screen, albeit, in a kind of orange phosphor against a black background. Or, you could have an orange background with text and graphics in black! (The screen dimensions were 1024 x 1024 pixels.)

A limited animation was possible with sprite-like objects about the size of a quarter. There was a shape editor in which you could make new shapes. Other features of the plasma panel included a touch-sensitive grid so that the user could select screen areas by pointing a finger at the screen. There was a remote-access projection system for microfiche; a feature of the plasma panel was that it could be used as a microfiche projector. (This was not used in the elementary math courseware.) There was also a remote-access audio system for "automatically selecting segments of speech or music under computer control." (This was used primarily in the reading component of the demonstration.) There was also an e-mail system as well as on-line help features. I point this out to show that the development of multimedia enviroments has been an inticement for computerists for a long time. Integrating different media into a system and allowing users to control them was not only a Logo dream but also a Plato dream.

Plato Elementary Math

Plato math demonstrated that the computer as *Interactive Textbook* can "place adequate emphasis on the creative and exploratory aspects of mathematics, and on various forms of social cooperation and interaction." Previously, the fear had been that the computer as an Interactive Textbook would "increase the emphasis on rote arithmetic, and diminish the role of creative heuristic analysis" [Davis 1977, 65].

Previously, many people "visualized one child, working alone at a terminal, cut off from social contacts with other human beings, so that their social development was retarded, and (perhaps worse) they did not learn to talk about the work they were doing, so that they failed to develop a 'meta' language for discussing mathematics" [Davis 1977, 64]. The opposite happened with Plato. Typically, within a classroom there was a cluster of four terminals. The children talked to Plato as they interacted with it, they talked to the other three children at the stations, and later they shared their experiences with their other classmates. Furthermore, the courseware encouraged sharing ideas and celebrating diverse solutions to a problem. Children talked while they were at the computer and afterwards about the mathematical activities they engaged in with Plato.

The courseware was divided into three strands: (1) whole number arithmetic, (2) fractions, mixed numbers, and decimals, and (3) graphs, variables, functions, and equations. The strands were fondly called whole numbers, fractions, and graphs. Strands are made up of lessons, which vary in style. Some are more didactic than others; some present new ideas; others offer practice.

Examples from the Plato Math Curriculum

The elementary math material relied heavily on graphical representations. The computer was an interactive textbook with graphics that changed as a result of the children's actions.

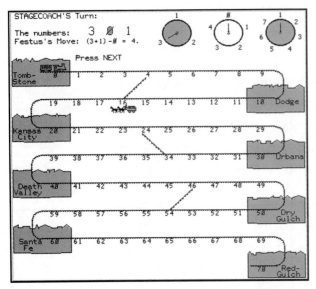

An early example from the Plato Madison Project: *How the West Was One + Three x Four* from UCI.

Example of Discovery Learning by a Challenge Strategy

In the following lesson from the whole numbers strand called *How the West Was One + Three x Four*, children discover the rules of the game as they play it. West captures the excitement and challenge of Madison Project's "Guess my rule" games. One of the most appealing of the Plato lessons, West is a two-player board game based on *Chutes and Ladders*, a very popular children's board game. The pieces are a stagecoach and a train engine. Players compute moves by using each of the numbers generated randomly on three spinners located in the upper right of the screen. There are certain dangers (players can bump one another) and bonuses (short cuts and jumps) in the game. The train and stagecoach race one another through eight towns with 71 board positions. The focus is to make a move by forming a true statement using each number once. Each arithmetic operator can only be used once. Parenthesizing is encouraged to group the operations.

West is commercially available on today's personal computers [Bonnie Seiler, Sunburst Communications, Inc. 1994; Macintosh version]. On the following page is a screenshot from this version.

Imagine you are playing the Sunburst version of West, and you are given the numbers 1, 2, and 4. Landing on 4 is the cool thing to do since it is a shortcut to position

17. So a reasonable goal is to get the sentence to equal 4. However, there are other sentences that might be better or acceptable. For example,

4 x (2 - 1) = 4

2 x 1 + 4 = 6

4 x (1 + 2) = 12

2 x (1+ 4) = 10

Wow! This last sentence is the one because if your piece lands on a town you get jumped to the next town.

Children aren't given a long list of rules to learn; instead they learn by playing the game. The game itself uses familiar ideas such as spinners, arithmetic, and Chutes and Ladders. The teacher doesn't have to stand over the children, but can be a resource for making optimal moves. (In the Sunburst version, the computer can act in this capacity.) Plato can also be a player and then set an example of how to play the game. Timid chil-

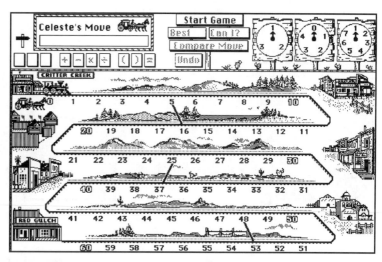

An example of *How the West Was One + Three x Four* from Sunburst.

dren who do not like to compete against other children enjoy playing against Plato. Moreover, some children might concentrate on making legal expressions out of the three numbers while others might focus on developing game-playing strategies; they might do this without any explicit instruction from the computer or the teacher.

In a sense, this game is a fancy way of getting drill-and-practice. Its duality of purpose, a drill-and-practice machine on a familiar topic and a challenging way to learn new things has made it particularly attractive. The game captures a certain spirit of doing mathematics and of being in a culture of doing mathematics that Davis particularly likes. It attracts people of all ages. The way many people found out about the game is through word-of-mouth.

Example of Discovery Learning by a Paradigm Teaching Strategy

In the Plato math curriculum children are introduced to fractions by the paradigm teaching strategy. You have already seen part of the lesson, *Sharing Jumping Beans*. Look what happens if you don't divide the beans fairly. You are reminded to fix the situation.

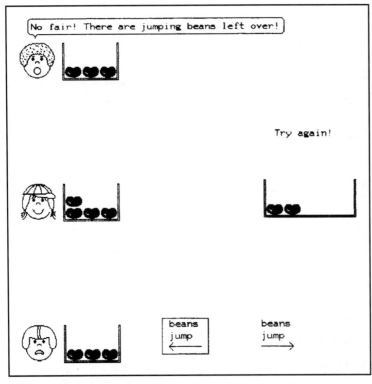

An example of Sharing Jumping beans with beans left over.

Another example, one that feels more didactic, is *Subtraction with Sticks*. This lesson is meant to emulate a Madison Project manipulative experience where tongue depressors are used to represent base-ten. One tongue depressor represents units. Ten tongue depressors bundled together in a rubber band represent tens. Ten such bundles are placed in a plastic bag to represent hundreds and so on. Children thus can physically borrow or regroup by breaking up the bundles into smaller components as needed. Instead of using tongue depressors, this lesson uses sticks. The child can unbundle them as needed. The physical representation of bundles of sticks is eventually stopped as the lesson continues. However, if the child needs help, the bundles of sticks can reappear.

Examples of Education and Entertainment

One of the Plato math lessons from the fractions strand, which was designed by Sharon Dugdale and David Kibbey, is a *Paintings Library*. The example that follows is from the *Paintings Library*. It shows a kind of playfulness. It is an example of children having access to other people's work and using them as models for their own work. This lesson capitalized on a networked environment not so much as a management device but as a showplace. Anyone could save work in this library and anyone could look at the work in the library.

The lesson itself is about fractions. Students can choose a fraction between 0 and 1. Then, using the touch panel as input, the student represents that fraction on a gridded rectangle by painting in the appropriate number of cells.

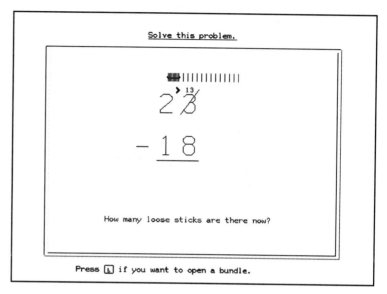

Subtraction with Sticks: an example of regrouping. (UCI)

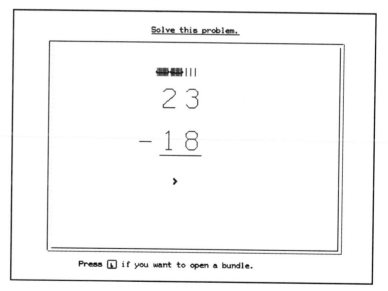

Subtraction with Sticks: an example of borrowing. (UCI)

STRENGTHS AND WEAKNESSES

One of the tasks of the Madison Project was to "devise suitable 'process' experiences, and to give teachers the necessary educational background to cope with the demands of this style of teaching" [Davis 1967, 1: 46]. Now *process* experiences had

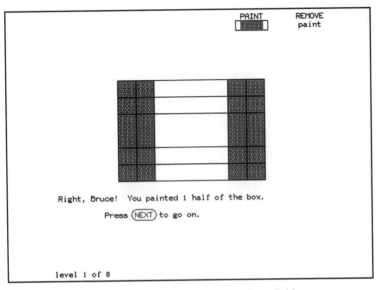

An example from the Plato Madison Project's Paintings library. (UCI)

A second example from the Plato Madison Project's Paintings library. (UCI)

to be found that would make use of Plato's features such as its graphics, animation, and touch input; that could be implemented on Plato; and that would preserve the Madison Project style of teaching. The two Madison Project staff that accompanied Davis to Illinois expected to develop materials in a similar way to their previous experience.

The procedure was developed of having a team of mathematically-competent people and educationally-sophisticated people work out a flexible and tentative lesson plan, try it out with children, discuss it, revise it and polish it, subject it to further trials, and—when it seemed to be in reasonably stable shape— teach it to children to whom it was a new lesson and record the interplay between teacher and children on film, video-tape, or audiotape. [Davis 1967, 1: 47]

The immediacy of the national demonstration, only two years from the inception of the project, and the style imposed by the Educational Testing Service evaluators created conditions under which the material could not be revised, even though actual experience in the classroom indicated places for revision.

After the demonstration, research funds were drastically reduced. The commercial costs of Plato were still too high to support its use in schools. Bitzer anticipated cost cutting by using cable or broadcast bands instead of telephone lines, but the FCC withheld its approval at that time. Furthermore, the authors retained individual ownership of the lessons they wrote. When funding was cut, many of the authors lost their jobs.

Perhaps, the most impressive part of this curriculum is its overall adherance to an integrity of design. There are certainly lessons that are exceptions. For the most part the exceptions stand out both to the casual observer and the active user. We need more models of this kind. Suppes' CCC material also stands as a monument to design integrity. But the difference here, is that the lessons are not uniform nor are they intended to be. They are based on the Madison Project. Different teaching tactics including drill-and-practice were used for different purposes, but they were all used in the spirit of learning as a creative process for student and teacher. Furthermore, the tactics were used within the framework of two strategies: building on what children already know coupled with challenging children to come up with solutions in new situations through the clever and consistent use of manipulatives.

Another aspect of Plato which needs some attention is the kinds of communications that took place through its remote tie-ins. The kinds of stories that circulate about the Internet were typical of the Plato communications where children and adults might be playing chess with one another or discussing issues of the day and not distinguishing age differences. These were informal, out-of-school experiences and often took place after hours, in non-peak time. The children in school had less opportunity to chat with the outside world, but they did use Plato during lunch, before school, after school, whenever there was free time. Records of their use of the strands indicated that many of them spent more than half an hour a day at the computer.

Davis, himself, is no longer adapting Madison Project materials as interactive lessons on a computer. The reasons for this were several: He had to run a high school as well as teach student teachers and he wanted to focus on high school. The politics of the situation at the end of the demonstration period made it unlikely that the material would be revised. The funding stopped and it would have required considerable funds to revise the material.

Today, Davis is based at Rutgers University where he is again videotaping children and teachers doing mathematics, Madison Project style. He continues to use computational ideas to talk about children's mathematical misconceptions and to champion innovations, especially computer innovations that children can use and manipulate in their mathematical activities. He continues to influence teachers and offer them models of constructivist practice through videotapes and his writing.

WHERE IS PLATO NOW?

Bitzer spent many years sorting through all the red tape involving the university and the lesson authors. By 1992, a company called NovaNET was formed with the rights to the Plato technology, including its courseware. (Bitzer is part of NovaNET and a professor in North Carolina and thus no longer on the University of Illinois faculty.) NovaNET, based in Tuscon, with the main computer in Urbana, now markets Plato and courseware to schools and colleges. Although the courseware has been revised, it maintains the look and feel of the original lessons. The *Jumping Beans* lesson used the touch panel and is no longer part of the courseware even though the *Paintings* lesson is.

NovaNET, using IBM clones or Macintoshes as delivery stations, is a private network. The people on it all access the same system through cable connections. The computer in Urbana contains all the lessons, the management system, and records of the students' performances. The advantage for the user is that bugs can be fixed quickly without additional costs due to delivery of the changes. The advantages to the company are ones having to do with control of the products. There is less likelihood of software piracy and so forth.

- Logo is a programming language, a computer culture, and a multimedia environment meant to help children learn in a natural way through rich formal and informal experiences.

- The environment provides concrete objects for children to think with and the culture offers models for talking about their play and constructions. The language allows the children to expand the worlds of these objects. Turtles are examples of such objects.

- Powerful ideas from computer science, such as naming things so that you can talk about them, procedurizing, and debugging, are made readily accessible to children in the Logo culture.

- Children can work on projects or problems—not exercises—with Logo. Their work is not bound by a class period and, in fact, the children might spend several weeks on a project.

- Logo research has always included testing ideas with children and making revisions based on feedback from such experiences.

- Drill-and-practice is seen as a clear example of the computer as an Interactive Textbook and acts like a very individualized and patient teacher who will lead a child at his or her own rate through a curriculum by a series of planned exercises.

- Drill-and-practice to teach elementary school math started as a university research project. Within three years it was converted into a commercial product. Research studies continue to improve and support the curriculum.

- The delivery system consists of the detailed organization of the subject matter and the sophisticated management of its dispersement.

- The system represents a behaviorist's analysis of the subject matter and good teaching strategies.

- The Plato elementary math project started out as a large-scale implementation. Over 100 hours of lessons for grades 4, 5, and 6 were created within less than 4 years.

- Plato Math represents an attempt to mold the computer as an *Interactive Textbook* to a constructivist's demands for learning to be based on children's everyday experiences.

- Discovery learning through Socratic dialog, a paradigm teaching strategy, and student challenges underlies the lesson implementations.

- Graphics is essential to the lesson material and the student interactions with the Plato elementary math system.

CD—ROM Edutainment

A girl reads from a computer screen, *"Mandalay, in northern Myanmar, was built in 1857, by King Mindon to fulfill an ancient prophecy that a center of Buddhist teaching would be built on the sight."*

"That doesn't give us any clues," says the boy to the girl.
"Let's phone the crime net then," says the girl.
"We're running out of time. Maybe we don't need the clue to find the crook," says the boy.
"We don't need it if we're sure he's in Malaysia, but he could be in Indonesia too."

"I don't know. Let's call the crime net," says the boy, as he selects a computer notepad entry. An official-looking report then appears on the screen. It reads, "Suspect reported monkeying around in the Borneo Rainforest with gibbons and orangutans..."*

"Borneo?" asks the boy.
"No clue, I'll look it up in the book. Borneo... Borneo... page 549... 549... 549. Here it is! Uhhhh... it says it's in Indonesia AND Malaysia. We still need another clue," says the girl.

"No choice, let's ask the musician," and with that, the boy selects another entry on the computer notepad. A cartoon character appears on the screen and says, "He promised me he'd have a ball on the island of Bali."

"Bali... page 549... Here it is! It's Indonesia!" says the girl.
"All right! Let's travel!" says the boy.

This brother and sister team, ages 10 and 12, have been spending the afternoon at the computer playing and learning with **Where in the World Is Carmen Sandiego?**

BACKGROUND

For years, children's games have lived outdoors in playgrounds or around kitchen tables at board games with dice and little wooden pieces. For years, children's stories have lived between the pages of books or in the imaginations of campfire storytellers. Today, children's games and stories still live in those places, but they also can be found on computers that offer a world of multimedia. Learning geography, history, or science while catching computer cartoon thieves is becoming as common as climbing a tree. *Pointing and clicking* at *hot spots* or *buttons* on a computer screen are becoming as common as turning pages in a book.

* To offer entertaining educational multimedia experiences
* To be a commercial success
* To establish tie-ins to films, books, television programs

goals

EDUTAINMENT : WHERE EDUCATION AND ENTERTAINMENT MEET

Today, the world of multimedia games, stories, and activities is a place where education and entertainment meet. It is a place that many have come to call *Edutainment*—a place that asks children to enjoy what they are learning with a combination of sound, animation, video, text, and images. By simply using a computer mouse to *point and click* on a particular picture, word, or button, stories and information come alive on a computer screen. Selecting a picture of a cat might offer an animated romp ending with a loud "meow." Selecting a word might offer a definition with additional text. Selecting a button might offer a view to a new room to point and click at new images and words.

Children can interact with characters in ancient fables or new original poetry. They can wander through animated reference materials that explain the scientific principles behind a zipper or a nuclear reactor. They can play games that take them back in time, out in space, or across the world. Edutainment offers children a way to wander through stories, information, or games at their own pace and in their own way. They can connect ideas in paths they choose, or investigate one particular idea among many.

No, this is not a world in which children can be authors of their own stories or games. This is a world in which they can wander freely among characters, places, and information that *others* author. This is a world that approaches information as an *Interactive Textbook*. Some would say children are best left to create their own worlds, rather than being confined to what paths others create. This is perhaps the equivalent of suggesting that children's books and toys are not necessary, because children can

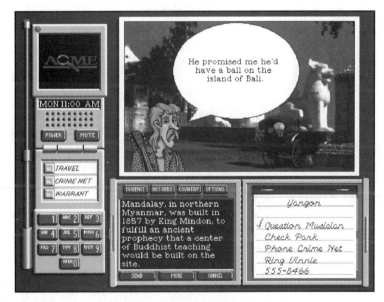

Example screen from *Where in the World is Carmen Sandiego?*

write their own stories with crayons or build their own games with blocks. To the contrary, children (and adults) need models to explore, to learn from, to take apart, and to understand. Once these models have been digested, children can go on to create their own multimedia experiences with authoring tools designed especially for them (see Chapter 4).

Children's Edutainment has become immensely popular and commercially success-ful with parents, teachers, and children. In the past, however, teachers and parents did not see the importance of Edutainment. They did not see how children's every-day play experiences could be a tool for learning. Educational researchers and psy-chologists have written extensively about the benefits of play as an integral part of children's learning. Professor Howard Gardner, a noted psychologist and researcher at Harvard University, has pointed out, "A child's play has its purposes: greater mas-tery of the world, more adequate coping with problems and fears, and superior understanding of oneself and one's relationship to the world … (in play), the child is free to experiment, to order, and to reorder objects, to try new combinations, to prac-tice, refine and ultimately master his actions.…" [Gardner 1982]

L.S. Vygotsky, a well-known Russian psychologist and researcher, also discussed the importance of play when he said, "The influence of play on a child's develop-ment is enormous…. The motivating nature of *things* for very young children is (considerable)… a door demands to be opened, stairs to be climbed, a bell to be rung…." [Vygotsky 1978]. Professor Marvin Minsky, co-founder of MIT's Artifi-cial Intelligence Laboratory, and a founding Professor at the MIT Media Lab has also pointed out, "Enjoyment, which has been banished to the realm of the enter-tainment sciences, may be the most powerful influence of all on how each person learns." [Minsky 1986].

Only recently have words such as these become accepted among the mainstream teaching community. Professor Robert Davis was one of the first educational comput-er researchers in the 1970s to demonstrate the power of bringing children's everyday play into the classroom. With the Plato Madison Project (see Chapter 1) he integrat-ed children's real life experiences (e.g., sharing a candy bar, playing *Shoots and Lad-ders*) into a mathematics curriculum. At a time when it was fashionable to use the computer to present glorified flashcards with numbers and words, Professor Davis offered children games with pictures and numbers. Today's multimedia Edutainment is a descendent of Professor Davis' approach to teaching and learning.

THE BUSINESS OF EDUTAINMENT

Edutainment is most commonly found on CD–ROMs which can hold up to 650MB of sound, images, text, animation, and video. CD–ROM Edutainment is part of a larger group of commercial multimedia software called *CD–ROM Titles*. These titles range from the *Southern Living Cookbook* to *Tank Commander* to *Plan Ahead for Your Financial Future* to *Dr. Health'nstein's Body Fun*. CD–ROM titles are as diverse as any collection of books for adults and children can be. However, when most people think of multimedia, they have come to associate it with Edutainment. This is perhaps due to its enormous commercial success and the extensive publicity given to it, throughout the news media.

Many industry analysts point to children's Edutainment titles as having fueled the success of today's growing commercial multimedia industry. In 1994 alone, over 50 million CD–ROM titles were sold, which was triple from the previous year's estimates [*New York Times* 1995]. According to the Software Publishers Association, over $1 billion worth of educational software was sold in 1994 [*Investors Business Daily* 1995]. Predications from analysts suggest that this trend will not let up thanks to the sales of new personal computers which all contain CD–ROM drives as standard components [*Indelible News* 1995].

It is no wonder, then, that people see multimedia Edutainment in bookstores, toy stores, computer and software retailers, catalogues, and on-line. Edutainment CD–ROMs are a big business. There are CD–ROM tie-ins to our movies, Saturday morning cartoons, and even our dolls. CD–ROMs range from IBM's *Hyperman* to Brøderbund's *Carmen Sandiego* to Mattel's *Barbie*. Some of our best-loved animated characters all now star in Edutainment CD–ROMs: *The Lion King*, *Casper the Ghost*, *Snoopie*, *Winnie the Pooh*, and *Peter Rabbit*.

The commercial multimedia industry has become a complex, ever-changing business to follow. As multimedia developers, we must understand not only the creative and technical aspects of the development process, but also the business of Edutainment. Movie producers have partnered with software companies; television companies have joined forces with toy manufacturers; and book publishers have bought software developers. All are in pursuit of that killer title which will make millions.

These unlikely partnerships are becoming the norm for two main reasons. Software developers are looking for *content* (e.g., movies, books, art exhibitions, television shows) to transform into an interactive multimedia experience. *Content providers* (e.g., museums, publishers, television, and movie studios) are looking for technical expertise to develop new products. In the old days, software developers created tools for people to write, draw, or compute numbers (e.g., paint programs, word processors, spreadsheets). Now it is much more common for software developers not only to create these tools, but to use them as well. Today's multimedia development companies no longer can survive with just two programmers hacking in someone's garage. They need people that understand visual art, music, sound effects, narrative storytelling, and content research,—not all previously a part of what we knew in the past as *software development*.

EDUTAINMENT CHALLENGES

You would assume that thanks to this growing new industry, children, parents, and teachers must now have access to an enormous number of quality CD–ROMs. Unfortunately, this is not the case. Instead, we have a staggering number of CD–ROMs to wade through, to find what is truly exciting. There are numerous multimedia Edutainment titles with little or no content, with annoying sounds, with boring animation, with too much or too little text, and with little flexibility to access the information that is needed.

Robyn Miller, one of the creators of *Myst*, a bestselling multimedia game for teenagers and adults, characterized the many challenges of multimedia development in this way: "The problem is, how do you create a non-linear story that's still a real story? You literally have to let people within a certain area go in any direction they want. If the area is too large, the person can become completely lost and not even know a story is happening. But if you confine that area a little bit too much, people can't go where they want and lose interest." [Sterngold 1995].

This is the fence that multimedia developers sit on every day. We must find that balance between immersing users in a point of view or narrative and enabling users to shape their own unique experiences. Numerous user interface questions arise when looking for that balance. For instance, there is the question of how many options, buttons, or *hot spots* to create. How many are too many? How many are not enough? Can users wander around the information (e.g., lin-

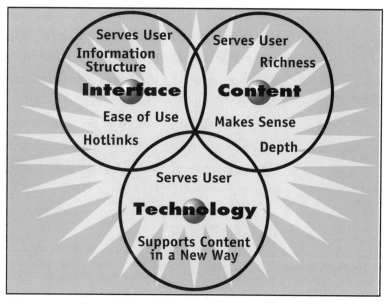

Diagram of interface, content, and technology issues.

early, hierarchically, randomly) in ways most comfortable to them? Can users find what they are looking for efficiently and easily using word searches, topic lists, or image maps? Does the interface enhance the content, or does it just get in the way of the information (e.g., too confusing, too slow, too hard to use)?

Besides the challenges of developing an interface, we as multimedia authors must consider the content of the multimedia experience. We must ask ourselves, does the content offer enough richness and depth to be interesting to users again and again? Does the content serve a purpose for users (e.g., children, teachers, parents)? A crucial question that must be asked in developing specifically for Edutainment is, how much "edu-" to offer versus "-tainment?" In other words, is there interesting, accurate information offered in a way that's engaging and enjoyable to learn or is the information a layer sitting on top of a *shoot'em up* game? On the other hand, if the multimedia experience is a narrative, does it go beyond what a book can be? Does it offer animation, video, or text in places that make sense and enrich the narrative content?

One final group of questions that we as multimedia developers must face concerns the technology we choose to present our message. Does the technology fit with the audience you want to reach? Are your users consumers that own CD–ROM drives? Are they connected to on-line services? Can the content be offered best on a CD–ROM, on-line, in a book, or in a video? All are thoughts that must be considered when starting the development process. As you can see, there are any number of questions that you must face as a multimedia author. These questions are not terribly unique to developing CD–ROM Edutainment; they can be asked in developing almost any other current form of multimedia.

THE CLASSICS

Today there exist thousands of CD–ROM Edutainment titles. When trying to decide which few examples to discuss in this chapter, I found myself asking three questions:

1. Which titles clearly represent at least one distinct strength of Edutainment?

2. Which titles represent one obvious style of an Edutainment experience?

3. Which titles have influenced the development of numerous CD–ROM titles by other multimedia developers?

The four examples that follow should answer these three questions well.

In the first example, I will discuss the Living Books Company's *Living Books*. They are simple, animated, interactive experiences based on well-known children's stories. They have inspired thousands of look-alike products from numerous commercial competitors. For me, however, their distinct strength is what can be done with them on and off the computer. Living Books products offer a *Framework* or teacher's guide which suggest numerous activities to explore on various topics. It is rare that commercial Edutainment products (most commonly sold for home use) so thoroughly consider the needs of teachers and students.

The next two examples examine two engaging Edutainment reference titles: *My First Encyclopedia* from Knowledge Adventure and *David Macaulay—The Way*

Things Work from Dorling Kindersley. In the Knowledge Adventure product, children are offered reference information, usually available to older children and adults, in a way that is incredibly intuitive to very young children. It is an excellent example of careful consideration for user interface issues. The Dorling Kindersley product is a unique example of transforming a bestselling book for older children into a compelling interactive experience. It offers humor and stunning visuals which are refreshing qualities not usually found in most reference titles today. In the case of both examples, numerous titles have been influenced by these works.

The last example represents a powerful learning experience in the form of an Edutainment game. Children have been playing and learning with Brøderbund's *Carmen Sandiego* series for over 10 years. *Carmen* has been so popular with children, parents, and teachers, it has spurred an enormous number of Carmen-like CD–ROMs as well as television shows, board games, and more. Not only is *Carmen* an excellent example of a playful learning environment for children, but it is also an outstanding example of how to expand one software product into a solid commercial business.

All of the examples are in part responsible for the incredible growth of the Edutainment industry in the last 10 years. I call them the *classics* of Edutainment.

EXAMPLES

These multimedia products offer users a wealth of information, entertaining stories, and quality visual, audio, and interactive experiences. They have been developed by companies well-respected not just for one product but for many. Much can be learned from the strengths and weaknesses each product has to offer.

THE LIVING BOOKS COMPANY: LIVING BOOKS

Hi, I'm Little Critter. Welcome to Living Books. To have the story read to you, press this button. To play inside the story, press this button. (Music begins and Little Critter starts to dance. He waves his arms, jiggles his belly, kicks his legs, all, while waiting for you to choose a button.)

[Living Books Company, *Grandma and Me*]

Welcome screen of the Living Book, _Grandma and Me_.

In 1991, a 12-page animated book named *Grandma and Me* quietly propelled Brøderbund into the center of the multimedia industry. Brøderbund brought to life a simple children's story with interactive animation and sound. *Grandma and Me* became the first commercial *Living Book*. There were no control panels, no video, and very little text, just charming illustrations that came to life at the click of a mouse button. Three *Living Books* later, in January of 1994, Random House book publishers and Brøderbund Software formed a partnership: The Living Books Company [Schlichtig 1995a].

Today there are 10 Living Books in all, whose titles range from Mercer Mayer's *Grandma and Me* to Marc Brown's *Arthur's Teacher Troubles* to Dr. Seuss's *ABC*. In each case the simplicity and elegance have enchanted millions of children and adults at home and in school. To wander through the stories, you simply move the mouse and click on an image on the computer screen. If that image is *hot*, a short animation will appear (e.g., select a chimney and a puff of smoke will rise; select a character and it will talk; select a word and it will be read aloud). An average of 10 *hot spots* can be found in any given screen.

Children (as well as adults) have a wonderful time exploring screen after screen to discover where each hot spot is and what it does. There are no roadmaps to what is hot; children must discover what is there. The youngest ones are stunned that they can actually make something happen with a simple press of a mouse button. The many young people that I have observed have loved *Living Books* because they feel as if they're "making their own cartoons." What I found most interesting, is that children love to select the same hot spots over and over again, long past the time when many adults have grown restless or bored. I have seen this same love of repetition when children watch a classic Disney video, such as *The Little Mermaid*. They can watch this video 43 times in one month before they grow tired and move on. It seems children love familiarity. It is a way for them to be comfortable learning what is new. However, they do not like it when *adults* ask them to repeat the same task over and over; but if *they* are at the controls, children love the experience.

While no formal assessment study has been done on how children explore each screen, Mark Schlichtig, the originator of *Living Books* and now the Creative Director of the Living Books Company, has observed hundreds of children playing with Living Books. What he has consistently found is that different age groups of children pick different hot spots. For example, four- to six-year-old children love to point and click on the words. They like to hear the words

An example screen of the Living Book, *Grandma and Me*.

and they like to form sentences. For the most part younger children select the words in the order they are found in the Living Book's text, while older children (seven years and up), who have mastered their reading skills, tend to jump around the sentences, selecting words and forming sentences of their own. Schlichtig has noticed that young boys tend to create the "grossest" sentences by randomly selecting certain words [Schlichtig 1995a].

Another observation Schlichtig has made is that adults seem to select different hot spots than children. For example, in *Grandma and Me*, there is a dog lifeguard who sits on a tall chair. Adults never seem to select the lifeguard chair, but children

● This is the story of the Tortoise and the Hare. The Tortoise was a friendly fellow who moved at his own slow pace. The Hare was a busy person who was always on the move.

An example screen from the Living Book, *The Tortoise and the Hare*.

always do. It is too bad because the Living Books designers created a wonderful galloping chair to enjoy. (I have to admit, being an unfortunate adult, I never saw the galloping chair until Mark told me that story!) The designers at Living Books take very seriously the kid-testing process they do with each screen page. When a few pages are developed of any given Living Book, they are kid-tested. Usually the testing offers a few surprises for product designers. For example, when children selected a hot spot in *The Tortoise and the Hare*, they were unhappy to find that the Hare ran out, read a newspaper, then crumpled it up and left it on the ground. Many children felt that the Hare was littering. So Schlichtig and his colleagues added a hot spot animation. Now, if children select the crumpled newspaper that the Hare has left behind, the Tortoise says, "Hey Hare, did you forget to recycle that paper?" [Schlichtig 1995b].

Since 1989 Schlichtig and his colleagues at Brøderbund, and now at Living Books, have been creating animated Edutainment. Back in 1989, Schlichtig was an unknown artist who had a great idea for a product. He presented his idea to the management at Brøderbund, in the form of a prototype *Living Book, The Little Monster at School.* They not only liked the idea, but also made also him a product designer and Creative Director for all *Living Books.* Since that time Schlichtig has been joined by upwards of 30 people with talents ranging from animation to sound to content design. For the most part, the traditional book authors (e.g., Marc Brown, Mercer Mayer) whose work has been adapted for the computer contribute minimally. Some have a few suggestions for hot spot animations, but in general they let the staff at Living Books steer the project [Schlichtig 1995a].

A recent addition to all of the Living Books products has been the *Living Books Framework.* These teacher guides suggest various ways that Living Books can be integrated into classroom activities. Developed by three former and present classroom teachers, these materials suggest everything from language arts activities to math, science, and music tie-ins. They offer possible thematic units to study when using Living Books (e.g., the ocean, grandparents, siblings, fables). For example, in *Arthur's Teacher Troubles*

An example of a *Living Books, Framework* worksheet.

Arthur has a difficult time with his sister. Therefore, children can use Arthur as a starting point to explore the theme of siblings. They can create sibling scrapbooks, role play disagreements with siblings, determine the percentage of siblings children in the classroom have, and read such books about siblings as *Waiting for Baby* or *My Brother John* [Ray 1994].

My favorites are the wonderful activity sheets that children can use to color Arthur, create their own puppets, or write their own stories in place of where the book's text was. These activities offer open-ended creative learning experiences for children. Their approach suggests that the *Interactive Textbooks* of Living Books can be an *Expressive Medium* to explore ideas ranging from our ocean to our grandparents. What is also quite useful for teachers is the volume of papers given in the overview section. They discuss other classroom teachers' experiences with technology. It is rare that such extensive educational materials are created for Edutainment CD–ROM products which started out for home use.

According to Lucinda Ray, a former classroom teacher and now the Education Product Manager for Living Books, the idea to create these types of materials was

An example screen in English of the Living Book, *Grandma and Me*.

An example screen in Spanish of the Living Book, *Grandma and Me*.

inspired by their customer base of teachers. She explained that teachers would constantly be sending ideas and examples to them of what they'd done with *Grandma and Me* or *Arthur*. So often when Ray was a teacher, she would see software and think, "That's neat, but I have 25 kids here... what should I do with it?" Materials such as the *Living Books Framework* offer a wealth of suggestions. Today the Living Books Company continues to listen to their customer base of teachers. *Living Books Framework II* offers worksheets in Spanish as well as English, again thanks to the suggestions of the teachers in bilingual classrooms around the country [Ray 1995].

The *Living Books Framework* is such a strong feature for the Living Books products that in the future I believe these materials should become a software component as well. It would be wonderful if I could type my own words into the actual software and create my own Living Books story on the computer rather than just on paper. Granted this might be more appropriate for older children, but given that many of them will have grown up on *Grandma and Me*, it would be an excellent activity. It would also be wonderful to see all of those Framework activity sheets on a disk so teachers can print out what they need, how they need it, and when they need it. Many teachers have better access to their own classroom printers than they do to a copy machine in the principal's office. In addition, it would also be rewarding to see annotated bibliographies with on-line references as well as books. Books are important tools for learning (this is stressed throughout the teacher-support materials), but in the future the Internet will be an important resource as well.

KNOWLEDGE ADVENTURE: MY FIRST ENCYCLOPEDIA

Welcome to My First Encyclopedia. It's a cool place to learn. A place where kids teach kids about things that are important in our world.

[Knowledge Adventure, *My First Encyclopedia*]

Since 1991 the staff at Knowledge Adventure has been creating *cool places* for children, as well as developing the underlying technologies for the authoring of them. Among other things, the staff at Knowledge Adventure has developed a proprietary compression technology which enables them to fit an enormous amount of media on one CD–ROM or a set of floppy disks. They have also developed a 3-D software technology that creates 3-D still images and movies using a standard PC and 3-D glasses. These technologies have enabled Knowledge Adventure to develop such popular multimedia Edutainment as *3-D Dinosaur, Isaac Asimov's Science Adventure,* and the *Adventurer* Series [Armstrong 1994; *CD–ROM Today* 1995; Knowledge Adventure 1995].

Besides its unique technological strengths, Knowledge Adventure has developed important ties to the world of media content (e.g., books, movies, television) thanks to a year of partnerships with various industry players. In the summer of 1994, Knowledge Adventure established an alliance with Random House (the same book publisher that started the Living Books Company with Brøderbund) to create Edutainment reference products for children. Also that summer, Knowledge Adventure established a creative relationship with Steven Spielberg to develop creative content for new products. In addition, Knowledge Adventure has named a new president, Ruth Otte. She was previously the president of Discovery Networks, which manages the cable Discover Channel and Learning Channel [Orban 1994].

With this diverse set of collaborators, Knowledge Adventure has recently developed some exciting new Edutainment products. One title which has redefined the *look and feel* of a multimedia encyclopedia is *My First Encyclopedia*. It throws away the traditional interface of layered windows, pull-down menus, and buttons in favor of a *tree*. Similar to the Living Books' *hot spots*, a tree of knowledge is offered to young children to explore and enjoy. In this tree there are children, animals, terrariums, swings, tree-top telescopes, and underground hideaways. By selecting any of the branches, the tree's children (*video kids*) guide young users to information about the stars, the food we eat, how our body works, the transportation we use, and more.

This simple visual interface was first developed by Roger Holzberg, director of Knowledge Adventure's Think.Games group. When Holzberg began his research, he went to daycare centers and preschools looking for children's input. He asked all the children he encountered, "Where do you most like to play after you go home from school or daycare?" Their most common replies were, (1) "play outside" and (2) "climb a tree." Holzberg took this information to heart and with his staff developed a tree of knowledge for young children ages three to six [Holzberg 1995].

In *My First Encyclopedia* there is little text for preschoolers to struggle with; instead, there are video kids that explain ideas and lead activities. An enormous amount of video is packed on this CD–ROM, undoubtedly due to Knowledge Adventure's video compression technology. The graphics and video are professional quality which reflects Holzberg's extensive background in Hollywood film writing, producing, and directing.

A tree of knowledge in *My First Encyclopedia* by Knowledge Adventure.

Having observed a number of young children using *My First Encyclopedia*, I can say that children seem to love pointing and clicking their way through the tree. It takes the youngest children (of three years) some time to understand the connection between selecting a part in the tree and the "learning area" activities they end up exploring (e.g., selecting the roots offers information and activities on how the earth works, selecting the topmost branches offers information

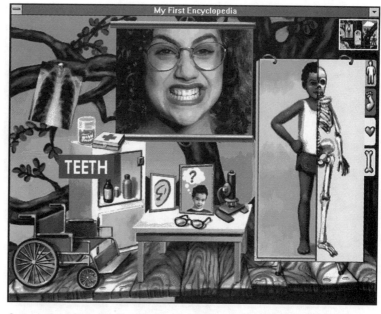

An example of the medical area in Knowledge Adventure's *My First Encyclopedia*.

and activities on astronomy). Once young children are in a particular learning area, they seem truly engaged, especially with the video kids that give them information. Occasionally, when one of the video kids gives an explanation that is longer than a minute, children seem to lose interest. Young users also seem to grow restless if they have spent most of their time listening to the video kids explain things, rather than working with the software's puzzles, coloring or drawing tools.

I found that the biggest strength of *My First Encyclopedia* was the variety of activities children could interact with. Children can explore the tree and learning areas. They can wander among maps, terrariums, scrapbooks of animals, and space-age control panels. There is an impressive number of ways to find information without reading screens full of text. Holzberg explained that the only reason the product offers a typical index was because parents, not children, wanted one [Holzberg 1995]. (I assume parents needed to feel comfortable that they, too, could find information in the software.)

An example of the art area in Knowledge Adenture's *My First Encyclopedia*.

Another strength of the product is *The Adventurers*, a software magazine of sorts, also on the CD–ROM. *The Adventure*rs gives children a way to meet numerous children from around the world. In a way, it's a digital kids club made up of Knowledge Adventures' young users (that also recently became available over the World Wide Web). Children can select among various video clips of other children, such as the clip of David from Long Island, New York: "My name is David and I will be eight years old in September. This is my LEGO Island and it took me a long time to build." [*My First Encyclopedia* 1995]. I found that the children I observed wandering through *The Adventurers* started to discuss what they would do if they had the chance to introduce themselves. They discussed their hobbies, their animals, their brothers and sisters. I found *The Adventurers* was a wonderful way for children to begin thinking about themselves.

Where *My First Encyclopedia* could be enhanced is in the types of activities it offers children to do. Keep in mind that I am an avowed *constructivist* and do have my biases, but I propose that the product would be all that much more engaging if it offered more open-ended games and activities. Instead of matching body parts or solving picture puzzles, or answering comprehension questions, children could use more coloring book or paint program options. For example, what if children were asked to draw what they'd learned about a particular subject area? What if they could create a slide show using images of places they'd explored on the CD–ROM? What if children could build their own treehouses of knowledge? Perhaps children could collect information and leave it on the tree for others to learn from and enjoy. *My First Encyclopedia* is such a strong product, that with a few additions, older children could benefit from this multimedia experience as well.

DORLING KINDERSLEY: DAVID MACAULAY THE WAY THINGS WORK

"Welcome to my workshop. As you can see, it contains a number of ingenious inventions. I've studied them all with the help of my loyal assistant the Great Wooly Mammoth. Everything is arranged on these shelves. I have hundreds of machines here, along with the scientific principles that underlie them, the history of their development, and the stories of their inventors. So be my guest, click on the shelves and explore my collection for yourself."

[Dorling Kindersley, *David Macaulay The Way Things Work*]

The Way Things Work is a very special Edutainment CD–ROM developed from a very special illustrated book by the prize-winning artist, David Macaulay. *The Way Things Work* is one of those rare cases in which a book has been brought to life quite successfully in a multimedia CD–ROM form. So often, using books as fodder for Edutainment titles ends up falling sadly short of what an interactive experience can be. Critics have described these titles as "coffee table books 10,000 pages long" or "interactive screen savers" or even "living wallpaper" [Sterngold 1995]. This is definitely not the case with *The Way Things Work*; and the strongest reason may lie in the original book.

In 1988, David Macaulay published the book, *The Way Things Work*, with Houghton Mifflin in the United States and Dorling Kindersley in England. It took Macaulay four years (with interruptions to finish another book) to create this book with exquisitely beautiful watercolor and ink illustrations, describing (for lack of a better way to say it) the way things work. The book was broken up into four parts: "The Mechanics of Movement," "Harnessing the Elements," "Working with Waves," and "Electricity and Automation." Within those chapters it contained short but numerous text descriptions such as: "Car Engine Crankshaft: Powered by the explosion of the fuel, a piston moves down inside each cylinder of a car engine. A connecting rod links the piston to a crank, which then continues to rotate and drives the piston back up the cylinder...." [Macaulay 1988].

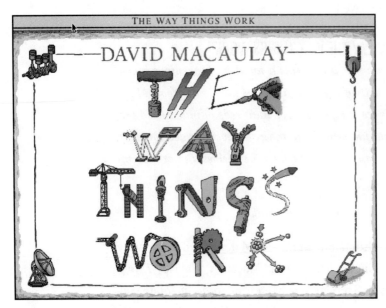

Opening screen from Dorling Kindersley, *The Way Things Work.*

To the uninitiated it may sound somewhat dry, especially for children. But take one look at the illustrations and you will understand the power of this book. It captures page-sized light bulbs, whimsical toilets, and a walk-through toaster, among other things. And every 10 pages or so an endearing character named the Great Wooly Mammoth humorously illustrates such points as heat, printing, pressure, light, and images. For example, one vignette entitled "On Mammoth Attraction..." discusses the magnetic attraction of objects: "One day I happened upon a mammoth whose hair had been lovingly combed... No sooner had the perfectly conferred animal stepped into the street, however, than a combination of litter, loose laundry, and stray cats flew into the air and secured themselves to the startled beast's freshly combed coat. It is common knowledge a well groomed individual is more attractive, but never have I seen this so forcefully illustrated [Macaulay 1988].

What is missing from this very special book? Movement and sound—the pictures just beg to be animated. I want to hear the suction of a vacuum cleaner. I want to see the helicopter's wings move. I want to hear the music of the woodwind instruments and I want to see the hot air balloon fly. Besides that, this book does not lend itself to being read from start to finish. It's a book that gives you short chunks of information. Therefore, I want to jump around. I want to find all the pages with the Wooly Mammoth examples. I want to learn about a laser, then skip over to a compact disc player, then wander over to a record player. These are all things I can do with the Edutainment CD–ROM version of *The Way Things Work*.

In 1992, Dorling Kindersley, a well-respected English publisher, decided to move into the growing world of multimedia. The publisher established a division to re-purpose its vast collection of books into CD–ROM titles. The company approached David Macaulay and asked if it could use his best-selling book, *The Way Things Work*. Macaulay was skeptical at first. He had such success with his book that the last thing he wanted to see happen was to create a spin-off product that would

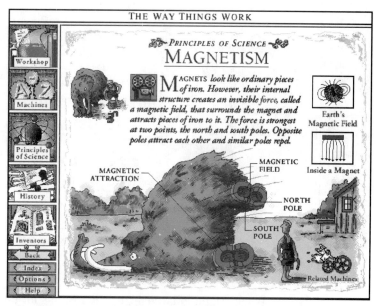

An example of "Animal Magnetism" from *The Way Things Work* **CD–ROM**.

reflect badly on his well-regarded work. The management at Dorling Kindersley convinced Macaulay that they had an excellent chance of equaling the quality of the book, so Macaulay agreed [Macaulay 1995].

For the most part, throughout the two years of development, Macaulay stood back as a slew of animators, graphic designers, musicians, content developers, and software technologists took a crack at recreating the *look and feel* of the book. Artists scanned, traced, modified, and added to the existing artwork. Software technologists developed new extensions to page layout software (QuarkXPress) to create better authoring tools for product designers to use. Animators fleshed out the Great Wooly Mammoth adventures and created 20 "movies" or animated vignettes. Content designers reshaped the chapters into six areas to explore: Macaulay's "Workshop," "Machines," "Principles of Science," "History," and "Inventors." All the while, Macaulay observed the process and was updated regularly. Macaulay saw his role as

The "History of Machines" from *The Way Things Work*.

protecting the integrity of the original book. When all was said and done, was he happy with the CD–ROM results? "Yes, the CD–ROM has an authenticity to it…. It has a strong voice, a continuity, and a point of view." [Macaulay 1995].

I can't agree more. The CD–ROM brings to life great science content, humorous storytelling, and yet offers a flexible path for exploration. Each screen has numerous *hot spots* to press that either offer a textual explanation, an animated example, a humorous Wooly Mammoth movie, or suggestions for other topics to explore. It offers timelines of history, scrapbooks of inventors, and even a workshop to noodle around in. Whatever way you feel comfortable looking for information, it's there for the using.

What's missing? Support materials; there are almost no printed instructions. All of the documentation is within the software product. That is fine, since the product is very simple to figure out how to use. But I do miss additional support materials that offer suggestions of what to do when I wander away from the computer. Should I take a house tour and take apart vacuums, tea kettles, or toasters? Should I build my own microphones, pulleys, or model helicopters? Should I draw and create my own books on the way our bodies work or on the way our minds work? In addition, while *The Way Things Work* is a beautifully done reference title, future Edutainment software environments could be developed which offer children (and adults) the ability to create their own machines on the screen. Children could learn the principles behind pulleys, gears, and motors by playing with them. Granted, these activities may be best suited for older children, but they are possibilities that could offer middle and high school students and teachers hours of learning and enjoyment.

BRØDERBUND: WHERE IN THE WORLD IS CARMEN SANDIEGO?

"Well kid, you've come out of training academy with flying colors, but this is the real thing. Have you got what it takes to be an ACME field agent?… Priceless treasures are disappearing all over the world. We're up against the most devious bunch of thieves we've ever faced… Get out of here and go after Carmen Sandiego and her gang. Who knows what kind of trouble they're causing at this very moment."

[Brøderbund, *Where in the World Is Carmen Sandiego?*]

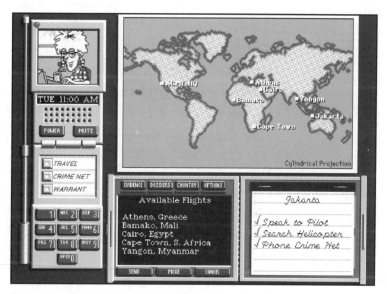

Since 1985, children have been trying to stop Carmen Sandiego and her gang of amusing thieves. Carmen has led children on travels around the world, out in space, and back in time. In the process, children have learned information about geography, history, and astronomy, along with sharpening their skills in problem-solving, information-gathering, and analysis. Today, over five million copies of the Carmen Sandiego series have been sold. Along with this,

An example screen from *Where in the World Is Carmen Sandiego?*

there is a Carmen PBS television series, a Saturday morning cartoon, and enough merchandising of Carmen T-shirts, boardgames, and books to allow anyone to forget Carmen started out as a software product.

This did not all happen overnight. In fact, in 1985 *Where in the World Is Carmen Sandiego?* ran on an Apple II platform and was not an instant success. However, thanks to a lack of product competition (there weren't 10,000 CD–ROM products competing for shelf space as there are today) Carmen Sandiego was given a chance to grow a following. At that time, schools had just begun to buy Apple IIs and needed software, and in the process teachers found Carmen. Back then there weren't any teachers' guides or educational editions; they were to come much later in Carmen's history. Instead, there was simply a software game children seemed to love; enough so, that children went home by the thousands and asked their parents to buy Carmen [Goldstein 1995].

By the late 1980s, Carmen Sandiego had become a phenomenon, with almost two million software copies sold. It was amazing when you consider that Carmen was a black and white software package with few images and a whole lot of text. The product did not really take advantage of multimedia until a few years down the road. What attracted people to Carmen then (and still does) was the entertaining activity of tracking down thieves, and in the process learning some interesting facts about geography or world cultures. Originally, Brøderbund envisioned Carmen as a one-person game to be played at home just for fun. What the developers at Brøderbund eventually found out, was that teams of children enjoyed playing, and not just at home, but in school as a part of a geography, history, or science activity [Goldstein 1995].

Within five years of Carmen's birth, Brøderbund had been approached by PBS to develop a television game show based on the product. It was every software publisher's dream. Carmen went from being a software product to being a business. At that time, few developers saw the business opportunities of tie-ins between television shows, movies, and software characters. Today it is a given. At that time, few people also understood the power of a software series. Today few people design multimedia products without considering what a series might be in the future. In the case of Carmen, there have been as many as seven different products in the series (e.g., *Where in the World...,Where in the USA...,Where in Space...,Where in America's Past...*, *Where in Europe..., Where in Time...*, and *Camen Sandiego Junior Detective Edition*). At one point, Brøderbund offered DOS, Windows, Commodore 64, Amiga, Macintosh, and Apple II versions of the products with an option for floppy disks or CD–ROM. Today, they have begun to standardize on Windows and Macintosh versions to pare down the number of Carmen products in the series. According to Ken Goldstein, Brøderbund's Publisher for Education and Entertainment Products, in the future they intend to enhance a smaller number of products with more media (e.g., video, animation) and more character development [Goldstein 1995].

Why have the Carmen products been such a popular success for over 10 years? It has to do with the actual activity Carmen promotes. It goes beyond the simple interactivity of the *Interactive Textbook* approach. Instead of randomly wandering around information spaces, it challenges children to use information, on the computer and off. Since 1985, children have been looking up facts in such books as Funk and Wagnall's *World Almanac* or

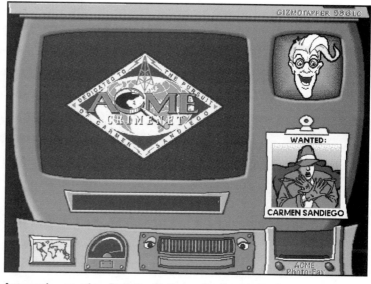

An example screen from Brøderbund's *Carmen Sandiego Junior Detective Edition.*

World Almanac of the USA. (The books are included right in the product box.) The Carmen products combine the on-screen challenges of gathering clues, with the off-screen process of information collection and fact analysis. Older children learn to use indexes, read maps, and decipher statistics. Not only are these valuable skills, but they become just plain fun when trying to track down crooks named "Hugh Stink" or "Robin Banks," using "Gizmotappers," or "ACME Crimestopper gadgets." It's a game; it's a learning environment; it's a simulated world.

What could be done for Carmen products in the future? The addition of on-line information sources (e.g., WWW addresses, gopher sites) could be quite fun and useful since our children in the future will frequently have to research information that can be found on-line. Imagine an on-line version of Carmen where maps, indexes, and statistics can all be found on a Brøderbund World Wide Web home page, updated weekly. Sources at Brøderbund suggest that their multimedia designers are currently exploring the use of local electronic databases. Brøderbund designers are also looking at different methods that would enable children to play Carmen on two separate networked computers.

The addition of expert levels would also be a welcome feature. For those older children (and adults), a more complex game level could be created with more difficult clues to decipher and more complex travels to wander. And finally, adding a product in the future that would enable children to create their own Carmen adventures would be an enjoyable creative learning experience. Imagine giving kids tools to author their own game travels, draw their own thieves, and design their own clues for others to use. Not only would children have a wonderful time designing games, but also they would have a more intimate experience with the information that the Carmen products offer.

STRENGTHS AND WEAKNESSES

Each of the examples I have just introduced to you represents one of the many possible strengths of Edutainment products. The *Living Books Series* represents what can be done with educational materials for Edutainment products that started out in the home. *My First Encyclopedia* represents what can be done with a simple graphic interface for large amounts of information. *The Way Things Work* represents what can be done when translating a book well-suited for multimedia interaction. The *Carmen Sandiego* products represent what can be done when designing into the product, interactivity on and off the computer.

All of these products have many more strengths than just those named, but for me, these are the strengths that stand out. Unfortunately, the majority of Edutainment products on the market today do not offer outstanding support materials, graphically intuitive interfaces, excellent books translations, or activities in books and on the computer. In fact, most offer screens of text, awkward inflexible interfaces, uninteresting content, poorly animated ideas—these weaknesses can abound in Edutainment products. How then can we go beyond these pitfalls? We need to understand what others have done in their development processes and consider what changes are in the wind for the future.

EDUTAINMENT PRODUCT PRACTICES

Among all the companies who have produced the products just discussed, there are similarities in four areas of the product development process. All take an interdisciplinary design approach; all integrate children into their testing and product development practices; all develop underlying technologies to support their multi-media authoring efforts; and all are commercial companies developing products to make money.

In terms of an interdisciplinary design approach, all these companies employ upwards of 30 to 50 people per project at any given time. These people's talents include content development, graphics and animation, sound design, and more. Some companies, such as Brøderbund and Knowledge Adventure, take an active role in partnering with others to enhance their depth, talent, and product distribution. It is interesting to note that professionals with visual design expertise seem to play a leadership role in the multimedia product development effort (e.g., Mark Schlichtig at Living Books Company, Roger Holzberg at Knowledge Adventure).

In the area of testing, all of these companies integrate children as a crucial part of their software development process. Children are asked for their feedback not only near the end of product development, but at the beginning formative stages as well. For example, Holzberg at Knowledge Adventure did research with children very early during the product conception stage. Schlichtig and his colleagues at Living Books work with children on every few screens that are developed. Not only do these companies ask for children's input, but they listen as well. Many animations or activities have been created or altered thanks to the suggestions of children.

- **Thousands of CD–ROM Edutainment titles are being produced**
- **New CD–ROM titles have higher product standards**
- **Enormous product tie-ins to TV, film, and books**

In terms of technology development, all of these companies have created additional software to aid in the authoring process. It is interesting to note that none of the development teams are using unaltered authoring software (e.g., *Macromedia Director*). Each has adapted bestselling authoring tools to suit its needs. The Living Books Company develops its products using *Director*, but then uses its own runtime engine for the final product which the company says speeds up the software interaction. Dorling Kindersley decided to adapt *QuarkXPress*, a page layout program, to suit its authoring needs since all of its printed pages were already in *QuarkXPress*. On the other hand, Knowledge Adventure has done extensive technology development that enables the publisher to add special features not regularly found in other children's titles (e.g., huge amounts of video footage, 3-D images, and video).

The final similarity that all of these companies have is that they develop commercial products that are meant to make money. Some would say that alone may keep them from taking creative risks. Others might say that this may promote taking shortcuts to save money in the development process. Yes, these are the hazards that come with making a commercial product for children. On the other hand, as the commercial marketplace becomes more and more crowded with what I call "me too" products, multimedia developers will *have* to take chances to be noticed. They will *have* to invest money in product quality to make money. Call me an optimist, but I believe that these factors will promote the development of even more exciting, more creative products for children.

THE NEAR FUTURE

If I look into my crystal ball to ponder the near future, I expect to see a number of business, design, and technology changes in the world of Edutainment. On the business side of the world, there will be broader distribution options (e.g., more retail stores, more on-line purchasing, more direct sales catalogues printed and on CD–ROM). This could mean nothing but good for developers who have struggled for shelf space, and consumers who have paid high prices due to lack of sales competition. On the product design side of the world, we will see higher quality standards in terms of entertainment and education. This will lead to higher customer expectations from the home and school markets (a daunting challenge at best). And finally, on the technology side of the world, there will be an expanded number of hardware platforms that will have the capability to run Edutainment software. We can expect that on-line environments and interactive television will be borrowing the lessons learned from CD–ROM development.

What I would like to see in the future, but am not sure if it is in the cards, are a number of product and design possibilities. I would like to see more open-ended Edutainment products; more concern for activities on and off the computer; more *Frameworks* for teachers and parents of Edutainment products; more original content developed just for CD–ROM as opposed to repurposing material that rarely does the content justice. What I would *most* like to see is more integration of children and children's ideas into the development process. So often they are asked for their opinions much later in the development scheme of things, too late to make significant changes. We must remember that these products are for children; therefore, we must respect their ideas as we would any adult user's. We would never consider developing a CD–ROM title for medical doctors without inviting a medical doctor to be a part of the development team. Therefore, why not invite children? As you will see later in this book (Chapter 7), design teams which include young designers offer the most amazing ideas for the future. If we start listening to our children now, we will see more exciting, creative products in the future.

- Today, the world of multimedia games, stories, and activities is a place where education and entertainment meet.

- In the world of Edutainment, children can wander freely among characters, places, and information that others author as *Interactive Textbooks*.

- Today's multimedia Edutainment is a descendent of Professor Robert Davis' approach to teaching and learning (see Chapter 1).

- CD–ROM Edutainment is most commonly sold through bookstores, toy stores, computer and software retailers, catalogues, and on-line.

- Software developers are looking for *content* (e.g., movies, books, art exhibitions, television shows) to transform into an interactive multimedia experience.

- *Content providers* (e.g., museums, publishers, television and movie studios) are looking for technical expertise to develop new products.

- *The Living Books Series*, *My First Encyclopedia*, *The Way Things Work*, and *The Carmen Sandiego Series* all represent the many strengths of Edutainment products.

- The *Living Books Series* represents what can be done with educational materials for Edutainment products that started out in the home.

- *My First Encyclopedia* represents what can be done with a simple graphic interface for large amounts of information.

- *The Way Things Work* represents what can be done when translating a book well-suited for multimedia interaction.

- The *Carmen Sandiego* products represent what can be done when designing into the product, interactivity on and off the computer.

• Unfortunately, the majority of Edutainment products on the market today do not offer outstanding support materials, graphically intuitive interfaces, excellent book translations, or activities in books and on the computer.

• Among all the companies discussed in this chapter, there are similarities in four areas of the product development process:
  • An interdisciplinary design approach
  • An integration of children into their testing and product development practices
  • Development of technologies to support their multimedia authoring efforts
  • All are commercial companies developing products to make money

Space Probe 449

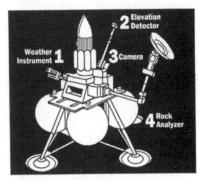

This probe is on or near planet

This probe is equipped with special tools that will tell you about the area around the probe. Use these tools to help you decide which Rescue Plan is best. Remember, it will cost you $500 to access each tool.

What the Tools Do

Weather Instrument: Reports on what the climate is like at the lost probe's current location, including temperature, wind speed, air quality, and water detection.

Elevation Detector: Gives height or depth of the lost probe's current location relative to its surroundings.

Camera: Displays recent events captured by the camera on board the lost probe.

Rock Analyzer: Reports how the rocks found at the lost probe's location were formed.

VIDEODISC
Problem-Solving Simulations

The class of fifth grade students do not sit quietly in their seats. Instead, dispersed around the room are groups of students that animatedly talk amongst themselves. One group of four students stands watching the monitor of a videodisc player.

"I think we passed the part with Emily standing on the scale," says a boy to the group.
"No, I think it's in another part of the story. Let's skip some..." says a girl in the group.
"But can't we do our plan without her weight?" asks another boy.
"Nahh, if Emily's gonna fly the plane to save the eagle, we have to know her weight." replies the girl.
"So if she's too fat, we have to come up with a better idea?" asks another boy.
"Shhhhh, here's the part in the video..." says the girl.

Across the room another group of students is drawing what looks like a map on the blackboard. Near the window four other students are discussing with the teacher how high an ultralite plane can fly. And near the door another group is flying paper airplanes. This is a fifth grade math class.

BACKGROUND

Since the beginning of time, teachers have shared stories and anecdotes with their students to excite and inspire them and to draw them into new learning experiences. These stories have captured ideas, people, and places not found within the walls of the classroom. They have engaged teachers and students in discussions, explorations, and problem-solving activities. Historically, these stories have consisted of verbal exchanges. In the last century, however, books with text and later pictures have become catalysts for classroom activities.

THE POWER OF STORYTELLING WITH THE CHALLENGE OF PROBLEM-SOLVING

Today, in a growing number of classrooms around the world, multimedia simulations have come to supplement conventional books. These simulations excite students about traveling in space, sailing the sea, or starting a business. With this excitement come group discussions, investigations, reflections, and problem-solving. Typically, these complex real-world challenges are confronted when students are shown video footage of a fictional dilemma. In the classroom example described at the start of this chapter, students watched *The Adventures of Jasper Woodbury: Rescue at Boone Meadow*. This simulation experience asked students to save a bald eagle that was shot. Their goal was to find the quickest way to transport the eagle to the local veterinarian. The students were divided into groups to work on the best plan for a rescue. In the process of devising a plan, the students used such mathematical concepts as *distance, rate, and time*. The simulation experience culminated in student group presentations and a class discussion.

These simulations combine the compelling power of telling a good story with the challenge and exploration of complex problem-solving. This type of multimedia experience is grounded in an *Interactive Textbook* approach to teaching and learning. It guides students in their experience, offering a set of preplanned paths to explore, with a right answer waiting for students at the end of their investigations. Yet, this approach also offers an additional exploratory nature, giving it shades of being an *Expressive Medium*. This is perhaps why these types of simulations are so popular with today's teachers. They combine the *safety* of knowing what framework the students will work within, yet there is the *exciting unknown* of how students will approach what is needed to be done.

In the past, simulations were much more likely to be found on a home computer rather than in our classrooms. In the past, only one child might have explored a problem-solving simulation rather than groups of children working together as a team. In the past, text and/or simple line drawings from floppy disks situated children in an adventure, rather than large amounts of video footage from videodisc players. In the past, these simulations might simply have been referred to as *games*. However, recently these simulations have found their way to our schools as educators have come to understand the power of confronting complex real-world challenges. Dr. Elliot Eisner, Professor of Art and Education at Stanford University has pointed out, "…Problem-centered tasks are tasks in which there is a problem to solve, one in which students care … they are invited to exercise the best of their analytic and speculative abilities. When the problem is one that is genuinely meaningful to them, they are much more likely to become stakeholders in the problem rather than people who simply execute the purposes of another…" [Eisner 1994].

goals

- To provide a rich context for multidisciplinary exploration
- To support problem-solving and problem-finding activities
- To facilitate cooperative learning and shared decision-making

Tom Snyder, founder and chairman of a company that has been focused on problem-solving simulations for years, has said, "With children you explain a list of stuff and they only remember some of it. But read them a story about a monster with red socks, and then read it again later and change the color of the socks, and the children will correct you…. Stripping our world of its social context and its story context is a fundamental mistake" [Snyder 1994].

The strength of this real-world, problem-centered approach has not gone unnoticed. Educators, researchers, multimedia developers, and even the federal government have come out in support of these learning experiences. From the National Council of Teachers of Mathematics (NCTM) to the National Research Council on Science Education, all have announced "new standards and guidelines" which support the use of "real-world related problems" to teach math and science [La Folletter 1993; Dublin et. al. 1994; Fox 1995].

Are these *standards* really new? No, these methods have been used for years in and out of classrooms, with and without technology. You need only to refer back to the work of Professor Robert Davis (see Chapter 1) to see the strategy of using children's everyday experiences to teach math. While the Plato Madison Project's computer experience did not include video footage, it did demonstrate that children can learn through informal discovery in a context familiar to them. What is new today is that these ideas are being readily accepted among the mainstream teaching community. And they are being accepted with the use of such multimedia technologies as videodisc integrated within the classroom.

TECHNOLOGY DIFFERENCES

A videodisc is a 12-inch platter, similar to the size of a record album. It contains information that is read by a laser in a videodisc player (which looks a lot like a VHS tape player). Videodiscs can contain one half hour of video per side and two sides can be used. With videodiscs, unlike video tape, it is possible to access any part of the videodisc information instantly. There is no need to *fast forward* or re*wind*; with one button press users can find their way to a specific section of video footage. While videodiscs are similar to CD–ROMs, what differs is how the information is stored on each. With CD–ROMs, the video information is translated into a digital format, unlike videodiscs in which the video remains in an analogue form. Another difference between the two is in the amount of information that each can hold. The surface area of a CD–ROM is much smaller than a videodisc and can hold less video footage. To get around this limitation, CD–ROM developers use special compression software that allows more video to be stored digitally. However, when video is compressed, its quality can be affected. This all may quickly change in the near-future as CD–ROM formats expand to accommodate increasing amounts digital information.

How do videodisc products differ from the commercial multimedia CD–ROM products discussed in the previous chapter? Some may say very little aside from the use of different technologies. However, others point out that the depth of information that is possible with videodiscs due to the quality and quantity of video footage far exceeds what is possible with CD–ROMs today. On the other hand, the video footage is less able to be integrated with the accompanying product software, allowing for very different interactive experiences. Another interesting difference between CD–ROM and videodisc simulations is in the depth and complexity of the product support materials created for teachers and children. With videodisc products a strong focus has always been in offering extensive support materials for classrooms, while with CD–ROM products these materials are far less common.

These differences may perhaps have more to do with *who* the developers of these products are than *what* technologies they are using. In the case of CD–ROM Edutainment simulations (e.g., *Carmen Sandiego*), they historically have been developed by commercial multimedia developers with little classroom experience. In many cases they have more intimate knowledge of the video game or entertainment industry than of classrooms. On the other hand, videodisc simulations have been developed by researchers and/or commercial developers with extensive classroom experience.

EXAMPLES

Three examples of videodisc work that has influenced a generation of multimedia developers come out of the Bank Street College of Education, Vanderbilt University's Cognition and Technology Group, and Tom Snyder Productions. Both Bank Street and Vanderbilt University have a long tradition of educational research and collaboration with classroom teachers. On the other hand, Tom Snyder Productions has a long history of classroom experience. Many of its principle founders and product designers spent many years as classroom teachers. Today, both Tom Snyder Productions and Vanderbilt University are actively researching and developing multimedia classroom simulations. In the case of the Bank Street College of Education, they are no longer involved in developing videodisc work. However, it was with Bank Street's *Voyage of the MIMI* that multimedia classroom simulations became a popular classroom tool. In the sections that follow I will discuss the videodisc work of each of these groups and the influence they have had on our classroom environments.

BANK STREET COLLEGE OF EDUCATION: THE VOYAGE OF THE MIMI

"How are we gonna get out of here? The ship's radios are shot. There's no way we can get help. And the Captain's sick!"

"The boat's in no shape to sail and we haven't got enough food. What are we going to do?"

"We'll take it one day at a time like we have been. That's all we can do."

[*The Voyage of the MIMI* video, Bank Street College of Education]

Back in 1981, before there was a *HyperCard*, before there was even a Macintosh, the Bank Street College of Education began developing multimedia materials for classroom experiences. Spurred on by generous funding from the U.S. Department of Education, Bank Street began developing math and science curricula for older elementary and middle school children. In the early 1980s they did not jump right into videodisc development. In fact, the videodisc materials were not to come until the start of the 1990s. The researchers at Bank Street began by developing a story that would be told on video tape in classrooms and broadcast on PBS television.

The team at Bank Street College, led by Professor Sam Gibbon, did not attempt this alone. They had many collaborators. Professor Gibbon, who was one of the original television producers for the Children's Television Workshop (CTW), brought in his colleagues to help with the original concept stage. They went out and surveyed children to find out what they were interested in. What they came back with were *dinosaurs* and *whales*. The researchers chose whales since they believed it was an easier subject matter to bring to life. Along with this, they believed that the appeal of whales was contagious among adults as well [Bank Street College of Education 1985; Marston 1995].

Once the subject matter was chosen, the researchers at Bank Street
began to look for technical consultants who would help to bring
whales, science, and math into
one exciting world for children.
In their search they discovered
Peter Marston, founder of the
Barn School in Gloster, Massachusetts. This alternative education program used a 72-foot sail-
boat name MIMI to offer hands-on
science and math experiences.
The Bank Street researchers spent

A videodisc image from the _Voyage of the MIMI_.

some time with students and teachers on the MIMI. With this experience they
were not only convinced that had they found a way to bring to life whales at sea, but
they had also found their captain. While Peter Marston had to screen test along
with other potential captains, he eventually became the well-known Captain
Granville [Marston 1995].

What these researchers developed were 13 half-hour video tape segments called
Voyage of the MIMI. Essentially the segments told the story of MIMI, her Captain,
and crew of students and scientists. Together they set out to study whales off the
coast of New England and in the process found their way into a storm, a shipwreck,
and a near-fatal experience on a deserted island. Not only does the crew end up sav-
ing the Captain from hypothermia, but they also find themselves foraging for food
and materials to repair the MIMI. This dramatic adventure shows real science being
done in real-life situations [Bank Street College of Education 1985].

In addition to the video footage, the researchers at the Bank Street College of Education developed print materials and software modules for the Apple II computer.
These support materials suggested ways for classroom teachers to extend the ideas

from the *Voyage of the MIMI* with student readings, discussions, experiments, and activities on and off the computer.

The strength of the *Voyage of the MIMI* was in its compelling story and outstanding production values. Professional actors were hired (except for Captain Granville), an enormous production budget was spent (similar to what a low budget movie costs), and television professionals such as Professor Gibbons, were brought in to develop the project. Along with this, researchers, educators, and professional maritime consultants added to the authenticity of the subject matter being shown. It clearly showed what could be done with a multidisciplinary team of professionals. Together, this team brought the principles of navigation, whales, and ecosystems to life. *Voyage of the MIMI* asked students to consider science in the context of real-world experience, rather than facts to memorize for a test.

However, what *Voyage of the MIMI* did not do was ask students to be participants in this drama. Students watched the adventures as they would read a good book. Students were not asked to help Captain Granville and his crew get off the deserted island. Students were not asked to help rebuild the MIMI. Instead, they had separate software modules that offered activities that were extensions of the MIMI experience. They could rescue a whale, locate sunken treasure, or use sensors and probes to collect information on light, temperature, and sound. All are perhaps worthwhile activities, but do not fully take advantage of the compelling video story. This lack of integration may be due to technology limitations and the time in which the software was developed. MIMI was originally created in the early 1980s, when video tape was a new media to be brought into the classroom. Developers did not consider taking advantage of the video footage in ways we might with CD–ROM today. Even when the video footage was later transferred to videodisc, it still did not offer students the active experience of what today's videodisc simulations do. What MIMI does show is the compelling nature of a good story told well in the classroom. At a time when precious few were using multimedia, *Voyage of the MIMI* offered classroom teachers a way to start.

What has happened since the first *Voyage of the MIMI*? There was a second voyage, where MIMI captain and crew explored Mexico and ancient Maya civilization. The software has been updated to be compatible with Macintosh and Windows platforms. And all of the video footage has migrated to videodisc distributed by Sunburst Communications. In addition, the Barn School and Peter Marston (a.k.a. Captain Granville), sponsor *MIMIFests* throughout the country. Marston and his staff offer hands-on activities for teachers and students that extend the *Voyage of the MIMI* classroom experience. In fact, this is what I find to be the true interactive multimedia experience behind the *Voyage of the MIMI*. These activities are a way to connect the classroom's video, print, and hands-on experiences.

When I asked Marston what advice he would give developers just considering creating problem-solving simulations, he said, "Use half your development budget and put it into teacher training." Why? Because the developers of the MIMI experiences found that *Voyage of the MIMI* was only as good as the teacher facilitating the activities [Marston 1995].

Will there be any more multimedia voyages for MIMI? As of today Marston and others are still fundraising. The government is no longer as generous as it once was and these video-intensive productions are far more costly than any CD–ROM budget today (to the tune of millions). They are also fundraising to refurbish MIMI, so she can continue to challenge sea-worthy students in the years to come.

VANDERBILT UNIVERSITY: THE ADVENTURES OF JASPER WOODBURY

"Come in Hilda! This is Jasper. I have an emergency. Come on in Hilda—or anyone. Repeat, this is an emergency!"

"I read you Jasper. This is Hilda. What's the matter?"

"I'm at Boone's Meadow. Someone shot a bald eagle here; it's hurt pretty bad."

"I copy, Jasper. What do you want me to do about it?"

"Call Emily Johnson; she'll think of something."

[*The Jasper Woodbury Series overview video: Rescue at Boone Meadow*, Vanderbilt University, Cognition and Technology Group]

For over eight years, the Cognition and Technology Group at the Peabody College of Vanderbilt University has been researching, developing, and assessing the value of new technologies in the classroom. This multidisciplinary group includes cognitive psychologists, content experts in math, science, and special needs, as well class-room teachers. *The Jasper Woodbury Series* has come out of a history of investigating the use of video-based problem-solving scenarios to teach mathematical concepts.

The Cognition and Technology Group began their work by using existing video footage (e.g., *Raiders of the Lost Arc*) to pose mathematical problems that would be meaningful to fifth grade students. In the case of *Raiders of the Lost Arc*, students had to use such math concepts as *distance* and *estimation* to find their way back to a rainforest to retrieve lost gold. Researchers soon found this to be a powerful envi-ronment for student problem-solving, but limiting in the breath and depth of mathe-matical concepts they could cover. This experience inspired the Cognition and Tech-nology Group to create their own videodisc prototype called *The River Adventure*. Again the group received excellent results from their research with fifth graders, and in turn received University and outside funding to create a "commercial quality production." While the work was considered outstanding research, it was faulted on its production quality. So, by 1988, with the help of film and video specialists, *The Jasper Woodbury Series* was born [McGilly 1995].

Journey to Cedar Creek, the first of the *Jasper Series*, established a set of criteria or a framework that the Cognition and Technology Group could use throughout the development of the series:

    1. Video-based format

    2. Stories with realistic problems (rather than a lecture on video)

3. Problem complexity (i.e., each story involves at least 15 steps, and in most stories multiple solutions are possible)

4. Generative format (i.e., students must generate and formulate the sub-problems comprising the major problem posed at the end of each story)

5. Embedded data design (i.e., all data needed to solve the problems is in the video)

6. Links across the curriculum (the use of pairs of related adventures in order to allow students to experience and discuss issues of transfer from one environment to the next) [McGilly 1995]

While these design principles were specifically developed for *The Jasper Woodbury Series*, you could easily use these as a generalized set of criteria for most of the video-based problem-solving simulations that are commercially available today. However, one design criteria is conspicuously absent from this list, even though the designers of the *Jasper Series* have come to expect it. This criteria is the support of cooperative or group learning. Researchers expect students to work together in teams to solve a given challenge.

The Jasper Woodbury Series today is made up of six different units: two of which focus students on trip planning (*Journey to Cedar Creek, Rescue at Boone Meadow*), two on business planning (*The Big Splash, A Capital Idea*), and two on geometric problem-solving (*The Right Angle, The Great Circle Race*). Six more Jasper adventures are in development as I write this book. Three will focus on these topic areas and three will focus on algebra. The ones that are commercially available today can only be purchased in pairs or more. The design team at Vanderbilt University felt it would be too difficult for students to generalize the mathematical concepts they used during just one Jasper simulation. By becoming involved in two or more episodes, students would be less likely to believe that one type of problem can be solved only in one particular situation or context [Barron 1994].

Each Jasper episode in the series situates students for an adventure they must solve (e.g., rescue the bald eagle, write a business plan, design a model of a playground).

Students must find the information they need either through the videodisc materials, the supporting computer software, group discussions, or mathematical problem-solving. Students are not passive observers and the multimedia materials are not separate, disconnected modules. They offer an interactive multimedia classroom experience. Of course, the videodisc materials are not as integrated into the computer software as you would hope, but as technologies improve this limitation will disappear.

What is more limiting from my standpoint is that when all is said and done, there still is only one right answer to a Jasper challenge. There is only one way to save the bald eagle. Imagine instead that Jasper and the eagle were stranded on a deserted island. The only way off is by boat. Imagine challenging students to build a boat for Jasper with what is on the island. There would be many ways to go about it. Students could not only take different approaches, but find different answers to a challenging problem. The experience is still a simulation, but one that becomes an *Expressive Medium* and a catalyst for student creativity, exploration, and fun.

Even with its limitations, *The Jasper Woodbury Series* has proven to be a very powerful tool in the classroom. Between 1990 and 1991, over 1,300 fourth, fifth, and sixth grade students participated in a one-year assessment program of the first few episodes of *The Jasper Woodbury Series*. What they found was that, "…at five different sites, located in five different states with varying curricula, and with varying levels of academic achievement, the children in classrooms where the Jasper program was implemented performed better than the children in non-Jasper classrooms on an array of attitude, conceptual and problem-solving measures" [Pellegrino et.al. 1991].

Not only that, but students really liked what they were doing. The researchers at Vanderbilt University have received many letters such as this:

Dear Vanderbilt,

I think it would be a good idea to expand Jasper into different grades. If you did this maybe kids would stay in school, they wouldn't be so bored, and they'd probably find it interesting.

For science maybe Jasper could be on the moon discovering the ruins of extra terrestrials. Or for social studies maybe Jasper could be in Saudi Arabia, in the war....

I hope you consider my ideas, and think them over carefully.

Sincerely,

Michelle..."

[Cognition and Technology Group 1994a]

What researchers also have found was that the, "...assessments were often less pleasant and informative for teachers and students than (was hoped); groups often functioned in a manner that was less than ideal; and we often failed in our attempt to help teachers understand and implement new approaches to teaching and learning..." [McGilly 1995].

Few studies of this scope and size have been performed on today's commercially available multimedia products. This study not only satisfied "traditional educational theorists" thanks to its exhaustive pre- and post-paper and pencil tests, but resulted in a commercial product release. The *quantifiable* results (rather than anecdotal or observable results), satisfied those educators who need studies that show relationships between variables. At the same time, however, the studies also pointed out that it is time to start changing the tests. If the assessment tools for creative new products are extremely intolerable for both students and teachers, it is unlikely that it is a true assessment. The researchers at Vanderbilt University have recognized this and have begun to address this challenging issue.

We, as designers of multimedia environments for the future, should pay attention to this study and the reactions to it by teachers, students, and the educational community as a whole. We must understand that today there is a bias in the educational community for quantifiable testing programs. Thanks to studies like these, many teachers feel comfortable accepting and happily integrating these multimedia simulations into their classrooms. Yet, it is studies like these that students (and teachers) do not like to perform. This is the complex nature of product testing and assessment that we will continue to face as we develop multimedia products for classrooms in the future.

What are Jasper researchers focusing their sights on next? CD–ROMs and more integrated software tools are on their list of research activities. They see that CD–ROMs not only offer them as developers more flexibility in the design of software, but also greater opportunities to reach more students in schools and at home. Researchers at Vanderbilt hope to transfer their videodisc simulations to CD–ROM in the near future. With this, they hope to add to the Jasper software tools already offered to students and teachers. They want to give students more ways to visualize their thinking as they work in teams and more ways for teachers to understand their progress [Cognition and Technology Group 1994b].

TOM SNYDER PRODUCTIONS: THE GREAT SOLAR SYSTEM RESCUE
Big Trouble in the year 2210!

Several valuable space probes have been lost in our solar system. A computer malfunction in the locator devices on each probe left them flying blind. We know that the probes are located somewhere in our solar system, but we don't know where...

Your job is to help locate and repair these lost probes quickly and as cheaply as possible.

[*The Great Solar System Rescue*, Tom Snyder Productions 1992]

For over 10 years, the development team at Tom Snyder Productions has been creating problem-solving simulations. Many of this team are past and present teachers. In fact, Tom Snyder himself, the founder and chairman of the company, first began creating simulations as a fifth grade science and social studies teacher in Cambridge, Massachusetts. Originally these simulations used very little technology (paper, pencil, calculator). As they evolved, so too did the technologies that were used. Eventually, Tom Snyder formed a company to continue what he had started in the classroom [Dockterman 1994].

The focus of Tom Snyder Productions has been to take the *best* of what teachers do and supplement it with technology. Their philosophy seems well summarized by a discussion of their goals for *The Great Solar System Rescue*: "We wanted (to create) a videodisc that offered much more than a selection of movies or a database of stills. We wanted (to create) materials that prompted more than passive viewing and at the same time was accessible to a classroom of students. We wanted (to create) an activity that generated interactivity… human interactivity" [Tom Snyder Productions 1992].

This perspective, while it seems quite obvious, is actually quite unique in today's race to create new technologies. So often, we as technology designers become focused solely on the technology itself. We become enamored with the *newest*, the *fastest*, the *biggest*. We forget about the people using our technologies. We forget that sometimes it is all right for people to focus on people, not the technologies they are using.

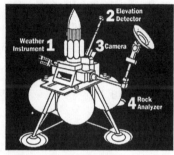

Space Probe 449

This probe is equipped with special tools that will tell you about the area around the probe. Use these tools to help you decide which Rescue Plan is best. Remember, it will cost you $500 to access each tool.

What the Tools Do

Weather Instrument: Reports on what the climate is like at the lost probe's current location, including temperature, wind speed, air quality, and water detection.

Elevation Detector: Gives height or depth of the lost probe's current location relative to its surroundings.

Camera: Displays recent events captured by the camera on board the lost probe.

Rock Analyzer: Reports how the rocks found at the lost probe's location were formed.

This probe is on or near planet

A Lost Space Probe from *The Great Solar System Rescue*.
Courtesy of Tom Snyder Productions

We forget that technologies can be wonderful tools to bring people *together* rather than isolate them. The designers at Tom Snyder Productions have not forgotten these important ideas and have found creative ways to address them in their products.

Tom Snyder Productions began in the mid 1980s to develop such problem-solving simulations as *Decisions, Decisions* and *Choices, Choices*. Still being developed today, these products combine role-playing, classroom debates, decision-making, and real-life dilemmas based on historical or contemporary issues. They focus on topics that include environmental issues, immigration, and even substance abuse. Groups of students are shown an initial dilemma with a simplistic graphic software presentation (e.g., should immigrants be allowed into the United States, and if so how many). Students must decide what they should do through a series of group or class discussions, supplemented with reading print materials prepared for the program. In the support materials there is said to be no *right answers,* but rather different points of view [Tom Snyder Productions 1986, 1991].

Recently, the company came out with a scoring mechanism for *Decisions, Decisions.* At the end of the simulation students are shown a score that evaluates the process of their problem-solving experience (e.g., did they follow the goals they set for themselves). Some teachers and students find this to mean that the simulation's designers believe there are *wrong* ways and *right* ways to make decisions. Some teachers choose either not to use the student scoring or to score the students and later discuss why it is or is not valid. Interestingly enough, however, many teachers have found that the scoring mechanism increased the students motivation and persistence at the simulation. Many times they will run a simulation experience a second time and compare the two scores.

These types of programs have been commercially successful and extremely popular with classroom teachers and students throughout the United States. Since 1992, Tom Snyder Productions has expanded on these types of products and offered videosdisc-based simulations. *The Great Solar System Rescue* was the first in a series of videodisc products now offered. As was the case with Vanderbilt University and the Bank Street College of Education, this work was developed by a multidisciplinary group of professionals. Tom Snyder Productions collaborated with the Chedd-Agier Production Company, a video development group recognized for its documentaries, museum exhibits, and educational multimedia work. Tom Snyder Productions also collaborated on this program with the Jet Propulsion Lab and NASA to assemble the outerspace images for the videodisc. The group also received support from the Massachusetts Corporation for Educational Telecommunications [Tom Snyder Productions 1992].

The Great Solar System Rescue is similar to Tom Snyder Productions' *Decisions, Decisions* and *Choices, Choices*; however, it emphasizes different aspects of the problem-solving simulation. One obvious change, which seems to be a more effective way of grabbing the students' attention is how the stage is set for the simulation activities.

In *The Great Solar System Rescue* the students are first shown quality video footage with music and sound, rather than the *Decisions, Decisions* cartoon drawings and text on a computer screen. Another difference in emphasis is the number of simulation outcomes. In *The Great Solar System Rescue* it is stated that there are *right answers*. While there are many different ways to solve each mission, there still remains only one correct result for the students to find in the end. "The probe is on planet…." If the probe is found

A videodisc image from *The Great Solar System Rescue.* Courtesy of Tom Snyder Productions.

by students, they are congratulated on their expert space skills and are offered the option of attempting another mission. But if a group chooses to go to the wrong planet, the students are told, "No probe here." Unfortunately, this reminds me a little too much of the drill-and-practice software with the words, "Wrong answer try again." Call me a bleeding-heart constructivist, but I would much prefer the possibility of different outcomes that students could explore.

On the other hand, this right-answer approach does offer some very valuable experience in cooperative learning. A continued emphasis in all the products developed by Tom Snyder Productions is on team problem-solving or cooperative learning. The printed materials in *The Great Solar System Rescue* strongly support this focus by offering roles for each student to be: *astronomer, geologist, historian, meteorologist.* Each student booklet contains different printed materials and only by working together can the group solve the mission. The designers at Tom Snyder Productions feel strongly that, "…true cooperative experiences involve ongoing interdependent relationships, shared goals, and shared decision-making" [Tom Snyder Productions 1992]. They feel that simply by placing students in a group does not guarantee that true cooperative learning will occur.

What are the developers at Tom Snyder Productions up to these days? They're making more videodisc simulations. They recently released a *Minds On Science* videodisc series that offers more role-playing experience in science. Students become scientists, presidential advisors, and industry leaders. Biotechnology, environmental issues, biology, and space are among the many content areas of these activities. As it turns out, these products were developed with materials from the Smithsonian's exhibit on *Science and American Life: Science and Society in the United States*. Again these videodisc materials offer another rich experience with a diverse set media.

STRENGTHS AND WEAKNESSES

Today, thousands of teachers in classrooms throughout the United States are using videodisc problem-solving simulations with their students. The most obvious strength of these simulations, as well as the most obvious weakness may not be found in the multimedia products themselves.

THE SIMULATION TEACHER

The quality of the simulation experience is strongly dependent on the classroom teachers. I have seen many cases where, if a teacher is disinterested and does not take an active role in supporting the students' team activities, students fight among themselves or are disinterested in completing the simulation. Students see the activity as only "...one more thing to get through for a grade...." On the other hand, if a teacher is *so* excited with the simulation that he or she must lead *all* the discussions and problem-solving activities, students come to see the simulation as another form of drill-and-practice. The teacher singles out students for the *right answers* and there is no cooperative learning or shared exploration among students.

Yet, on the other hand, I have seen many cases where teachers enabled students to explore the simulation's issues at their own pace and in their own way. Teachers

were facilitators, advisors, and team participants. They nudged students in directions that didn't seem possible to them, they settled arguments when team dynamics
were at risk, and they supplied additional information when the students asked for it.
Teachers used the simulations as reasons to take class field trips to planetariums,
zoos, and airports. And in turn, students were excited, involved, and took an active
role in the subject matter.

Perhaps, this may be the case with almost any technology integrated into the classroom. So often we forget that teachers can be as important an ingredient as the
multimedia technology's user interface or quality of content. Company's like Tom
Snyder Productions have understood this important factor and their support materials for teachers strongly reflect this. The written materials give teachers not only an
understanding of what the product does, but also suggestions for integrating it into
classroom activities.

As you can see, videodisc problem-solving simulations do not stretch or change significantly the activities we have come to know in the classroom. Students are given
problems with a predetermined right answer. This is not terribly surprising since
the best known researchers and developers are firmly grounded in the classroom
experience. While it is important for designers to be well acquainted with the people
and environment they are creating technologies for, sometimes this intimate knowledge may constrain designers from taking risks into uncharted territories.

Critics of these videodisc problem-solving simulations say that they do not go far
enough. They do not enable children to be *authors* of their own environments;
rather, a pre-selected path to travel is defined for the students. The only thing the
students discover is what the software designers have hidden from them. Critics
also point out that this type of multimedia approach generally does not promote student access to technology except in short doses. (Groups of students take turns at
the computer during the simulation process, but rarely get more than a few sus-
tained minutes at the computer. Little time is left for students to gain any expertise in
using new technologies.)

On the other hand, supporters of videodisc problem-solving simulations suggest that they are a compelling way to teach and learn that seem to produce excellent results with very little computing power. When having only one computer in a classroom is more the rule than the exception, videodisc simulations are easily integrated into today's classroom activities and enhance what is already there.

CD–ROM VERSUS VIDEODISC

Another aspect often hotly debated is whether these videodisc-based simulations are any different than what we see with today's CD–ROM Edutainment like *Where in the World is Carmen Sandiego?* As CD–ROMs become more powerful and as common as floppy disks in the future, it is likely that videodisc products will migrate to CD–ROMs. However, today there are still differences between the depth, complexity, and quality of information made available on videodiscs versus CD–ROMs. The extensive use of quality video imagery, as well as support materials specifically created for the classroom, set these videodisc-based products apart from commercial CD–ROMs. This is not to say that today many commercial developers aren't attempting to supplement what they offer to schools. *The Living Books Framework*, previously described in Chapter 2, is just one example.

- Funding focused on new multimedia problem-solving simulations for schools
- CD-ROM spin-offs are in progress for the future
- New on-line and interactive TV projects are being developed

Once these products do migrate to CD–ROMs, a greater integration of computer tools with video-based presentation will hopefully be developed. Currently, the software tools are not emphasized in these products. They feel quite separate from the videodisc materials, which may be more a result of technological limitations than considered design. However, if more use of simulated software measurement tools could be used to examine *crime scenes* or measure *weather patterns*, the simulation experience could be a richer, more complex learning environment. The integration of on-line communications should also be considered in future simulations activities. Imagine working with support materials on the World Wide Web, or working in cooperative teams via email. All could offer excellent ways to share simulation experiences.

In the future, researchers of new technologies (e.g., Interactive Television, Virtual Reality, Immersive Environments) may harness the power of simulation experiences. Tomorrow's multimedia simulations may not be on videodisc or CD–ROM. They may be found in whole rooms people can interact with or special helmets worn on people's heads. Wherever they may be found, simulations are a compelling, powerful way to involve children (and even adults) in exciting learning experiences.

- Videodisc problem-solving simulations combine the compelling power of telling a good story with the challenge and exploration of complex problem-solving.

- These simulations are the catalyst for group discussions, investigations, reflections, and problem-solving activities.

- This type of multimedia experience is grounded in an *Interactive Textbook* approach to teaching and learning. Yet, this approach also offers an additional exploratory nature giving it shades of being an *Expressive Medium*.

- Educators, researchers, multimedia developers, and even the federal government have come out in support of these learning experiences.

- Three examples of videodisc work that has influenced a generation of multimedia developers came out of the Bank Street College of Education, Vanderbilt University's Cognition and Technology Group, and Tom Snyder Productions.

- *Voyage of the MIMI* brought to life the principles of navigation, whales, and ecosystems by telling the story of MIMI and her crew that set out to study whales off the coast of New England.

- Today, *The Jasper Woodbury Series* is made up of six different units: two of which focus students on trip planning (*Journey to Cedar Creek, Rescue at Boone Meadow*), two on business planning (*The Big Splash, A Capital Idea*), and two on geometric problem-solving (*The Right Angle, The Great Circle Race*).

- *The Great Solar System Rescue* takes students out in space to look for lost probes and, in the process, students come to understand the solar system with cooperative problem-solving experiences.

- The quality of videodisc simulation experiences is strongly dependent on the actions of classroom teachers.

- Videodisc problem-solving simulations do not stretch or change significantly the activities we have come to know in the classroom.

- On the other hand, supporters of videodisc problem-solving simulations suggest that they are a compelling way to teach and learn that seem to produce excellent results with very little computing power.

- As CD–ROMs become more powerful and as common as floppy disks in the future, it is likely that videodisc products will migrate to CD–ROMs.

- Tomorrow's multimedia simulations may not be on videodisc or CD–ROM. They may be found in whole rooms people can interact with or special helmets worn on people's heads.

All these shapes
This is what I am

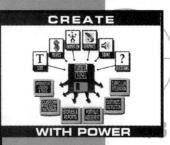

CREATE

WITH POWER

8 = 1/2 =

4/8 = 1/2 =

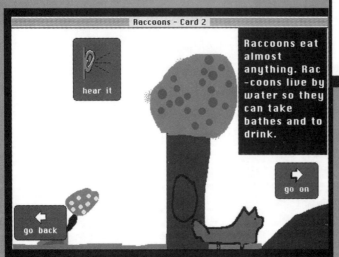

Raccoons - Card 2

hear it

Raccoons eat almost anything. Rac-coons live by water so they can take bathes and to drink.

go on

go back

CHILDREN'S
Multimedia
Authoring Tools

Two girls sit looking at a computer screen.
The one closest to the keyboard types the words,
"PRESS THE FIRST WORD TO HERE"

The other girl asks, "Wait, is that the right spelling?"
Her partner suggests, "Maybe it's H-A-I-R?"
"Nahhh, it's H-E-A-R..." says a third girl working nearby.
"Ohhh..." says the typist as she corrects her spelling.

"OK, now, where do the words go on the screen?" asks
her partner.
"We want people to see them...'cause it would be bad if they
missed hearing the sounds. So... I think the words should go
in the middle."
"...the middle?" asks the girl's partner.
"Mrs. Cushing always puts important things in the middle,"
explains the girl.
"OK, sure..." says the other as she moves the words to the
center of the screen.
"So people read the words, press the button, and it goes to
the next card..."

"How about a dissolve to a baby jack rabbit?" asks one to the other.
"That's cool!"

These multimedia designers are second grade students using an authoring tool called *HyperStudio*.

BACKGROUND

How can children be visual artists, researchers, content experts, interface designers, teachers, and technology users—all in one afternoon? Ask them to be multimedia authors and you will see them consider the design of a screen, question whether a button is easy for another person to use, or discuss what content should be included in a project.

LEARNING BY DESIGN

Children's multimedia authoring tools give young designers the opportunity to create their own multimedia presentations and interactive experiences. Video, animation, sound, pictures, and text can be combined using these authoring tools created specifically for children. With these tools, they can create such multimedia projects as slide shows that feature the growth of a plant, interactive notebooks that highlight sports across Europe, music videos that animate the parts of the body, and interactive simulations that take you back to the time of the Civil War. With multimedia authoring tools, children aren't limited to prepackaged multimedia experiences that someone else designs; they can create their own.

With this hands-on design experience, the relationship children can have with information is changed. Information becomes something to learn and use for a reason, rather than a test. It becomes immediate, intimate, and involving. At the same time, the computer becomes a tool or an *Expressive Medium* for children to explore ideas and subject matter through paths that they choose. As Professor Seymour Papert has said, "The best learning takes place when the learner takes charge" [Papert 1980].

We, as adult software designers, know how exciting it can be to create something for others to use. That is why many of us devote most of our waking hours to staring at a computer screen. We also know how much we can learn about different subject matter when we are designing CD–ROMs on sailing or scientific notation. It seems only fair that we should create tools that enable our children to have these same experiences.

A Second grade student's project created with *HyperStudio*.

Unfortunately, all too often in our classrooms today, multimedia authoring tools become the *thing* to be learned, rather than a tool for creating and learning *other* things. Instead of learning to make a button for the sake of showing how a cell grows, children learn to create a *button* for the sake of learning a computer program. Obviously, this is important in a world that is becoming increasingly dependent on technology, but it becomes a less meaningful learning experience for children. It is as if we are asking them to memorize a list of spelling words for a test on Friday, as opposed to learning to spell words in the process of writing a story of their own. This is not a unique problem in introducing children's authoring tools to classrooms. Many educational Logo researchers have pointed this out as a common difficulty in any environment that gives children and teachers an open-ended tool such as a programming language like Logo [Carver 1987; Papert 1985].

In fact, much of what we have come to understand about children's learning, in the context of designing something concrete with the computer, has come from three decades of Logo researchers (see Chapter 1). Since the late 1970s, researchers have struggled to introduce children to programming and design in a way that supports children's *constuctivist learning* or as Professor Papert now calls it *constuctionist learning*. When children create programs that other children can use to create poetry, geometry, or understand fractions, the path to learning is designed by children for children.

- To provide tools for children to create their own multimedia experiences
- To provide an expressive medium for children to explore ideas and subject matter
- To support the exploration of visual, audio, textual, and interactive design

goals

Dr. Idit Harel, a Logo researcher, recently finished her doctoral work on the impact of this type of learning environment on children. She explored what happens when fourth grade students designed software with Logo to teach third grade students the concept of fractions. In her book *Children Designers*, she discusses the four months and 70 hours of programming the students accomplished: "When children were designing software for fractions they were certainly engaged in mathematical ideas and their representations. But they were no less engaged with the expression of ideas in words (they did writing and reading), in pictures (they did art), and in moving images (they did animation). They were engaged in thinking about teaching... They were engaged with thinking about design... Thus the project was... transdisciplinary" [Harel 1991].

According to Dr. Harel, learning through a design experience has become much more common in the mainstream educational community since the early 1990s. In the past, most researchers and educators were less concerned with learning by design, and either concentrated on developing/using an *Interactive Textbook* approach to software or focused on enhancing programming strategies for the sake of learning to program. In classrooms of the past, that meant using such software that followed the *Drill-and-Practice* model, or using such programming languages as *Basic*, *Pascal*, or *Logo* to teach programming. What happened to change people's approach? Dr. Harel informally polled a group of educational researchers; what she found out was that they believed that the software and hardware technologies had changed to make a difference. New technologies had become more accessible. Many researchers referred to the *Macintosh* and *HyperCard* as the reasons for change. They felt that these technologies offered classroom teachers and children an easier, quicker path to creating more "media-rich" classrooms [Harel 1991].

After reading this, I decided to conduct my own informal poll to see if this was still the case four years later. However, I went to the users on the front lines. I polled classroom teachers in the state that I had recently moved to, New Mexico. What I heard mirrored the results of Dr. Harel's researchers four years earlier. These teachers confirmed that they had moved away from only using a programming language or *Drill-and-Practice* software. More frequently they used the combination of both commercial multimedia software and multimedia authoring tools. Why? They "...now have more Macs in their classrooms," they have

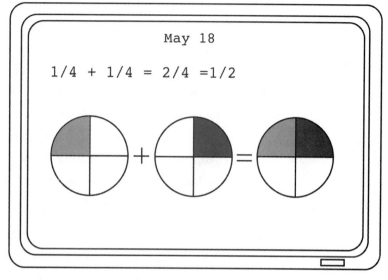

An example of a fourth grade student's fractions project from *Children Designers*. Reprinted with permission from Ablex Publishing Corporation.

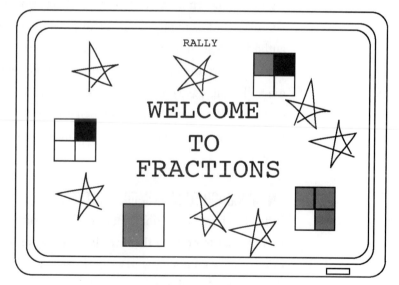

An example of a fourth grade student's fractions projects from *Children Designers*. Reprinted with permission from Ablex Publishing Corporation.

"... authoring software that runs on an Apple IIgs," and they "...feel comfortable with the multimedia tools" [Druin 1995].

On the other hand, many die-hard Logo teachers and researchers would point out that nothing has changed. The Logo community has been actively demonstrating the process of learning through design for years. Many would say that multimedia authoring tools have not been the only catalyst for change. They might also add that in comparison to programming environments, today's multimedia authoring offers less powerful tools for creating truly complex, rich environments. This may well be the case, however, if you glance at today's most powerful commercially available Logo, *Microworlds*; you will notice the influence and similarity to many multimedia authoring environments. (This was not previously seen in Logo before the popularity of such authoring tools as *HyperCard*).

Programming versus multimedia authoring; English language notations versus graphical menus; impassioned technologists could debate the strengths, weaknesses, and similarities until next century. Unfortunately, that discussion will have to wait for another book. Let me simply say that both programming and multimedia authoring offer children the power to create their own environments. While programming languages may give them powerful tools to create more complex environments, authoring tools may give children quicker, simpler paths to begin designing. Today it may be hard to decide where a programming environment begins and a multimedia authoring environment ends. Whatever the case, both are important tools for children, no matter what their style of learning, strength, or weakness. Students can approach the design process in a way most meaningful to them and construct their own paths to learning.

AN APPROACH TO MULTIMEDIA AUTHORING

When teachers first acquire multimedia authoring tools, many times they are uncertain of what to do with them in their classrooms. They know that these tools can offer a powerful new way to explore diverse subject matters, but they are not sure where to begin with these new tools. The written materials that accompany a majority of these authoring tools include *How To* guides on menus and buttons, rather than a discussion of how this technology could be integrated into a learning environment. Therefore, let me take a moment before delving into the chapter's product examples, to give you one model of an approach to multimedia authoring. Some may call it a *whole language* approach, others a *problem-centered* approach, and still others a *constructivist* approach. Whatever the name, it is an example of how one second grade teacher and her students used multimedia authoring tools in their classroom to learn about animals in their local community.

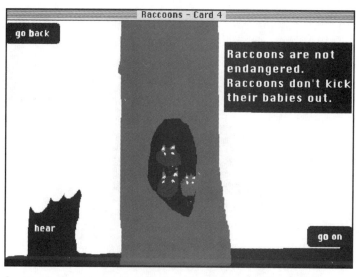

An example of a second grade student's project created with *HyperStudio*.

A southwestern elementary school teacher began by asking her second graders to become immersed in learning about local animals by reading books, examining magazine articles, and observing their local neighborhoods. From there, the children formed teams and selected one animal to focus on (e.g., jack rabbits, bobcats, snakes, porcupines). The teams then wrote research papers to familiarize themselves with their animals. After which, the class discussed how they could teach other people about this information. They suggested

An example of a second grade student's project created with *HyperStudio*.

such projects as quilts, puzzles, puppet shows, masks, and computer presentations. Each group selected one type of project along with preparing for a multimedia computer project. While they worked on their puppets, quilts, and puzzles, the children also began creating storyboards for their computer presentations [Cushing 1995a].

An example of a second grade student's project created with *HyperStudio*.

Each team used the information they had previously found and restructured it for their various projects. For three to four hours a week, over a three-week time period, the children worked on computers with their teacher and classmates. They made use of the school's computer lab with 12 Macintosh LCs, as well as their own classroom Macintosh. They designed screens, added buttons for interactivity, and included sound effects and verbal descriptions. They didn't create multimedia projects that offered multiple paths to information or a tree structure. And they didn't include any video or animation, but these second graders made projects that told a story with all the media and expertise they had. Eventually, they presented their work at an open house for their parents, at a school technology fair, and at a *Sharing Session* with their sixth grade partners. It is interesting to note that usually the sixth graders share with the second graders a particular activity, but in this case, the second graders were the technology experts sharing with their sixth grade partners [Cushing 1995b].

The impact these multimedia activities had on this second grade class reached across many different disciplines on and off the computers. Among other things, these students' art, spelling, technological expertise, knowledge about animals, team design, research, and problem-solving skills all could be seen to improve. How did this second grade teacher know this? She asked her students. Before their unit on animals began she asked them to fold a piece of paper in three parts. On one part she asked them to write about what they already knew about their chosen animals. On the next part she asked them to write what questions they had about their animals. And on the last part, she asked them to leave it blank. When their multimedia activities were completed, she asked her students to write what they thought they had learned. What follows is one example assessment written by a team of two girls who focused on jack rabbits:

What We Know: *rabbits, furry*

We Wonder: *If they have teeth? Mean or nice? Come in difrent [sic] colors? What do they eat? Where do they live? How did they get there [sic] name? If they smell? How old they get? What color are eyes? How long hair gets?*

We Learned: *They have teeth, long ears, jump very far, eat juicey [sic] leaves or stems, got there [sic] name from four kinds of large hares, they live in the Desert, [sic] and grassy areas, in the winter they dig a hole under ground to keep warm, they can have 5 litters in one year and 7 babys [sic] in one litter. They come in difrent [sic] colors, brown, gray, black, and white. When they are born they are born hairless, blind and helpless.* [Cushing 1995b]

After the students had completed this assessment, the teacher led a class discussion. She asked her students, "…why they had done the evaluation in three parts and what it showed. They responded with 'It shows what new facts we have learned about our critters…' 'We found answers to some of the things we wondered about…' 'We can see a difference in what we knew at the beginning and what we know now.' When asked if that is all they learned during the project, there was a resounding 'NO!' Then (she) asked them (what) they had learned besides facts about their chosen animals. A list of those responses follows: how to look for information… where to look for information… how to use the CD to find information and print it… learning to read better… deciding how to choose only certain facts… having patience because it takes time to find things… learning more about HyperStudio… putting buttons where people would notice them… doing the sound over 'til it sounded right… working together and making decisions was hard; sometimes you didn't get your way…" [Cushing 1995c].

This example does not necessarily show the extent to which these children in second grade learned only because of their computer experience. Comparison assessments with teachers who *do not* use technology, or *only* use technology, will have to be left for other educational researchers. However, what can be said about this approach to multimedia is that these children enjoyed learning a new content area and a new way to do research. According to this second grade teacher, "Many things could be evaluated in this project, but most could not be measured by numbers or lists. The process of learning was evident in each step the students took to complete their projects and present them. We all experienced growth in our own way. When I asked the kids about the amount of time spent on this project, if perhaps it was too long, they replied, 'No, let's do it all again with another animal or another topic.' We will" [Cushing 1995c].

Many teachers around the country are discovering this same approach to integrating technology into their classrooms. Unfortunately, for every second grade teacher such as the one I have just described, there are many more teachers who use these same multimedia authoring tools to the exclusion of all other learning tools and media. They leave out the books, art projects, and outdoor research. Along with these teachers, there are also those who instruct children to use authoring tools to design *true* or *false* or *fill-in-the-blank* tests (an activity that to me asks children to build their own jail cells). And there are still other teachers who won't even offer their students a multimedia authoring experience until "they are old enough" (older than second grade).

Professor Papert described this issue with a well-placed metaphor, "Does good wood produce good houses? If I built a house out of wood, and it fell down would this show that wood does not produce good houses?... Everyone realizes that it is carpenters who use the wood, hammers, and saws to produce houses... and the quality of the product depends on their work" [Papert 1985].

Clearly, both *good wood* and *good carpenters* are needed to create quality learning environments for children. The examples that follow are, for me, the *good wood* of children's multimedia authoring tools. This *good wood* can be used by creative carpenters or shortsighted ones. Teachers, parents, product designers, children—we all have the choice of what kind of *carpenter* we can be. We also have a choice of what *wood* to use. If we make thoughtful, informed decisions, the environments we build can be sturdy and nurturing places to learn, work, and play.

EXAMPLES

Multimedia authoring tools for children can be described in three different ways. The first category of tools is what I call *multimedia resources*. These tools offer examples of media (e.g., video, sound, graphics, or animation) that children may want to use in creating their own multimedia experiences. Apple Computer's *Visual Almanac* is an excellent example of one of the earliest multimedia resources commercially available for children and teachers. The next category of authoring tools creates what I call *multimedia presentations*. These tools offer children the ability to develop their own video or slide show presentations. Brøderbund's *Kid Pix Studio* is a well-seasoned application for children to create these types of presentations. Finally, the last category of multimedia authoring tool enables children to create what I call *interactive multimedia*. With a tool such as Roger Wagner's *HyperStudio*, children can create multimedia experiences that offer *their* end-users an interactive experience. All three types of multimedia authoring tools will be described in the section that follows.

MULTIMEDIA RESOURCES—APPLE MULTIMEDIA LAB: THE VISUAL ALMANAC

In 1987, a group of researchers at Apple Computer began developing examples of what could be done with multimedia technologies. At that time, black and white computer screens were the norm, CD–ROMs were experimental, and videodisc players were generally not used with classroom computers. Also at that time, *Hyper-Card* had just been developed; interactive date books and rolodexes were the most common examples of *HyperCard* experiences. The world still wasn't sure what multimedia could do for them. This was the time in which a group of researchers came to be called the Apple Multimedia Lab.

From 1987 to 1992, this lab of researchers included graphic designers, videographers, educational researchers, software technologists, teachers, and content experts. Together they brought a number of new interface strategies to the world of multimedia. These researchers explored what could be done with visual maps or multiple representations of stories and information. They created simulations (e.g., *The Mystery of the Disappearing Duck*) that asked children to point-and-click their way through an adventure. They repurposed existing video footage (e.g., *Donald in Mathmagic Land*) and developed an interactive multimedia experience with it. They even developed a dance activity for young children (e.g., *Dancing Stories*) that asked people to dance with the computer rather than type or mouse click [Hooper 1988].

One of the most powerful tools to come out of the Apple Multimedia Lab was the *Visual Almanac*. This videodisc and *HyperCard* software offered teachers and children a way to author multimedia presentations. While most authoring tools today emphasize the *glue* they give to combine different forms of media, the *Visual Almanac* emphasized the types of *media* that can be glued together. Back in 1987, there weren't the dozens of CD–ROMs that we see today full of clip art, audio, animation, and video (clip media). These researchers in the Apple Multimedia Lab understood that to create multimedia environments, people needed media.

It took from 1988 to 1990 to bring together 12 collections of images, video, and sound on a videodisc that covered everything from historical events to everyday physics. Researchers worked with classroom teachers and children to understand what activities were usually difficult to capture and bring into the classroom. Flying through space, zooming through an electron-microscope, wandering through time—all were important perspectives to capture in different media [Hooper 1988; The Multimedia Lab 1991]. In comparison, the clip media we find today has 14 images of gum balls or two of cows and 10 of bicycles. All may be useful, but do not thoughtfully consider the types of thematic projects that teachers and children explore in a learning environment.

Kristina Hooper Wolsley, an educational researcher and the Apple Multimedia Lab's past director, has pointed out, "The goal we've always had is to try and have people become more articulate about thinking about learning… What we're hoping is that these visual elements lend power to that. Where people can start to understand things they didn't understand before, or get closer to something because they're now controlling it, manipulating it, and composing with it. So we want people to increase the activeness of that process. And so having a resource available will let people engage those things with a little more depth" [Apple Computer 1991].

The *Visual Almanac* included 54,000 videodisc frames of images as well as *Hyper-Card* authoring tools. With the authoring tools students and teachers could collect various media on different subject matter, organize it into a subcollection or scrap book, then bring it into a *HyperCard* workspace that created buttons to represent and play the media clip. Also included was a diskette of activity software. Children and teachers could find already created collections which considered such concepts as time, physics, and motion. Teachers and children could begin by using these collections which suggested directions for them to create their own multimedia collections. Teachers and students using the *Visual Almanac* have created collections that focus on everything from Japan to Martin Luther King, to even the letter "B." One classroom resource specialist collected all the pictures that contained the images that started with the letter "B." In this way she helped her young children understand what the the letter "B" sounded like [Apple Computer 1991].

While the *Visual Almanac* is an exceptional tool for its time, it dates itself due to its videodisc format, limited *HyperCard* tools, and Macintosh-only format. The Apple Multimedia Lab no longer exists and the researchers are no longer updating the material. The *Visual Almanac* is still being distributed today through the multimedia publisher Voyager. However, when I attempted to order the product, a company representative informed me they had none in stock and weren't sure when or if they would have any again. It is a shame. With some updating to the software and technology, numerous teachers and children could benefit when using this tool. By enhancing the interface to take advantage of color, expanding the authoring tools to allow more complex interactivity, making it *Windows*-compatible, and transferring it to CD–ROM, an already strong product could become that much better.

Commercial multimedia developers have also found it to be a valuable authoring resource as well. In the past few years, a number of products have since been developed by alumni of the Apple Multimedia Lab, using the *Visual Almanac*. While these new products are interesting in their *Interactive Textbook* approach, they are far from the groundbreaking *Expressive Medium* of the *Visual Almanac*.

MULTIMEDIA PRESENTATIONS—BRØDERBUND SOFTWARE: KID PIX

"I'm a flying sea otter with a hundred toes and a pickle in my nose and I rock the house… Draw Me." This unique thought comes out of *Kid Pix Studio*, a very unique painting, animation, and slide show product. This program was first developed in 1989 by Professor Craig Hickman, an art professor from the University of Oregon. He initially created *Kid Pix* for his three-year-old son Ben, when he realized how little there was on the computer that resembled crayons for children. Professor Hickman began by giving *Kid Pix* away to people as *shareware*. A fan of the software suggested that *Kid Pix* deserved a wider audience and that it should find a home at a well-respected children's software publisher such as Brøderbund. Hickman took this advice and sent a copy of *Kid Pix* to the product submission group at Brøderbund. This software soon caught the eye of Harry Wilker, now senior vice president of product development. Within eight months, Hickman, along with both a product and a sound designer from Brøderbund, expanded and re-released what the world came to know as *Kid Pix* [Wilson 1995; Hickman 1995].

Today there are numerous multimedia presentation products available for children (e.g., Microsoft's *Fine Artist*, EA's *Kid Art Center*, Micrografix's *Crayola Art Studio*). Back in 1989, few people could guess this type of product was needed. The staff at Brøderbund began to realize this need after their first *Kid's Day*, a weekend testing day that asked 20 children to try-out *Kid Pix*. The Brøderbund staff made sure to offer their testing crew juice and cookies for a break, as well as a *crafts* table with paper, glue, and glitter—just in case their testers got bored. As it happened, no one seemed to get bored. In fact, the Brøderbund staff had a difficult time convincing the children (or parents) to leave when the day was over [Wilson 1995].

Kid Pix was enormously successful and it still is today. Why? I believe it has to do with attitude. It's a program with a sense of humor that enormously appeals to children and adults. It has all the typical paint tools (e.g., brushes, geometric shapes, undo), but it has silly sounds, animated erasers, and more. The sounds you can turn off if you choose, but rarely do because it is too much fun to hear. The paint drips, or the eraser blows up, or the letters talk to you. If you ask children if they're drawing or playing music, many times they can't decide. It's all part of the same experience. Along with the sounds, there are animated effects that blender-ize your movies or crack your page into a million pieces. *Kid Pix Studio*, released in 1994, also offers *Moopies*, *Stampimators*, and *Digital Puppets*. All recent inventions of Professor Hickman's, they turn any child's drawing into an animated image with a life of its own. Not only can children create a multimedia presentation, but just using the *Kid Pix* tools is a multimedia experience in itself.

However, it's not just the sounds or animated tools that give *Kid Pix* their wacky fun. Such creative features as *Draw Me* ask children to draw a silly picture by offering a suggestion in words they see and hear: "I'm a hairy eyeball ten feet tall in the dry hot desert and I'm covered with feathers... Draw Me." What makes *Kid Pix* an exceptional tool is its combination of open-ended fun and guided activities. Often enough, parents will ask children to draw them a picture. But 10 minutes

An example drawing done using Brøderbund's *Kid Pix*.

later, parents will find children coming back to ask what they should draw. With options such as *Draw Me, Color Me,* or *Silly Stamps,* children are given a nudge to get started if they want it. Once off and running, it's amazing how quickly they move on to create their own pictures.

Kid Pix has spawned a slew of competitors with the *loudest* painting tools children could want. Unfortunately, few seem to have found the same balance of the wacky fun

An example drawing done using Brøderbund's *Kid Pix*.

A screen from Davidson & Company's *Multimedia Workshop*.

and simple straightforward tools that *Kid Pix* offers. In contrast, *Multimedia Workshop* by Davidson and Company, is a well-regarded recent entry into the multimedia presentation tools arena. It is a more sophisticated, quieter tool for older children that offers video, paint, and writing studios. Its video tools resemble the professional tools of *Adobe Photoshop* and its paint tools are exceptionally powerful as well. Even its writing studio offers such nice touches as a thesaurus. While *Multimedia Workshop* doesn't offer the full-featured authoring tools that can be found in similar adult programs, it does offer simple, good tools for older children.

What are programs like *Kid Pix* and *Multimedia Workshop* missing? I believe it is interaction—the ability to create a screen with buttons that will lead to many other screens in a nonlinear way. When children create slide shows, the slide shows' viewers aren't offered a choice of skipping to another part or just seeing all the information on one subject. A slide show is what the author has made it to be. There are very few interactive options for its viewers. This is not to say that video, slide shows, and desktop publishing aren't all valuable forms of expression for children. In fact, these multimedia presentation tools offer a design experience that children can learn from. However, they can go further. They can offer more for children than an automated bulletin board. *Kid Pix Studio* and *Multimedia Workshop* are powerful creative tools that ask to be even more powerful and creative in the future.

INTERACTIVE MULTIMEDIA—ROGER WAGNER PUBLISHING: HYPERSTUDIO

In 1988, when the world was just beginning to notice Apple Computer's Macintosh authoring tool, *HyperCard*, the Roger Wagner Publishing Company began offering *HyperStudio* for the Apple IIgs. Many people, including some within Apple Computer, thought that *HyperStudio* would not amount to much. The developers at Apple had made a conscious decision not to create *HyperCard* for the Apple IIgs. The

future of the hardware platform was uncertain and it was questionable whether it was worth the trouble to wrestle with the complex operating system of the Apple IIgs, just to give away the software as Apple had already done with *HyperCard* for the Macintosh. The Roger Wagner Publishing Company chose to wrestle and chose to charge money for the product. Today, there are over 300,000 copies of *HyperStudio* that have been purchased worldwide for the Apple IIgs and Macintosh platforms [Wagner 1995b].

An example of a second grade student's project created in *HyperStudio*.

Roger Wagner, an ex-science and math teacher, started his company with designers, technologists, and fellow teachers in 1978. Today this 16-person company is devoted to producing one product: *HyperStudio*. According to Wagner, "*HyperStudio* is designed as a multimedia authoring tool for kids, poets and grandmothers" [Wagner 1995a]. The product's goal has not been to compete with such professional multimedia authoring tools as Macromedia's *Director*. Instead, it has always been meant to be a tool that a fourth grader could use to create a class project on whales or an interactive family tree with his or her grandmother at home [Wagner 1995b].

HyperStudio is based on the metaphors of *HyperCard*. A screen is a *card*. A *card* can contain images, text, video, and sound. And media can be triggered by pressing a *button* or *hot spot* on the *card*. Many cards linked together form a *stack* on a particular subject matter. The main difference is that with *HyperStudio*, the multimedia author uses icons and graphic menus to create the multimedia project. With *Hyper-Card*, the user must learn, to some extent, a simple English-based *scripting* language called *HyperTalk*. *HyperStudio* is not written in *HyperTalk*, but in the C programming language. That is why developers were able to more easily create versions of *HyperStudio* for the Apple IIgs, Macintosh, and Windows platforms. It is interesting to note that *HyperStudio* does not offer a *HyperTalk* scripting language for children, but a version of *Logo*. This comes out of Roger Wagner's respect for the rich history of *Logo* in the classroom and an understanding of how important a learning tool Logo can be.

Perhaps the biggest strength of *HyperStudio* is that it does run on most of the platforms found in schools today. Children who create *stacks* on the Apple IIgs in school can work on homework using their parents' PCs. It is possible to create a *stack* on an Apple IIgs in the United States and send it to an English classroom to run on an Archimedies computer (a hardware platform common in most English schools). While cross-platform compatibility is an important feature, it may perhaps be a limiting one for the future. Eventually, the types of tools that the Roger Wagner Publishing Company may want to create for more powerful machines will undoubtedly become incompatible with software for older hardware models. This trade-off is something developers must continually wrestle with throughout the lifetime of a popular product.

This cross-platform capability is not a feature found in many of the newer multimedia authoring tools today. For example, *Digital Chisel*, a 1994 product produced by

Pierian Spring software, has chosen not to be compatible with the Apple IIgs. This very popular newcomer to the field of multimedia authoring instead opted to include more power tools to their program (e.g., an extensive library of clip media, hotlinks for text). They also offer (which are not to my taste, but may be to others) a number of templates that automate a user's *true-and-false* or *fill-in-the-blank* testing. In doing so, *Digital Chisel* requires a minimum of 4MB of memory, which is more than most Apple IIgs platforms have. Even using much more than 4MB of memory on my Macintosh (I have a PowerMac with 36MB), the program still ran slower than I expected.

Both *Digital Chisel* and *HyperStudio* have one important thing in common—they are authoring tools that you can use to create an interactive experience. Many authoring tools offer the user tools to create a multimedia presentation, but few offer the ability to create a branching, richly complex interactive experience. *HyperStudio* and *Digital Chisel* give the multimedia author options to design a story with many possible endings. They give the author the ability to create a multimedia

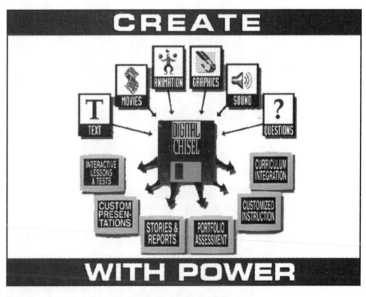

An example screen from Pierian Spring's *Digital Chisel.*

experience that another person can shape when using their stack or project.

STRENGTHS AND WEAKNESSES

Today, multimedia authoring tools can be found in homes and classrooms from Los Alamos, New Mexico to London, England. They are tools that are being used along with books, crayons, and glitter. Their strengths as well as their weaknesses very much depend on how teachers, parents, and children choose to use these authoring tools. These open-ended tools need road maps or models for people to understand what is possible. With multimedia products which lean more towards an *Interactive Textbook* approach (e.g., Simulations, Edutainment), the guidance is built right into the multimedia experience by the developers. This is not generally the case with multimedia authoring tools. While this is an important strength which enables these tools to be an *Expressive Medium* for many different purposes, it is an important potential weakness that must be addressed by multimedia developers of these tools.

MODELS FOR TEACHERS

Included with every multimedia authoring product are *How To* guides on *button-pressing* and project examples of other children's work. While this is extremely useful in jump-starting users, many of these authoring products are missing crucial information. What they don't explain is how teachers and children get from the *button-pressing* to their final projects. How did other teachers organize their classrooms (e.g., in teams, individual work)? What resources did the teachers and children use besides the multimedia authoring tools (e.g., books, on-line information, field trips)? How long did the project take to complete (e.g., one month, one week, one semester)?

- New authoring tools are emerging on the market
- Multimedia authoring tools have been a catalyst for change in classrooms
- Children explore multimedia subject matter on and off the computer

There are magazines and journals (e.g., *Multimedia Schools, Learning and Leading with Technology*) and there are books such as this and others (e.g., *We Teach with Technology, The Technology Age Classroom, The Official Kid Pix Activity Book*) that offer models of what can be done in classrooms. But teachers or parents should not have to depend solely on whatever third-party information sources they can find. Our multimedia products should include suggestions and guidance from the people who may know the product best, the developers.

In the past, developers did not include content experts, graphic designers, or teachers. Today, in almost all the examples I have presented, interdisciplinary design teams are the norm. Therefore, the resources exist within today's multimedia development groups to suggest ways in which to use these new technologies. Written material, videotapes, and on-line tips could all be offered. Perhaps the best examples of this come out of The Living Books Company (see Chapter 2) and Tom Snyder Productions (see Chapter 3). However, developers should be careful not to offer guidance that sounds too much like strict rules as opposed to *rules-of-thumb*. Developers may end up limiting the creativity they are trying to inspire from teachers and children. Given a careful balance, these models can serve to nudge teachers and children in directions they never thought possible.

MODELS FOR CHILDREN

Giving children powerful tools to create their own learning environments is a wonderful start. However, without models or examples of what is possible when using authoring tools, children may not understand the true potential of authoring. This does not mean just showing them examples of what other children their age have done. This also means showing them outstanding examples of what adult authors have done. It would be as if we only gave chil-

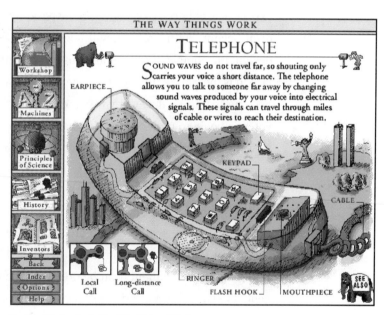

Dorling Kindersley's *The Way Things Work*.

dren their own simple stories to see and read, as opposed to offering them the classic works of Mark Twain or Lewis Caroll. Children will go no further than what they see—they must be given models that ask them to reach beyond what they know into new creative territories

Within the product boxes that contain our multimedia authoring tools today, children are not offered the classics. They may see examples of what others have done in classrooms or homes, but professional multimedia products such as *Grandma and Me* or *The Way Things Work* are not there. These classics need to be shown to children authors, just as much as they need to be shown to adult ones. If our authoring tools cannot offer such examples bundled within their products, then written support materials should point out where the great examples may be found. Ideally, it should not be a product endorsement for whomever a company does business with, but a thoughtful guide to outstanding work.

In whatever way children are exposed to these models, they need to be exposed before they begin to author *and* as they are authoring. At the start of their authoring experience, children may simply be inspired by these outstanding products. As children become authors, they will begin to acknowledge the beauty of the screen design, the complexity of the information structure, or the consistency of the interface. It is the same with any discipline; at first you are awed by the whole, then as you become an informed viewer you come to appreciate the pieces. In other words, once you can begin to understand what happens backstage, you can become a different viewer of the activities on center stage. It is the best way I know of developing knowledgeable designers and developers, that are children or adults.

MODELS FOR DEVELOPERS

What this book as a whole attempts to do for you, as a multimedia developer, is to offer some models to chew on. Once digested, it is my hope that new, more powerful multimedia environments can be created for children. In this chapter, I have presented to you a few authoring products specifically developed for children. What we as designers should not overlook is that there are other powerful models of multimedia authoring tools that exist right under our noses. They are the tools *we* choose to use to create multimedia environments.

Such professional authoring tools as Macromedia's *Director* and Apple Computer's *Apple Media Tool* offer examples of powerful metaphors that can be incorporated into children's environments for the future. For example, in *Director,* the idea of authoring a multimedia project with a *Cast* is a simple yet effective idea. *Director* suggests that a user pull together different media (e.g., sound, images, video) into a visual palette or *Cast* which can be used in different projects. This, to me, is much more descriptive than a list of *Objects* or *Elements* that other programs ask users to define.

Another powerful metaphor that could be applied to children's multimedia authoring environments is the flowcharting feature of the *Apple Media Tool.* Again, it is a wonderfully visual way of authoring. By seeing the connections between the screens you are creating, there is no confusing what information is connected where. By visually drawing lines between boxes which represent screens, authoring complex tree structures becomes easily understandable.

Macromedia *Director's Cast* Window.

This is not to say that all the metaphors you will find in professional multimedia authoring tools would be excellent for use with children. In fact, some of these metaphors are confusing for adults. For instance, I have never found the *Score* metaphor in *Director* an easy way to author. Its

Macromedia's *Director's Score* Window.

scrolling grid interface relies on users to decipher, among hundreds of small squares, what the structure is of an interactive experience that is being created. I much prefer the flowchart connections of the *Apple Media Tool.* The *Score* is a metaphor that works nicely when, in a previous life, *Director* was named *VideoWorks* and was simply an outstanding animation program.

What we as multimedia designers must learn to do is ask why a product has become as commercially popular as it has. Perhaps it became a bestseller because it came out on the market first, or had excellent distribution channels, or even had excellent tools. We must see through market-share and ask ourselves what models make sense to us in what we see. Once we can understand these models, more powerful products can be developed in the future.

THE IMPACT OF MULTIMEDIA AUTHORING

I'd like to end this chapter where I began, with the profound impact that these authoring tools can have. They can be a catalyst for change within our classrooms, as well as a catalyst for learning within our children. Multimedia authoring tools can promote active, creative, meaningful use of information by children. Young designers can learn subject matter as diverse as European culture or southwestern animal life. They can consider representing ideas visually, verbally, or interactively. At the same time, children can become expert technology developers and users. These are the most important strengths of multimedia authoring tools.

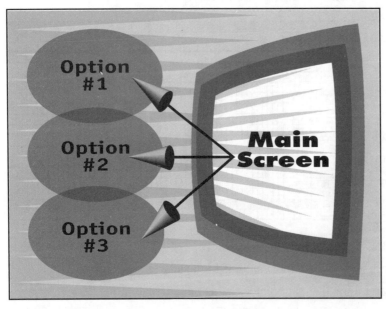

Flow-chart tree structure.

The power that these tools offer for change in the dynamics of classrooms is profound. Since 1985, a research project sponsored by Apple Computer (ACOT, the Apple Classrooms of Tomorrow) has examined the impact of computer saturation on teaching and learning. These researchers associated with universities from around the country studied elemen-tary, middle school, and high school classrooms to understand the effects that com-puters can have on these learning environments. In the late 1980s, researchers' initial reports discussed classroom activities with *Interactive Textbook* software pack-ages. By the early 1990s, they began to discuss how children could learn by creating their own environments with authoring tools such as *HyperCard* [Sandholtz, Ringstaff, and Dwyer, Apple Computer 1990]. What they found was that by using these tools in the classroom, certain activities became more common:

- *More project-oriented work*

- *More group work and cooperative learning*

- *More interdisciplinary activities…*

- *Giving students choices*

- *A reduction of lecturing…*

- *No more "teach a skill, test a skill"…*

- *Introduction of student portfolios…*

- *Less structured classroom—students more independent…* [David 1992]

Therefore, we can see an impact not only in *what* children learn in the classroom, but also in *how* children learn. While this is just one study, it does reflect much of what other teachers and researchers are currently finding in classrooms around the country [David 1990; Collins 1991; Sheingold 1991; Ringstaff, Sterns, Hanson and Schneider, 1993].

Where can this lead in the future? It is hard to say. As classrooms continue to change, teachers and students will expect their tools to develop and change. Hope-fully, these authoring tools will become more powerful, more flexible, and easier to use in the future. Perhaps these authoring tools will not just live behind our comput-er screens, but also be able to control common physical objects or media throughout a room (see Chapter 6 for a full discussion). What is certain is that multimedia authoring tools have a place in our learning environments. They offer teachers a valuable tool to enhance and change their classroom activities. They enable children to express what they know about their world. They offer children and adults the chance to create something new.

chapter thoughts

- With children's multimedia authoring tools, students can create such multimedia projects as slide shows that feature the growth of a plant, interactive notebooks that highlight sports across Europe, music videos that animate the parts of the body, and interactive simulations that take you back to the time of the Civil War.

- By using children's multimedia authoring tools, information becomes something to learn and use for a reason, rather than a test. It becomes immediate, intimate, and involving.

- Unfortunately all too often in our classrooms today, multimedia authoring tools become the *thing* to be learned, rather than a tool for creating and learning *other* things.

- There are three types of multimedia authoring tools:
  1. Multimedia Resources: libraries of multimedia sound, images, video, and so forth.
  2. Multimedia Presentations: tools to create slide shows, movies, animation
  3. Multimedia Interactive Authoring: tools to create interactive nonlinear multimedia

- The *Visual Almanac*, *Kid Pix*, and *HyperStudio* are examples of different approaches to multimedia authoring for children.

- While most authoring tools today emphasize the *glue* they give to combine different forms of media, the *Visual Almanac* emphasizes the types of *media* that can be glued together.

- *Kid Pix Studio* is a paint, animation, and slide show program with a distinct sense of humor that appeals to young children (and adults).

- *HyperStudio* is a multimedia authoring tool that a fourth grader could use to create a class project on whales or an interactive family tree with his or her grandmother at home.

- Our multimedia authoring tools should offer road maps for teachers that include written materials, video, or on-line tips suggesting activities for the classroom.

- Children need models of outstanding multimedia work to inspire them to reach beyond what they already know and explore new creative territories.

- Such professional authoring tools as Macromedia's *Director* and Apple Computer's *Apple Media Tool* offer examples of powerful metaphors that can be incorporated into children's environments for the future.

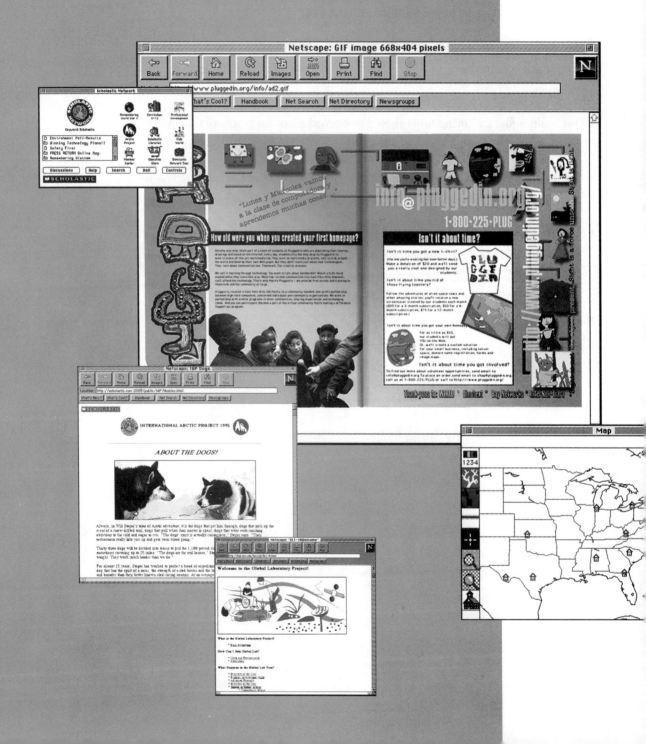

ON-LINE
Multimedia Environments

"...We live in Fairbanks, Alaska. It gets very cold here, but we can stand it, because we're tough. In case you're wondering we don't live in igloos, or ride dogsleds to school. We live in a normal town with McDonalds and Kmarts." (http://ww2.northstar.k12.ak.us/schools/upk/here/here.html)

"...My neighborhood is really terrible now. It's not safe for anybody to walk down the streets of East Palo Alto. There's drug dealers, lots of gangs too. And the drug dealers even leave their drugs hanging around so little kids can just come and either eat it, poke their selfs (sic.) with it, or put it in their mouth. I'm trying to tell you I want all the violence in E.P.A. to stop ..."
(http://www.pluggedin.org/ckp.html)

"...I have been living in Europe for three years now. Our tour ends this summer. Germany is the best place I have ever lived and if I had my way, I would stay here the rest of my life. The best things about living overseas is you get to learn more about foreign cultures, feasts, drive on the Autobahn, and just have plain old fun."(http://192.253.114.31/Web/Web_team.html)

These are the words of students from different parts of the world. All share their thoughts with millions of people, in words and pictures, using an on-line multimedia environment called the World Wide Web.

BACKGROUND

In Minnesota, children are creating *virtual museum exhibits* about space, atomic energy, and dinosaurs for the Franklin Institute. In Finland, children are following weekly journal entries via the World Wide Web, written by true Arctic explorers as they make their way from Russia to the North Pole. In Australia, children are collaborating with children in Russia and the United States as they collect, analyze, and share global information on air quality. What do these children have in common? They all are making use of on-line multimedia environments.

ON-LINE MULTIMEDIA ENVIRONMENTS: WHERE ARE THEY? WHAT ARE THEY?

Thanks to the press, industry, and government hype, on-line environments have been called everything from *cyberspace* to *virtual communities* to the future's *information superhighway*. Mixed in and mixed up in this hype are such technologies as the *Internet*, the *World Wide Web* (*WWW*), and *commercial on-line services*. What do these all mean? Some say that an on-line environment can be a *place* where you can share thoughts and information with vast numbers of people just a computer away. Some say that it is a *technology* that enables you to share information with any part of the world. I think it might be something in between.

A Place

An on-line environment seems to be more than its mere parts. Yes, you use lots of software, on lots of computers, connected together with lots of cables and modems. But that technology can connect millions of people to enormous quantities of information all over the world. Perhaps some of that information is not visually stunning or may be inappropriate for minors, but it feels as if you've wandered into a library the size of our planet. That technology also connects tens of millions of people to tens of millions of others. Perhaps, some of those people may not be whom your mom hoped you would meet, but it feels as if you have an infinite choice all the same. And that technology can enable you to create your own sights, sounds, and words to show to millions of others. Perhaps the world may not need more multimedia, but it's wonderful to feel that if you want to, you can author a multimedia message and publish it to millions of people in just a few moments. Together, these feelings about on-line environments can add up to give you a sense of being in a place with lots of people.

Some have come to call this sense of place *cyberspace*. It is an expression first used in the 1984 science fiction classic, *Neuromancer*, by William Gibson. In his novel he explains, "Cyberspace. A consensual hallucination experienced daily by billions of legitimate operators, in every nation, by children being taught mathematical concepts... A graphic representation of data abstracted from the banks of every computer in the human system. Unthinkable complexity. Lines of light ranged in the nonspace of the mind, clusters and constellations of data. Like city lights receding..." [Gibson 1984]. Today's on-line multimedia environments may not be exactly as Gibson envisioned, but some people believe it's just a matter of time.

goals

- To offer children immediate access to large amounts of electronic information
- To offer collaborative learning experiences with peers in distant parts of the world
- To offer a multimedia authoring environment that can be used to publish to a world-wide audience

Today, it is also not uncommon to hear people refer to an on-line environment as a *virtual community*. This can be a place where people come to know each other not by bumping into one another at a corner store, but by sharing ideas in words and pictures across a computer network. Eric Utne, founder and editor of the *Utne Reader*, wrote the following in a special issue of the magazine entitled *Cyberhood Vs. Neighborhood*: "Community is one of those terms that six people in the same conversation might use differently without knowing it. What is 'real' community? Must it be connected to a place or a neighborhood? Can it exist in cyberspace? Does it?… It isn't necessary to come to a final definition of what 'community' means to understand that in an increasingly fragmented society, it's important to find ways to support one another…" [Utne 1995].

This term *virtual community* seems not only to confuse people, but to worry them as well. As Howard Rheingold, author of the book *Virtual Communities,* has pointed out, "Many people are alarmed by the very idea of a virtual community, fearing that it is another step in the wrong direction, substituting more technological ersatz for yet another natural resource or human freedom. These critics often voice their sadness at what people have been reduced to doing in a civilization that worships technology… (finding) their companions on the other side of a computer screen…" [Rheingold 1995].

I am not sure I can agree with those critics. I happen to believe that on-line multimedia environments can give people an important chance to know one another thanks to their thoughts and creative expressions. All too often, we meet people based on what we look like or what car we drive. On-line environments offer a bigger, wider world based on ideas and interests.

Besides the presence of people within these virtual communities, there is also a landscape, not of buildings or trees, but of information: text, graphics, video, sounds from all parts of the world. Some see this information as an important part of our future. Vice President Al Gore first popularized the term *information superhighway* in 1991. Then, he was a Senator focused on what it would take to build critical resources that could support enormous quantities of information. Since then, the media attention given to those two words, *information superhighway*, would lead you to believe that such a highway already exists. In fact, it does not. The Internet is only a beginning. We are only now starting to pave the way for a highway that can carry all the world's information on-line. Until such a time, a highway metaphor is an excellent one to help us grasp future possibilities. Danny Goodman, author of the book *Living at Light Speed*, explains: "Perhaps the most important similarity is that both kinds of highways link between people and places. By themselves roadways contribute nothing to society. They're no more than inanimate concrete and asphalt ribbons. But place some vehicles carrying goods and people on those roads and suddenly we have commerce, travel, and interactive exchanges amongst people. The same can be true of an information highway…" [Goodman 1994].

A Technology

Virtual communities paved with information superhighways must be built from something. That something or somethings are the underlying technologies being used today and developed for tomorrow. Today's on-line environments are for the most part resting upon the structure of what's called the *Internet*. The Internet is not actually one hardware or software technology, but a network of thousands located around the world's governments, universities, and industrial sites. This loosely connected network of computers first began in the United States in the 1960s as ARPANET, a tool for university, government, and military research. Eventually researchers (not just scientific or military ones) began to use the Internet. Not only did they find it an important source of information, but also an equally important way to communicate. It became a forum for discussion where individuals could write to other individuals and have their electronic mail delivered in a few fleeting moments. It also became a place where individuals could post messages to whole groups of people with a particular interest (e.g., chemistry, biking, teaching, cooking) using what people call ListServes or Message Boards. The Internet also became a place to publish timely information (e.g., newsgroups).

Since the Internet's beginnings, the way people communicate and publish information has been for the most part in a text form. In recent years, graphical interfaces have been developed so that people wandering the Internet need not remember cryptic text commands. Commercial on-line services such as *America On-line*, *Prodigy*, *e-World*, and *CompuServe* offer (for a price) the same email, newsgroup, and bulletin board options as was made popular with the Internet's text interface of UNIX. Instead of typing commands to see or transfer files, you can mouse click or drag folders of documents. While this has been an important step forward in making on-line environments more accessible, the documents themselves and the way we communicate to one another have still been text-based for the most part.

In recent years, an important new graphical addition to the Internet has been the *World Wide Web* (WWW). It offers people the ability to publish screens of text, graphics, sounds, and video to other people on the Internet (using the appropriate viewing software). For the first time, the possibility of a true on-line multimedia environment has become available. By mouse clicking on certain highlighted or underlined words or pictures, it can take you to another screen full of words and pictures: a *Web page*. These Web pages can be your own or other on-line multimedia authors' from Alaska to Turkey. By linking together pages in this way, it has become a web of information, not a hierarchy of order. The best description I've seen recently of how *untidy* the Web can be, is from an on-line user: "It's as if the Library of Congress had exploded in midair. There's all kinds of information strewn over the countryside approximately laid out according to its logical relationship. If you want a particular piece of information, it's probably not there, although some corpuses of data have landed intact. And the professional librarians haven't arrived yet to sort out the mess" [june@hotwired.com, 1995].

In actuality it may not be quite as difficult as all that. With a growing number of search engines available on the WWW, you can search by keyword or content area and receive thousands of pointers to information. Sorting out those thousands of entries is another story. At times the Web is painfully slow (especially if the page has a great deal of graphics on it) and frustrating in its unevenness of quality. Anyone with anything to say (e.g., children, teachers, parents, professionals) can create a *Web page*. And within minutes, if they have the appropriate hardware connection and software, they can publish what they want, when they want. It is an exciting, yet scary democratic process.

THE EDUCATIONAL POSSIBILITIES

With access to vast quantities of information and vast numbers of people on-line, a wealth of learning possibilities has emerged in recent years. Children can share multicultural experiences; they can pursue research activities; they can publish multimedia documents; they can investigate complex problems; and they can explore interdisciplinary content area. Yes, while all of these activities can be made possible using more traditional technologies, it seems that these qualities are amplified when children use on-line tools. This is due to the quantity of information and people available through these on-line technologies.

For example, the ability to share our experiences on-line cannot be understated. Traditionally, children have enjoyed discussions with their parents, teachers, and friends in their local community. They have also taken advantage of the telephone to talk with distant friends and family. And many times children have written to pen-pals in other countries. With on-line technologies, children have the opportunity for much more immediate communication with many more diverse individuals. Not only is it easier to find connections with like-minded individuals, but it is also easier to be anonymous if they so choose. Two such examples of this can be found in the electronic mail of two different boys. One boy, a 10-year old who is also a four-year college graduate explains, "One of the greatest things about the Internet is that no one has to know who you are... There have been times people my own age may not be interested in what I'm interested in, and, at the same time, people who are older than I am, who might be interested, don't always want to spend time with someone so much younger than they are. But if you are on the Internet, things like age are unimportant—or invisible, anyway, if you want them to be..." [Long 1994].

Another boy has explained, "I am 15 years old. I came to terms that I was gay last summer and aside from some depression, I'm OK. I am not in denial about being gay. I would like to write to someone that I can talk to about issues I can't talk about with my friends..." [Silberman 1994]

On-line environments are important places to connect with other people. These environments can also go beyond personal letter-writing exchanges. They can become a way to collaborate and share learning experiences with others many miles away. With the Global Laboratory project developed by TERC (Technical Education, Research Centers), classrooms of students share not only their classroom experiences verbally, but also their research findings on air pollution and ozone depletion.

Ultimately, they share their data so that children across the world can graph, map, and analyze trends in the global ecology. These on-line tools are not the core of what is being learned, but they are an important tool for problem-solving and interdisciplinary investigations (I will further describe this in a later section).

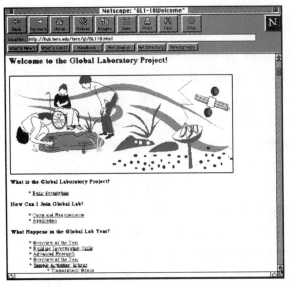

TERC's *Global Laboratory* WWW page.

The examples I have just shared with you are primarily based on textual communication. However, in the future it will become commonplace to use graphics and sound to exchange ideas in real-time on-line. People will soon be able to verbally discuss ideas, in a simulated three-dimensional environment. Imagine, your voice is your own, but the visual character you display to the world is a fanciful dragon, movie character, or comic book hero. One such system is now being developed by the Starbright Foundation in collaboration with software, hardware, and film producers. With this system children who are hospitalized for serious illnesses will be able to visit with other children in other hospitals. But instead of wandering through sterile hospital environments, children will be able to explore with others simulated jungles, caves, or even clouds. Steven Spielberg, a creative force behind this project has explained, "For a sick kid, having fun means lots of different things… It means letting the imagination run wild when the body can't. Or controlling the switches when the pain starts. Or just being taken seriously for a few moments as a kid" [Lewis 1995].

For children and adults who are not in hospitals, a portion of these fanciful worlds are available on the WWW by Worlds Inc., the developer of the 3-D simulation software for the Starbright project (http://www.kaworlds.com/). Today, with this system, it is only possible to communicate with text as your character interacts with others. In the future, real-time sound interaction will be added. If, however, you are interested in real-time sound and video, but no simulated worlds, you can use the technology *CU-SeeMe*, developed by Cornell University (http://cu-seeme. cornell.edu/). Using additional hardware and software people can now converse on the WWW using real-time video conferencing. Unfortunately, if there are a great deal of people using the WWW at a given time (which is usually the case), the video connection can be excruciatingly slow. Dropped frames of video and delayed sound can make it quite difficult to communicate with others in this way. It is almost enough to send users back to their keyboards for faster exchanges of information.

Besides using the graphical on-line worlds of others, children can publish their own on-line multimedia. In the case of the WWW, schools across the world are creating Web pages containing text, graphics, sounds, and video. In the process, children are offered multimedia authoring experiences as well as a way to explore numerous content areas: geography, history, science, math, and social studies. In addition, these on-line multimedia projects offer a chance for children to collaborate and receive feedback from a global audience of their peers, content experts, and educators.

Patch High School's Berlin Wall WWW Page.

One outstanding project, which focuses on the fall of the Berlin Wall, was recently started by Patch American High School students (http://192.253.114.31/Berlin/Introduction/ Berlin.html). This school, located in Stuttgart, Germany, for the families of American military personnel, decided to examine the fall of the Berlin Wall five years later. To do so, they asked via their WWW page for collaborators from European, American, or Department of Defense Dependent Schools. Their hope is to create a virtual museum which will cover different topics related to the fall of the Berlin Wall: the Cold War, WWII, the history of Berlin, personal stories, and even a place for CU-SeeMe video conferencing discussions. It is a year-long project that is still being developed as I write this book. But from the looks of what they have published already, it is an impressive start. While they are still working on integrating more pictures and video, the text portions relate a rich understanding of history from a global perspective. Along with this, the students have used their knowledge of the WWW to become strong designers, collaborators, and on-line publishers.

This powerful learning experience is not unique to American students living in Germany. Low-income kids in East Palo Alto, California, are experiencing the same powerful activities. In a nonprofit, after-school program called *Plugged-In*, children and their families are using the WWW to develop collaborative community projects. In their "HTML Shop," Plugged-In offers the local and global community the service (for a small fee) of creating a WWW page for anyone in need. Not only do the Plugged-In students come to better understand the outside community, but this activity provides valuable part-time jobs for kids who have little chance of finding them. In East Palo Alto, where street crime, drugs, and violence are the norm, Plugged-In and the WWW are making a difference.

MAKING SENSE OF THE NOISE

These are just a few isolated examples of the learning opportunities available using on-line multimedia environments. Some use the WWW and some use commercially developed on-line software. Whichever the case, there are thousands of educational efforts being spear-headed by teachers, researchers, commercial professionals, and children throughout the world. Unfortunately, for every Patch High School or Plugged-In after-school program, there are thousands of trivial, unimaginative uses of on-line multimedia. As with any other form of multimedia that we have previously discussed, new technologies can be taught for the sake of teaching technology or they can be powerful tools for exploring many different disciplines. As with others, these tools can offer children another form of an *Interactive Textbook* or another *Expressive Medium*. The choice is up to designers.

When trying to make sense of the vast number of approaches to creating on-line environments, I found that who creates these environments, what different technologies are used, and how these on-line environments are use, all influence what is developed. What follows is a further breakdown of these three influences:

1. On-line activities are designed and developed by three groups:

> Grassroots users
>> (e.g., children, teachers, schools, nonprofit organizations,
>> universities)
>
> Commercial industry
>> (e.g., magazine, book, or software publishers; film, television,
>> or radio producers)
>
> Governments
>> (e.g., service agencies, information archives, political
>> organizations)

2. These developers either use existing on-line technologies (e.g., the WWW, com mercial on-line services) or they develop their own software or hardware tech nologies (e.g., TERC's Alice Network Software, AT&T's Learning Network)

3. When these on-line environments are created, there are differing amounts of support materials and activity structure available to users.

In the previous section, I described examples of various grassroots efforts of small on-line educational projects. In the section that follows, I will describe two examples of commercial on-line environments which integrate a number of on-line activities within one environment. These environments offer children the ability to communi- cate on-line, to access information, to share information with experts in a particular field, and to investigate interdisciplinary content areas with complex real-world pro- jects. All of these separate activities can be found in one form or another in numer- ous areas of the Internet developed by many different people. However, it is less common to find integrated environments with a range of tools and activities designed specifically for educational purposes.

EXAMPLES

The two environments I will describe next have been developed by two well-respected organizations in the field of education. The first is TERC (Technical Education Research Center) which has been developing educational technologies for over three decades. The work they have done in developing on-line environments for children uses their own software technologies. The second example is Scholastic Inc., a well-respected publisher of educational magazines and books, which uses existing technologies for their on-line environments. Both organizations offer some important examples of what can be done with children and on-line actvities.

TERC (TECHNICAL EDUCATION RESEARCH CENTER)

In April 1988, more than twenty-thousand scientists throughout the world joined in an unprecedented effort to explore the acid rain problem, sharing the results of their investigation with scientists at the Acid Deposition Study,... the organization in the U.S. responsible for monitoring acid rain. In October of that year, the same scientists again shared data, this time about weather phenomena. The next spring, they began collecting data on the lead (Pb++) content of water in the nation's public schools, relaying their findings to the U.S. Environmental Protection Agency. While topics being studied were not out of the ordinary, the 'scientists' were. They were all elementary school children. These student scientists were fourth, fifth, and sixth grade students who participated in curriculum field tests of the TERC Kidsnet project..." [Tinker 1993]

For over 30 years TERC, a nonprofit research organization based in Massachusetts, has been exploring new ways of teaching and learning. In 1986, when people were just considering the possibilities of multimedia, they began the development of an interdisciplinary science curriculum that took advantage of on-line technologies for scientific collaboration. This was unheard of, especially among elementary school teachers and children. Few, if any, classrooms had phone lines. UNIX was the on-line tool of choice among Internet wanderers. And the WWW had not yet been born.

By 1989, seven curriculum and software units were developed by TERC researchers, educators, and developers, with the support of the National Science Foundation and the National Geographic Society (NGS). At that time these units became commercially available through the NGS. These units make up what have come to be called the *National Geographic Kids Network* (or *NGS Kidsnet*). These units offered elementary school students the opportunity to explore solar energy, nutrition, acid rain, water, weather, trash, and more. They asked students to design and build their own rain collectors and measure the acidity of the local rain water. They asked students to analyze the foods in their lunches for the nutrient content. They asked students to build solar collectors and measure solar radiation levels. These seven units contained engaging classroom science activities for elementary school students.

So where in all these noncomputer activities were the on-line technologies? The on-line tools were used to support the sharing of information with other classrooms around the world. Students would discuss with other students in Texas or Russia or Alaska, the experiments they were working on in their classrooms. They would also discuss their work with a *unit scientist*: an adult expert in a related field. Once each classroom of students had

An example screen from the National Geographic Kids Network Software developed by TERC.

collected their local information on acid rain or solar energy, they would send their results to a central computer (at TERC) to compile the information. After which, students would then receive a summary of their work and their on-line collaborators'. From this compiled information or data, students would analyze the results using graphing and mapping tools provided in the *Kidsnet* software package. According to Dr. Candace Julyan, former director of the NGS Kidsnet project at TERC, "The basic premise of these curricula is that students can and should be scientists, that they can and should converse with real scientists about their work, and that computers can enhance this enterprise. Students conduct experiments, analyze data, and share results with their colleagues using a computer-based telecommunications network…" [Julyan 1995].

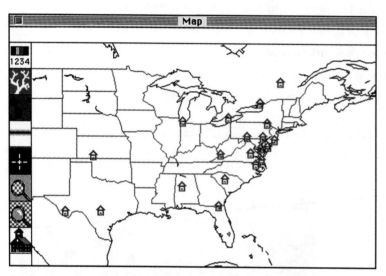

Map

An example screen from the National Geographic Kids Network Software developed by TERC.

It is a very powerful model of how students can explore a content area, on and off the computer. Students are not relegated to only computer activities. They are asked to do hands-on, real-world experiments and bring this back to the computer. In reality, *Kidsnet* is truly a multimedia environment bringing the physical and virtual environments into one activity. What is exciting about these activities is that the students are not looking for the "right answer." Using the information they collect in hands-on experiences, students can draw their own conclusions. It is not an *Interactive Textbook* approach with fabricated problems that must to be digested and regurgitated on weekly tests. Students are asked to tackle real science issues as real scientists would. The tools that support students' research are an *Expressive Medium*, that enable them to observe and explore in a particular content area. Bob Tinker, a physics educator influenced by the work of Seymour Papert, is the driving force of this educational approach at TERC. He has pointed out: "The idea that kids are measuring something for others and that the results matter, transforms the classroom. Students become committed, careful, articulate, and surprisingly intense. Along the way they learn large amounts of mathematics, science, technology, experimental procedures, geography, and communication skills in a way that will probably last a lifetime…" [Tinker 1993].

Over the years, several hundred schools in over 30 countries have collaborated in the NGS *Kidsnet* programs. Not only have they offered important learning experiences in many different content areas, but also they have had an important impact on their local communities and schools. It is not uncommon to hear about a Kidsnet classroom such as this:

After six weeks of study on the quality of the local drinking water, a class of sixth graders in the Midwest prepared its final presentation. In their studies the students had explored the pH of water, including why and how cities alter the pH of drinking water. They had also examined their own drinking water for pH and lead levels. They had discovered that if lead is present in any water pipe, low pH... can affect how much lead leaches from the pipe into the tap water. Their investigation led to the discovery of unsafe lead levels in the school's drinking fountains...

The students invited the superintendent of schools to their final presentation. The audience also included representatives from the water company... as well as parents and other members of their school community. In addition to presenting what they had learned about water in general, the students reported their findings on the school's water. They asked that the superintendent act on their findings by commissioning an in-depth study of the drinking water..." [Julyan 1993a]

This is just one example out of many Kidsnet classrooms that have made a difference in their local communities. Thanks to the profound results of the Kidsnet program, TERC began developing the *Global Laboratory* project and *Kidsnet for Middle Schools* in the early 1990s. Both learning environments offer older students similar project-based explorations that take advantage of on-line tools for data collection, analysis, and collaboration with other students. However, in the case of the Global Laboratory, students are given a year-long program with more open-ended experiences that can result in original publishable research. This program asks students to begin by selecting a site to study (e.g., a nearby forest, river, playground, classroom). Students then collect data on their site performing some simple introductory experiments, then share them with their on-line collaborators. The second half of the year, students are asked to design their own more advanced projects using the same methodologies.

With the Global Laboratory, as opposed to Kidsnet, students work with more sophisticated measuring tools to collect environmental information (e.g., probes, sensors, digitizers). TERC, in collaboration with local engineers, has even developed a *Total Column Ozonometer* (TCO) which measures the total amount of ozone found directly above an observer. These instruments are reasonably accurate, surprisingly low cost, and easy for secondary students to use [Feldman and Nyland 1994].

What has also come out of this work is a software technology called the *Alice Network Software*. Essentially, it is an upgraded and more enhanced version of the original software developed for Kidsnet. It offers word processing, data tables and graphing, mapping and telecommunications software. With these tools students can do scientific research without the distractions of other on-line environments. It is a self-contained software package created specifically for doing network science. Since 1993, the *Global Laboratory* project and the *Kidsnet for Middle Schools* have been using the *Alice* software. Today TERC is freely distributing *Alice* in hopes that it will be helpful in starting new "grassroots research efforts" by educators who want to use on-line technologies to explore different content areas. Such projects that study energy consumption and water quality have already begun using the Alice Network Software [Feldman and Nyland 1994].

The success of TERC's efforts in developing on-line multimedia environments is a result of many different strengths in the development process. To begin with, TERC's initial *Kidsnet* prototypes were assessed and evaluated with over 5,000 children worldwide, before they were ever available for sale. Few commercial products can boast of such an extensive assessment program. Throughout the field testing, educators, technologists, and designers at TERC received valuable feedback and direction from the Kidsnet classroom teachers, students, and unit scientists. For example, in the original Kidsnet *Hello* unit which introduces students to the data collection and telecommunication processes, students were asked to collect and analyze information about where they were born. While this information was fascinating for adults to see where immigrant populations emerged, the students were less interested. With this feedback, TERC developers quickly changed the unit so that students would instead collect and analyze information on the types of pets they owned. The students became much more motivated when exploring this content area [Julyan 1993b].

Other changes and additions have been made by the TERC staff, thanks to their work with teachers, students, and content experts. As the WWW has gained in popularity and accessibility in schools, teachers and students have asked for tools that would take advantage of this technology. TERC has listened by developing, as an addition to *Alice,* WWW tools to access subsets of data compiled by collaborating science classrooms. In addition, TERC has also begun developing more sophisticated data-querying tools for students when accessing different databases. For example, students will be able to ask for all the information on acid rain collected in the Southwest since 1992, as opposed to only being able to access all the information on acid rain collected by all Kidsnet classrooms [Feldman and Nyland 1994].

Another strength of the TERC work has been in the integration of activities, on and off the computer. So often, when we become enamored with technology, we forget that little else exists. This has not been the case for researchers at TERC. Their interdisciplinary design team began with a content area that they thought was important. Only after they were satisfied with the content did they look for tools and activities to support this learning environment. This is unique in today's world where typically you can hear developers say, "Kids need to learn how to use the Internet. Let's make up a project that helps them learn to use it."

However, with these strengths also comes some drawbacks. For one, TERC has focused on only one approach to scientific exploration: Take measurements and analyze them with graphs and maps. There are other ways to go about investigating a scientific problem. For example, scientists also examine problems qualitatively and attempt to build new technologies to support a given solution. It would be exciting if TERC were to develop new science units that asked students to design a bridge, or a greenhouse, or even a solar-powered car. Each would offer students interdisciplinary challenges in engineering, ecology, earth sciences, mathematics, and more. Each project would also benefit from the research and collaboration between worldwide classroom partners.

Another area that TERC has already begun to address, is the integration of more media into the learning experience. With the addition of WWW tools and other graphical drawing options, TERC's on-line environments will be richly enhanced. In addition, sound would also be a useful medium to take advantage of in the future. Not only would that add to the texture of the learning experience, but researchers could also make use of sound as a content area to teach within a science curriculum.

Finally, TERC's science activities are so rich that, sadly enough, teachers find it difficult to keep up with the project schedule. Many teachers find it necessary to begin using *Kidsnet* or the *Global Laboratory* as an after-school activity or independent study project for a few students. Once educators come to understand the value of these activities, there have been many cases in which whole classroom curricula have been restructured to accommodate these TERC programs. While it is a drawback that the average classroom teacher cannot easily support these activities, it is also a strength. TERC's on-line science activities ask for classroom change. They ask for more time to be devoted to exploring earth sciences, math, technology, biology, and chemistry (among other things). If our children's on-line environments ask for more interdisciplinary time within our schools, we could be faced with worse challenges.

SCHOLASTIC

A different approach to developing on-line multimedia environments can be seen with the work of the Scholastic Corporation. Best known for over 70 years for its educational magazines, books, software, and videos, Scholastic recently entered the world of on-line multimedia development. In 1993, Scholastic created the *Scholastic Network* using the commercial on-line environment of America On-line. And in 1994, they created *Scholastic Central*, using the WWW. As opposed to developing new on-line technologies, Scholastic chose the route of using what was there. They also chose to use two different on-line technologies to offer users a wider range of on-line capabilities.

While Scholastic offers a variety of on-line activities similar to TERC (e.g., on-line collaborations with classrooms, on-line discussions with experts in various fields), Scholastic's activities show the roots of its publishing history. Among Scholastic Central's WWW pages are on-line literary magazines and field trips to the Arctic.

These WWW pages bring to life with text, graphics, and sound, living, breathing people in places around the world. It is an *Interactive Textbook* in the finest sense, that can lead to additional classroom activities in science, literature, geography, and social studies. The strength of Scholastic's on-line environments is in their timeliness. They are constantly being updated. In the case of Scholastic Network, each month special events are offered from on-line field trips to study dinosaurs or the North Pole, to on-line discussions with civil rights leaders or past presidents. My favorite was the recent Arctic exploration offered on both Scholastic Network and Central.

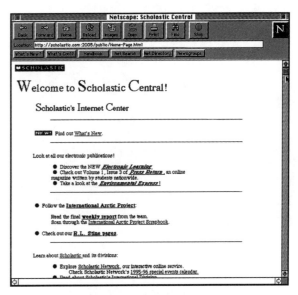

The Scholastic Central WWW page.

With this field trip, weekly updates were written by the actual team of explorers crossing the Arctic Ocean by dogsled and canoe-sled. From Russia to the North Pole students were able to follow these people's real-life adventure in words and pictures.

March 8, 1995

Daily Report #3

...Our first night of camp! The whole team and all 33 dogs were flown by helicopter to our starting point just east of Cape Artichesky. This trip was done in two loads, with myself, Takako, and Martin on the last load with two dog teams. Finally our flying is over and we look forward to the dogsledding portion of our expedition. Everything is going very well and the ice looks safe...

June 9, 1995

Daily Report #68

...Another day of slow progress because of leads and deep snow. Victor has a challenging time finding the best route. The snow continues to be heavy...

June 15, 1995

Daily Report #72

Position: 83 deg 37.3 min N, 81 deg 59.9 min W

Temperature: 0 to 5c

Weather: partly cloudy

Wind speed: 0-3 meters per second

Wind direction: NW

We have spotted land! The mountains of Ellsmere are breathtaking, especially since we have not seen anything but ice and water since leaving Russia at the end of March. It was good to see the sun again today, although fog settled in shortly after noon. The day's travel included both smooth ice and ice that was broken in thick angular chunks...We hate to say good-bye to the dogs—they seem to know something's up. The resupply plane is due to arrive tomorrow.

[http://www.scholastic.com/]

With these on-line journal entries students can be right there with explorers, following with maps and pinpointing their positions. They can even send electronic mail to the Arctic asking a specific question. It is a rich opportunity to expand beyond the walls of the classroom. On-line field trips do not offer the words of dusty textbooks. Rather, they offer the words of people living today, sharing their thoughts interactively. Many other on-line environments have begun to offer similar "field trip" experiences (e.g., following America's World Cup Challenge boat race), but few offer the support materials and suggested add-on activities that Scholastic does. Students can write their own travel journal; they can analyze the pollution in their town's local snow; they can learn the history of past Arctic explorations; they can create their own computer-simulated Arctic adventure. There is a wealth of opportunity in these on-line materials.

What do developers need to think about when creating on-line multimedia environments such as these? Scholastic's Webmaster, Eadie Adamson explains: "You need to keep it fresh! It isn't over, when it's over. You need to keep updating pages to keep people coming back. You also have to make the most out of the interactivity available to you with the WWW. It's not easy since it can be so slow especially when using a lot of graphics. But the most amazing thing about the Web is that you can build a page with links to many other pages. Hotlinks are an important part of what makes this on-line world so interesting..." [Adamson 1995].

Scholastic Central's Arctic Exploration WWW page.

While Scholastic's *Interactive Textbook* approach is well done, unfortunately these environments are limited by the existing on-line technologies that Scholastic designers are using (as opposed to TERC which has complete control of the environment it has developed and can chart its own course for the future). On the other hand, there are benefits to using existing technologies. The distribution and the audience for Scholastic's environments are already there. Little overhead needs to go into technology development or distribution. Instead, Scholastic can focus on content creation. But this content is limited due to the capabilities of the WWW and America On-line. With *Scholastic Network's* use of America On-line, limited graphics can be offered to users, but interactive chat sessions and bulletin board postings add to the richness of the experience for students and teachers. With *Scholastic Central's* use of the WWW, limited forms of interaction are currently available, but a rich combination of media add to the information published.

In the future I would love to see Scholastic Central take advantage of *CU-SeeMe* video conferencing for more interactive discussion sessions. I would also love to see the simulated worlds of Worlds Inc. used to enhance the already exciting on-line field trips. I would also love to see more shared writing experiences between children from different parts of the world. And I would love to see a better integration of the activities of *Scholastic Central* with *Scholastic Network*. The wealth of resources that Scholastic brings to the world of on-line environments for children is exciting. The future will bring more resources with more on-line options for creative educational experiences.

STRENGTHS AND WEAKNESSES

When developing on-line multimedia environments, certain design considerations need to be addressed that are different from Edutainment CD–ROMs or multimedia authoring tools. Unless you are developing your own software technologies (e.g., TERC), your work will not be contained in a little world of its own. You will not be able to fully control the vision of the on-line environment you are developing. Many millions of people with their own on-line vision will be a powerful on-line distraction that must be acknowledged. There is also the difficulty of having access to on-line technology. Most of today's schools barely have computers, let alone a phone line for modem communications. And at times on-line environments will slow down due to enormous network traffic jams, making on-line interactions with graphics and sound seem almost impossible. In the sections that follow, I will briefly discuss the various strengths and weaknesses that I've seen in different on-line projects.

POWERFUL LEARNING EXPERIENCES

The most profound strength of on-line environments is the ability to collaborate with tens of millions of different people. An enormous number of educational activities can make excellent use of this strength, such as collecting global science information, role-playing historical events, writing collaboratively, debriefing professionals in a particular content area, creating virtual museum exhibits, and following the activities of politicians, explorers, or sports figures—the list of possibilities is endless. However, with these shared multicultural collaborations comes difficulties. There are distinct differences in languages, customs, expectations, and even school calendars. Negotiating these differences may be an important, but difficult learning experience for students when using on-line environments. Designers must be sensitive to these differences and develop activities that support a true multicultural learning environment.

While there are numerous on-line activities already emerging as powerful learning experiences, designers must keep in mind that not *all* educational experiences necessitate on-line technologies. It is important to understand if an educational activity is any better thanks to the use of on-line environments. The design strategy that has well-served TERC researchers, begins with discovering the educational purpose or content of an environment. Then they consider what tools would work best in a given situation. If those tools are CD–ROMs containing Edutainment or multimedia authoring tools, then so be it.

Designers should also keep in mind when creating on-line environments that there are enormous numbers of competing on-line environments with quality that is uneven at

- There are enormous numbers of people using on-line environments
- There are an ever-increasing number of on-line environments being developed
- Our schools have begun to address on-line activities

best. There are now millions of new on-line designers with little experience or sensitivity to educational issues. The on-line world was not created first with school children in mind. Therefore, students can easily be accosted with on-line commercial ads and screens of what many would call pornographic material. Shortly, there may be rating systems or filters that will help educators to weed out distracting information. But who decides what is rated PG and why are difficult questions for our future.

CONNECTIVITY

What is unique to on-line multimedia environments is the limitations of the technology. For example, when using any media beyond text on the WWW, the technology is slow (especially if many people are accessing the same area at the same time). It can be frustrating, because it won't help to go out and buy a faster hard disk or CD–ROM drive. There is little the average user can do except to wait for less on-line traffic. In the mean time users can waste enormous amounts of valuable time. The good news is that development of WWW pages is off-line. The bad news is that debugging a page needs to be done on-line. At times it may be difficult to know whether something that is slow is because you have programmed that into your WWW page or because the on-line traffic is congested.

Perhaps a more difficult limitation of on-line technologies is that educators and students have a problem getting access to the stuff. In public schools today, there is one desktop computer for at least every 12 students. Unfortunately, only 15 per cent of our nation's public schools have access to on-line environments. It is not uncommon to have the only phone line in the principal's or school nurse's office. And of those 15 per cent of schools with resources, a very small portion of them have the software or hardware capability to make use of on-line multimedia environments [Meyer 1995]. The future will change; this is something to be certain of. How much, and when, is up for grabs.

THE USE OF MEDIA

Few of today's on-line environments take full advantage of the wide range of media available. As technologies become faster, media limitations will fall by the wayside. Sound, which is usually the last form of media thought of by multimedia designers, will play a bigger role in our future on-line environments. On-line discussions will eventually truly be on-line verbal discussions. However, today's on-line designers must keep an eye to the future, but be mindful of what works today. People (especially children) become so impatient with slow screen refreshes and alike. Designers must try not to add to this slowness by placing 14 photographic images on one WWW page. The graphic browsers will just not take it.

VISUAL DESIGN

With such easy access to on-line publishing tools through the WWW, more people have the ability to visually accost many other people. As with any other form of multimedia, too many fonts, not enough space between lines of text, poorly scanned pictures, or an insensitivity to color will hurt the end result. If the visual design is used to say what the environment means, then the power of the educational experience will come shining through. If the visual design lacks a clarity of thought or is insensitive to readability, the message will be lost behind the media. On-line designers need to distinguish themselves amongst millions of other on-line multimedia publishers. Good visual design is an excellent way to do it.

INTERACTION DESIGN

In the future we must look for more innovative ways to interact on-line. If mouse-clicking from screen to screen is all we can expect to do, it is hard to say how interactive our on-line multimedia environments truly will be. This type of electronic page-turning will quickly become boring and tedious without other types of interactivity. On-line designers need to think about what makes Edutainment CD–ROMs and multimedia authoring tools interactively exciting and borrow a few lessons. Unfortunately, the WWW authoring language does not make designing complex interactions easy. HTML is a text-based language, more difficult to master than commercial multimedia authoring tools with windows, menus, and icons. To author WWW pages with interesting interaction, multimedia authors must become fluent in yet another cryptic language. Shortly, however, it is expected that easier interfaces to authoring with HTML will be offered. How powerful a tool will these be? What sorts of exciting WWW pages can novice users create? That remains to be seen.

As with other forms of multimedia, on-line designers must also consider whether the interaction makes sense to users. Is it easy to use? Does it add to the educational experience? All are questions that designers can hope to answer with extensive field testing and feedback from users. Without collaborating with teachers and students, designers will have little chance of developing solid educational experiences with on-line technologies.

QUESTIONS FOR THE FUTURE

As I ponder the future, I have more questions than answers about on-line environments. What types of software will be offered on-line? Will local storage devices (e.g., CD–ROMs) disappear because of our on-line environments? Will designers of educational environments make the most of what on-line environments can be? With all of these questions I can be certain of one thing, on-line environments will be at the very center of change and controversy in the years to come.

chapter thoughts

- On-line environments offer children the ability to share thoughts and information with vast numbers of people just a computer away.

- Children can author a multimedia message and publish it on-line to millions of people in just a few moments.

- Children can investigate complex problems and can explore interdisciplinary content area with on-line multimedia environments.

- On-line environments can offer children multicultural exposure to different languages, customs, and personal experiences.

- Schools have difficulty getting access to on-line technology.

- At times on-line interaction can be painfully slow, if many people are accessing the same area at the same time.

- The quality of on-line information is uneven at best.

- On-line activities are designed and developed by grassroots users, commercial industry, and governments.

- Developers either use existing on-line technologies or they develop their own software or hardware technologies.

- Both TERC and Scholastic offer some important examples of what can be done with children and on-line activities.

- When creating on-line environments, designers should consider how to keep information and activities timely.

- Designers should also keep in mind that on-line environments should be visually sensitive and interactively creative.

Chapter Six - Allison Druin

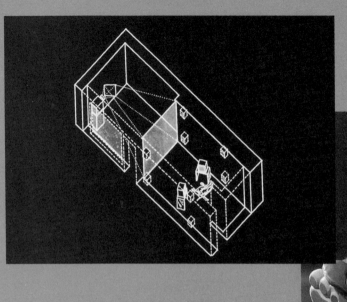

PHYSICAL
Multimedia Environments

"Hey, I'm sitting in a computer!" announced the six-year-old boy.

This was not far from the truth, because the boy sat in the lap of a five-foot tall stuffed animal that looked like a large "Muppet" with a computer in its belly. However, the boy did not sit there for long. Moments later, he jumped from the stuffed-animal's lap and ran around it. On his second time around, the boy squeezed the animal's large stuffed tail and he heard a sound.

"Now the computer is talking!" said the boy. He then ran to the front of the stuffed-animal and pointed at the screen in its belly. "Look, I changed the cartoon animal's tail! Wait, I can do that again!" And he did. The boy ran to the tail and squeezed it again. A new sound could be heard, and a new tail could be seen on the screen's cartoon animal.

"OK, now I'm gonna change his ears!" and with that the boy began climbing the stuffed-animal to squeeze his ears.

BACKGROUND

In the future, children's multimedia environments may not have to live in hard plastic boxes that sit on desktops with keyboards, mice, or the occasional joystick. Multimedia environments in the future may look like any familiar room, stuffed animal, or toy block. However, these multimedia environments will be responsive to a child's movement, touch, sound, or even gesture. By lifting an object, touching a wall, or walking in a particular direction, a child might turn lights on or off, make video appear, or perhaps trigger a sound. These multimedia environments will not replace a child's familiar physical surroundings; rather, they will become a seamless part of them, enhancing what is already there.

- To go beyond the conventional key boards, mice, and screens

- To enhance a child's familiar physical surroundings

- To create more engaging accessible multimedia for children

goals

BACK TO THE PHYSICAL WORLD

This description of the future may sound like pieces of a far off vision, but in fact it exists today and has existed for many years in computer research labs around the country. The six-year-old boy described at the start of this chapter is now a teenager in high school. And the five-foot stuffed-animal computer was my master's thesis, created at the MIT Media Lab between 1985 and 1987. This piece of the future was developed using a Macintosh Plus, 20MB hard drive, and 2MB of memory. The sensors in each of the stuffed animal's limbs were nothing more than keyboard keys embedded in foam and fur. While not technologically earth-shattering, it did enable children to interact with a computer in a intuitive way: by squeezing a stuffed animal [Druin 1988].

For over three decades there have been many such examples of what we have come to call *physical multimedia*. These places have redefined *where computers and people meet* [Bolt 1984]. People so often forget that children meet a computer from the moment they see it, to the moment they touch it, not just from the moment they interact with the software. As we look towards the future, we as technology designers must not only concern ourselves with the comfort and beauty of our technology's furniture, but with the structure and integration of walls, floors, and even lighting. We must consider the entire technology environment. As Professor Nicholas Negroponte, director of the MIT Media Lab, has pointed out, "The human interface with computers is the physical, sensory, and intellectual space that lies between computers and ourselves. Like any place, this space can be unfamiliar, cold, and unwelcoming. But it can also be like some other places, those we know and love, those that are familiar, comfortable, warm and most importantly personal" [Bolt 1984].

These ideas are gaining acceptance with many computer researchers today, and a growing number have begun to focus their energies on physical multimedia environments for the future. A pivotal summary of this work was highlighted in July of 1993, in the *Communications of the ACM*, "Computer Augmented Environments: Back to the Real World." It contained 12 articles by researchers from around the world developing physical multimedia environments for our work places, homes, and schools.

MIT Media Lab's *NOOBIE* with child.

While the technological research community has come to embrace this direction, so too, has the entertainment industry. If you look at our amusement parks, science and children's museums, art exhibitions, and even children's play toys, you can see physical multimedia environments at every turn. These objects and places now include physical interactivity that enables you to touch, move, and even talk to technologies. One commercial example was developed by World's of Wonder, a toy manufacturer. Best known for talking bears such as *Teddy Ruckspin*, this same company produced a doll named *Talking Julie*, over five years ago. Contained within Julie were sensors that were sensitive to light, temperature, touch, motion, and voice. When a child hugged Julie, the doll said, "I love you too." When it became colder in a room, Julie said, "Brrrrr, it's cold here. Is it time for Winter?" When it became darker in a room, Julie said, "I think it's bedtime. It's getting dark out." And when a child talked to Julie using any of the *keywords* Julie knew, such as *music*, Julie would sing, "Twinkle, twinkle, little star…"

Julie is a simple yet engaging example of what can be done with 124K of memory and five sensors. Today's physical multimedia environments are taking advantage of similar technologies, perhaps more powerful, but no less compelling. By recognizing multiple forms of communication, Julie establishes a relationship with a child which is truly a multimedia experience.

According to Jodi Levin, a spokesperson for the Toy Manufacturers of America, "…the choices are growing quickly: the market for hand-held and tabletop electronic toys and learning aids grew from $375 million to $500 million last year alone…" [Lippert 1995].

Another example of a physical multimedia environment that is finding its way into our children's world is a new kind of playground designed by TERC (the same research organization developing *KidsNet* and the *Global Laboratory*). TERC researchers are designing, "…new equipment that provides opportunities for children to explore their own movements and get immediate symbolic feedback in the form of numerical or computer-driven graphical displays. This equipment allows children to test questions about time, rate, and the fundamentals of motion, momentum, and force. Sample design ideas include: a large digital clock, strategically placed on the playground where it can spawn many games about time; a jungle gym that shows the forces children exert as they climb, stand, hang or jump…" (http://hub.terc.edu/terc/).

By offering real-world objects and places enhanced with technologies, physical multimedia environments can offer more powerful and involving learning experiences for children. The educational research and teaching community has acknowledged the importance of multiple forms of media in our classrooms. According to Professor Elliot Eisner, Professor of Art and Education at Stanford University, "…Both the presence of different forms of representation and a context that encourages their imaginative use are important features of educationally effective settings" [Eisner 1994].

Today researchers, educators, artists, and environmental designers are among the many professionals pointing in the direction of physical multimedia environments for the future. To date, much of this work has *not* been done for children exclusively. From sensor-driven public toilets in New York City to home automation and environmental monitoring, all use the technologies of physical multimedia for different purposes. Where these ideas and inventions may lead to in our future is difficult to say. You can be sure, however, that these ideas and inventions will not hide in hard plastic boxes, under mice, or behind glass. They will be rich physical spaces in which our children may someday take advantage of to live, learn, and play.

EXAMPLES

The examples I will discuss in the next sections were created for a range of users. One of the environments, *LEGO TC Logo* was specifically developed for children. The other two, the *Media Room* and *Immersive Environments* were not, but I believe they have enormous potential for children in the future.

THE MEDIA ROOM

You enter the Media Room. "It is about the size of a personal office: eight feet high, ten feet wide, and roughly thirteen feet long. The front wall is entirely a display screen on which images can be created by a projector located behind the screen. (You) sit at the center of the room wearing a microphone wired to an automatic speech recognizer. The recognizer... has a vocabulary of 120 words. (You) also wear a wristwatch band to which a small plastic cube is attached... (It is) effectively a wrist-born pointer." You are now ready to create objects on the display screen by talking and pointing. [Bolt 1985]

MIT's *Media Room* is one of the better known examples of early room-sized computer-controlled spaces. This physical multimedia environment was developed in the late 1970s by MIT researchers led by Professors Richard Bolt and Nicholas Negroponte of the Architecture Machine Group (a precursor to the MIT Media Lab).

In the *Media Room*, people did not use a traditional mouse or keyboard, rather they *told* the computer what they wanted to do, by looking in a particular direction, saying a short phrase, or even gesturing with their arms. However, in order to accomplish this, researchers asked users to wear special glasses to track eye movements, special sensors on their arms and hands to track gestures, and a microphone to understand speech. Joysticks, touch-sensitive screens, and a small keypad supplemented these input devises. With different combinations of these, users could manipulate virtual maps, books, a calendar, telephone or calculator on a wall-sized screen in the *Media Room* [Bolt 1984].

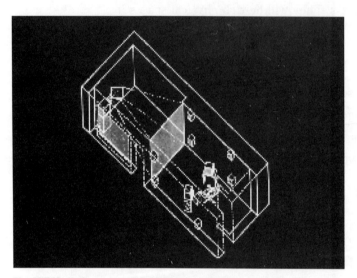

The *MIT Media Room.* Copyright MIT Media Laboratory, used with permission. Photo by Christian Lischewski.

What researchers found was that the combination of different forms of communication with the computer (e.g., speech and gesture) could amplify and clarify the meaning of the user. One form of input alone was not as precise a tool as multiple forms. (This, of course, could be said of any person-to-person communication as well.) What researchers also found was that having to *wear* multiple forms of sensors did not allow for a great deal of intuitive motion. While today's technologies are much less bulky, we still see people's aversion to wearing head-mounted displays for such activities as Virtual Reality gaming.

The *Media Room* did not go further than being a profound demo. It was never adapted for children, yet imagine if it were. Imagine if the *Media Room* were the *Media ClassRoom*. Children could explore new worlds by using wall-sized maps to zoom to other places. They could explore another planet or another country by pointing and saying where they wanted to go. They could visit with children in other *Media Class-Rooms* to share ideas and collaborate on new multimedia experiences. The technologies for this environment exist today, but *Media ClassRooms* are not yet a reality. Today, we use video conferencing equipment for teachers to give lectures in an *Inter-*

active Textbook approach. However, with the same technologies we could have *Media ClassRooms* that offer *Expressive Medium* to children and teachers that are exciting, powerful places to learn.

Today the *Media Room* does not exist per se at the MIT Media Lab. The eclectic mix of talented researchers focused on video technologies, gesture and sound recognition, as well as human interface design—all still are an integral part of the work being done at the MIT Media Lab today. The ideas found in the *Media Room* have influenced generations of researchers within MIT and beyond. The notion that an entire room could be your computer input and output was groundbreaking. The idea that you could interact with a computer with your eyes, voice and/or body was quite startling for 1976, and remains quite important for future research. Today's *Immersive Environments*, *Virtual Reality*, and *Computer Augmented Environments* all owe their beginnings to the *Media Room*.

LEGO TC LOGO

John, a fifth grader... had an alarm clock next to his bed at home... Often when the alarm went off, John simply shut off the alarm and went back to sleep. John was determined to invent another solution. His goal: to design an alarm clock that could not be ignored. John started by playing with the LEGO optosensor. He placed the optosensor by the window, so the computer could 'know' when the sun came up. But what should happen at sunrise? John had an idea. He built a small LEGO bed, with a small LEGO person on top. Underneath the bed, he placed a hinged platform so the bed could tilt from side to side. Along side the bed, he built a conveyor belt. Then he wrote a Logo program. When the optosensor detected light coming through the window, the program turned on two motors. One motor made the LEGO bed tilt to the side, making the LEGO person slide off onto the conveyor belt. The other motor turned on the conveyor belt, carrying the LEGO person out the door..." [Resnick 1993]

Other powerful examples of physical multimedia environments can be found in the Logo research led by Professor Seymour Papert of MIT. Since the 1970s, this group of researchers has been exploring concrete ways for children to use what they intuitively understand about the physical world. This constructionist approach combines Logo with *mechanical turtles*, LEGO gears, motors, and *Programmable Bricks*, for children to create their own physical multimedia environments. Instead of manipulating and creating objects solely on a computer screen, children are asked to manipulate and create familiar physical objects in their environment. By doing so, children not only begin to understand the technologies behind what they are using, but they begin to internalize complex concepts from geometry to the physical sciences [Bederson and Druin 1995].

LEGO TC Logo.

A popular use of Logo in the 1970s involved a *floor turtle*. It was a simple mechanical robot connected to the computer. Children programmed the floor turtle using the Logo language to move forward, back, left, or right. Children could be found imagining themselves *to be the turtle*. With this method, they could better understand how to program the turtle to move in the geometric patterns they so desired [Papert, 1980].

Today, *floor turtles* have been replaced with *LEGO TC Logo* and *Programmable Bricks*. Again, children need not create worlds only on a screen, but rather they can build their own interactive physical multimedia environments. With LEGO bricks that include gears, motors, sensors, and Logo computation, children can create simple mechanical models. For example, in a 1993 summer workshop for female students ranging from grades three through eight, students created everything from a boat, to a helicopter, to houses with lighting cycles, to amusement park rides. One popular project was an elf cookie factory that used a refrigerator to store cookie dough and was connected to a conveyor belt that transported the dough to the microwave to bake cookies [Hutchinson and Whalen 1995].

Another teacher at the Dalton School in New York used LEGO TC Logo as a meeting place for the arts and sciences in the classroom. "…we used the LEGO motors and Logo commands for rotating optical designs… As we built objects which rotated, we added colorful pieces to them. We discovered that the mixing of colors could be studied in a surprisingly different manner. Mixing colors by motion, we could make colored optical designs…" [Adamson, 1993].

Programmable Bricks go one step further by incorporating a very small programmable computer right inside of the LEGO brick (about the size of a deck of cards). This enables a child to create more complicated behaviors without the need to connect to any desktop computer. Some examples of what children could do with these *Programmable Bricks* were described by Professor Mitchel Resnick, from the Learning and Common Sense Group of the MIT Media Lab. In his list (compiled with Randy Sargent) "Of Twenty Things to Do with a Programmable Brick," he suggests such ideas as: "…Build a LEGO creature you can interact with. Program the creature to act in different ways when you clap once, clap twice or shine a light in its *eyes*…." Professor Resnick also suggests, "…Take a Programmable Brick with you to measure the pH level of the water in local streams, or the noise level at a local construction site…." Yet another suggestion is to, "…Create LEGO musical instruments. The instrument might have buttons like a flute or a sliding part like a trombone… (then write) a simple program so the Programmable Brick plays different notes or melodies when you move different parts…" [Resnick 1993].

All this and more has been done with *Programmable Bricks*. Researchers at the MIT Media Lab and LEGO Dacta have been working with teachers and children for years to understand what can and should be done with physical multimedia environments. They have come to understand that by building and programming physical structures, children gain a deeper understanding of programming, engineering, and mechanical control systems. These physical multimedia environments have children researching how vacuum cleaners work, when hamsters sleep, and how houses are built. These environments offer children *Expressive Medium* to explore the mechanics of everyday objects.

Perhaps, the biggest strength and limitation of LEGO TC Logo and *Programmable Bricks* lie not in the technologies, but in the classroom teachers who use them with children. As was the case with other forms of multimedia that are *Expressive Media*, teachers strongly impact how technologies are used in the classroom. The more open-ended and flexible a technology, the more influence a teacher has on its use. The more prescribed a technology activity is, the less room there is for varying outcomes.

Today, the LEGO TC Logo environment is used in thousands of elementary schools throughout the world. It is a strong example of a technology partnership (between LEGO Dacta Inc. and the MIT Media Lab) that has resulted in a commercial product grounded in solid, thought-provoking research. Not only does LEGO TC Logo challenge children to interact with computer environments in new ways, but it enables them to create their own visions of the future.

IMMERSIVE ENVIRONMENTS

You enter a room and see two "parents" projected as a video on a wall. The video parents thank you for agreeing to baby-sit, and they ask that Junior, their baby, be asleep when they return from the movies. You soon find out this is somewhat difficult, since various household appliances periodically turn on, making an enormous noise. You soon realize that each time you turn off an appliance in the room the baby stops crying, at least until the next appliance turns on. You run from one side of the room to the other, turning off a vacuum cleaner, a blender, a television set. Eventually the video parents return. If the baby is quietly asleep, they give you a big tip and thank you for your services. If the baby is crying and the appliances are still turning on, then they yell at you and say that you're a bad baby-sitter. [Druin 1993]

Another example of physical multimedia environments is in the area of *Immersive Environments*. Similar to, and influenced by the *Media Room, Immersive Environments* are room-sized computer-controlled spaces. However, instead of placing the input sensors on a person's body (e.g., eye-tracking glasses) the sensors are embedded into the physical surroundings. When these sensors are triggered by a person's movement, touch, sound, or gesture, information can be offered through changes in the environment's sound, video, lighting, and so forth. While in the *Media Room,* a person could not generally affect much more than a wall-sized computer screen; in *Immersive Environments*, the entire physical space has the potential to be manipulated [Bederson and Druin 1995].

Examples of this work have been developed at several places including MIT and NYU. Since 1992, numerous examples have been created and presented to the public by researchers led by Professors Glorianna Davenport and Larry Freelander at the MIT Media Lab, and Professor Ken Perlin and myself at the NYU Media Research Laboratory [Druin and Perlin 1994].

An *Immersive Environment* at the N.Y.U. Media Research Laboratory.

For the most part, these Immersive Environments have been works of interactive fiction. For example, a person may walk into a room which triggers a voice that describes where s/he has just entered. A video projected on the wall may be triggered by moving to the back of the room. A spotlight may be illuminated on an object if a person has picked it up. As the experience continues, a person may find out s/he is suspected of murder and must clear her/his name. Or in another experience, a person may find out that s/he is a baby-sitter and must keep the baby content until the parents come home.

All are Immersive Environments that ask the *user* to become an *active participant* in an experience. These types of Immersive Environments are similar to today's videodisc simulations; however, the Immersive Environment participants wander through physical spaces and interact with concrete objects. Participants are situated to solve real-world problems in a *not-entirely-real-world* environment. The depth of problem-solving in Immersive Environments has been far less complex than the videodisc simulations offered today. This is one important educational issue that must be addressed by Immersive researchers in the future.

In the years to come, Immersive Environments may come closer to an *Expressive Medium* similar to LEGO TC Logo. Immersive environment researchers are looking towards the day when they can offer children simple sensors to embed in any everyday object, and a programming language or authoring environment that will enable them to create their own whole room experiences. In this way children in the future may be able to explore astronomy, history, or geography by creating their own environments to learn from and enjoy. Imagine one day in the future when children will be asked to create multimedia experiences where they can learn about other countries by building those environments. Imagine being able to bring together the sites, the sounds, and the feel of another place. This all may be possible one day in the future with Immersive Environments.

STRENGTHS AND WEAKNESSES

The strengths and weaknesses of physical multimedia environments are similar to those of more *traditional* multimedia experiences on a screen with a keyboard or mouse. All of these forms of technology experiences must consider the educational approach, the visual design, the ease of use, and the content of the experience. If any of these design factors are weak, the environment will suffer. If they are carefully thought out, with a sensitivity to detail, they may be exciting new interactive experiences.

What *differs* with physical multimedia environments is in the size and scope of the design team, the approach to prototyping, and the type of content that may be suitable for a more *physical* experience. What follows is a discussion of those differences as it relates to the strengths and weaknesses of these physical multimedia environments.

THE INTERDISCIPLINARY DESIGN TEAM

Designing physical multimedia environments that utilize the power of new technologies, media, and physical spaces invites the collaboration of diverse talents. People are needed who understand computer science, environmental design, robotics, film/video creation, instructional design, and today's *traditional* multimedia. Since it is understandably rare to find one person who is proficient in all of these areas, an interdisciplinary research and development approach is of paramount importance [Perlin and Druin 1994].

The strength of this interdisciplinary team approach is perhaps the strength of physical multimedia environments. Bringing together many varied talents invites enormous possibilities

- Science and Children's Museums
- Art Exhibitions and Galleries
- Amusement Parks
- Children's Toys and Electronic Books

for creative changes in technology. By rethinking how we design and who we design it with, we may find more visually beautiful, interactively unique, and powerfully expressive technological experiences. Not only will the products of these collaborations benefit, but the team design participants may as well. By being exposed to many different people with numerous talents, the opportunities to learn from, and to be influenced by others become apparent.

The weaknesses of this approach is that physical multimedia environments *cannot* be created without an interdisciplinary team design. A budget that includes one or two people for design and implementation cannot hope to cover the development costs of an entire physical multimedia environment. Many different talents are needed which, in most cases, will cost more money than a traditional software development team.

THE PROTOTYPING PROCESS

Besides the cost considerations of an interdisciplinary team approach, you also need to consider the challenge of the team dynamics. By bringing together diverse people who might normally have little to do with each other, but must now work together, the design and development process becomes more complex. Communication between technical and nontechnical, visual and nonvisual designers may be the most challenging of the design process. Any breakdown in communication can result in adding more costly time, revisions, and expense to an already difficult development process.

One technique that I have found that can help the communication between design participants is the prototyping process. Traditionally, designers *sketch* an idea, whether it be on paper storyboards or simulating it on a computer screen. Unfortunately, these two-dimensional prototyping methods fall short from describing what a physical multimedia experience might be.

The Immersive Environment work at NYU addressed this area by developing a *physical prototyping method*. This process I have come to call *A Day in the Life Approach* (for more description see Chapter 7). The prototyping process begins by finding or creating physical objects that would represent what designers anticipate the environment will contain. Then the interdisciplinary design team *acts out* the environment by designating different people to be different environmental input and/or output. For example, in a physical prototyping exercise, lifting a bowl might trigger a spotlight to turn on or a voice to be heard. Therefore, one student might be designated to turn on a flashlight when the bowl was lifted and another might be designated to read aloud the words, "This porridge is too hot" [Druin and Perlin 1994].

It was in this way that we at NYU *walked through* a typical multimedia prototype. From this method we were able to tell if the logic of an experience held up, and if the inputs and outputs were well-timed or appropriate. And it was in this way that we initiated communication between technologists, visual artists, instructional designers, and more.

THE VIRTUAL VERSUS THE PHYSICAL WORLD

The last and perhaps most important area in considering the strengths or weaknesses of physical multimedia environments is in the experience itself. Many researchers have raised the issue of whether a physical experience is truly necessary or potentially more powerful than a software-only experience. Supporters of physical multimedia environments refer to the consistent findings in literature on media in education. The research clearly supports the superiority of multimedia over single-medium presentation [Schram 1977].

However, critics question whether this research can also extend to physical multimedia environments. Whether critic or supporter, the issue arises—how much information is possible to contain in a physical multimedia environment? We know it is possible today to access enormous amounts of information using such software tools as databases, text editors, and visual simulations. Can this same amount of information be accessible through physical multimedia environments? The answer is not clear. Much more research and analysis is needed in the future before answers can crystallize. If it becomes apparent that there is a limit to what quantities of information can be accessible, then it may be questionable if physical multimedia environments will be found in our future. If, however, it becomes apparent that the quantity and quality of information is just as accessible, then the future of physical multimedia environments for children can be certain for years to come.

- In the future, children's multimedia environments may not have to live in hard plastic boxes that sit on desktops with keyboards, mice, or the occasional joystick.

- Multimedia environments in the future may look like any familiar room, stuffed animal, or toy block, and may be responsive to a child's movement, touch, sound, or even gesture.

- People so often forget that children meet a computer from the moment they see it, to the moment they touch it; not just from the moment they interact with the software.

- By offering real-world objects and places enhanced with technologies, physical multimedia environments can offer more powerful and involving learning experiences for children.

- Today researchers, educators, artists, and environmental designers are among the many professionals pointing in the direction of physical multimedia environments for the future.

- The *Media Room, LEGO TC Logo*, and *Immersive Environments* all have enormous potential for future physical multimedia environments for children.

- In the *Media Room*, people did not use a traditional mouse or keyboard; rather, they *told* the computer what they wanted to do by looking in a particular direction, saying a short phrase, or even gesturing with their arms.

- Children can create their own physical multimedia environments when the Logo programming language is combined with LEGO gears, motors, and sensors.

- Instead of placing input sensors on a person's body, with *Immersive Environments* the sensors are embedded into the physical surroundings.

- Designing physical multimedia environments that utilize the power of new technologies, media, and physical spaces invites the collaboration of diverse talents.

- Enormous possibilities for creative change in technology can happen when you bring together computer scientists, environmental designers, robotics engineers,film/video producers, instructional designers, and today's *traditional* multimedia artists.

- Communication between technical and nontechnical, visual and nonvisual desigers may be the most challenging of the design process. One technique that I have found that can help is the prototyping process.

- There are still questions about whether a physical multimedia environment in the future will be as powerful as a software-only experience.

Rapid Prototyping

Product

Concept

Implement

redo prototype

Quick Prototype

discard prototype

Evaluate

Waterf...

Product Speci...

System D...

...pl...

ACTIVITY of Innovation

A group of four 10-year old boys and five adult men and women are gathered around a drawing of a human skull.

"We need to have room for the cottonball brain," points out one of the boys in the group.

Model

tion Document

"But we need to draw an ear on him, so why don't we put it a little lower, to make room for the cottonballs?" says a man to the group.

gn Document

"But what is this robot going to teach?" another man asks.

"...how to order pizza!" says a boy very proud of the giggles from the group.

ent Product

"You know, there could be an image of pizza in the robot's visual cortex," says a woman in the group.

er Test

Just then a 10-year old girl wearing balloons taped to her clothing walks over to the group and asks, "Can I trade some pipecleaners for some more balloons?"

Product Release

"Sure, we're making a 'Brainiac' robot and don't need 'em," says a boy in the group.

"Thanks!" says the girl scooping up a handful of balloons.

She then walks over to her group of adults and children, and exclaims, "Look what I got!"

"Great!" says a woman in the group, "but I think your kidney fell off when you were trading."
"Nothing a little tape and balloons won't fix," says another woman.
"Hey, who's making the VR glasses?" asks a girl in the group.
"I am," says another girl working on the floor with pipecleaners, "but someone has to help with the 'Sensor Gloves'."
"I'll help," says a man in the group, "but where did we say the sensors and probes were going to be in the gloves?"

This is a prototyping design session at a recent conference on computer-human interface design (CHI'95). Seventy adults and children worked together in teams of nine or ten to create prototypes of multimedia environments for the future.

BACKGROUND

How do we find great ideas? There is always the romantic notion that an apple will fall on our head and we will cry, "Eureka!" There is also the ever-popular *garage theory*, that by tinkering in a suburban garage, we will start a billion-dollar company with an apple logo. And then there is the warm and fuzzy *weekend-painter story*, that by programming up a little something for our kids on Saturdays and Sundays, we will stumble on a million-dollar product idea.

THE PATH TO PRODUCT DEVELOPMENT

The previous scenarios all make for good business folklore, but unfortunately they are the romantic exceptions rather than the real norms. The majority of today's CD–ROM Edutainment, multimedia authoring tools, and on-line multimedia environments are designed and developed in teams. Sometimes a single person may conceive of an idea and a design team will enhance, redefine, and/or visualize a direction for development. Other times, the interaction of a group (of three or more) may find a starting point. These product or research teams look for innovative answers to familiar questions: What will a product do? How will it look? How will a user interact with it? Each team brings to life their ideas in very different ways. The dynamic of each team varies as do the tools used to capture ideas. Make no mistake, the path to product development is littered with bruised egos, discarded prototypes, and a lot of compromising. It does not reflect a neat, tidy list of *10 easy steps to multimedia* that you can read aloud in the latest *How to* books. It is a messy, creative process where ideas build on other ideas.

In this chapter, I will look at this design process: how it has changed through the years; what tools people use in design; and the strengths and weakness of different design approaches. Now that you have made your way through chapters of multimedia examples for children, I'd like to take one step back and ask you to consider how *you* might design *your* multimedia environments for the future. To give you a first-hand feel for the design process, I will later discuss one example, in depth, of team design with children.

goals

- To find a common language or tool for teams to generate innovative ideas
- To capture and record ideas for the eventual process of development
- To foster a collaborative, productive team design process

THE DESIGN TEAM

Different disciplines have different priorities, different styles, and different values. When people from different disciplines get together, values collide. What one person finds valuable, others do not even notice. And they do not notice, they do not notice.

[Kim 1990]

Multidisciplinary design can be one of the most productive and creative processes. Yet, it also can be one of the most frustrating, painful experiences to live through. Many different people bring to the team many different perspectives and offer a wealth of resources to get the job done. On the other hand, imagine asking five people to work together, who might ordinarily have little reason to speak to one another. Not only do they have to find a productive way to work together, but they also must stumble upon great ideas in the process. This is no small task to accomplish.

Take a moment to consider building a design team that includes a computer programmer, a graphic designer, a classroom teacher, a sound designer, and a 10-year-old child. Imagine if they were all to evaluate the same piece of multimedia software. The computer programmer may be fascinated with how the underlying code works, but may find the look of the software unimportant. On the other hand, the graphic designer may see the colors, icons, and fonts of the screen layout, but may not be concerned with the sound or music quality. The sound designer, however, may notice every sound effect and music bit chosen, but may find the content of the product unimportant. The classroom teacher may be concerned with how this software is to be used to teach geography, but may find it of little consequence if the software is entertaining to use. Finally, the 10-year-old child may care whether the software is fun to use and may care that someone cares to know.

Together the team can see, hear, evaluate, and build a software product. One is sensitive to what the other is not. Each one has expertise in some part of the development process. No development company would ever consider *not* gathering together a team such as this to create a solid multimedia product for children. What varies from product to product is the participants on a given design team. If a database is needed for doctors or a spreadsheet for financial analysts, you can be sure a 10-year-old child will not be included on the design team. However, if the product is for children, then a child or some number of children should be included in the design process. (This may be an obvious point to make, but unfortunately is not obvious to most multimedia developers.)

With so many differences among members of a design team, a common ground must be found. There must be a way to offer a common language, where different points of view can be understood, and concrete compromises can lead to creative decision-making. To find this common ground, different teams use different design processes and tools.

THE DEVELOPMENT PROCESS

Team design demands "...the full spectrum of problem-solving activities, including stating the goal, ideating (sic.), structuring, evaluation, selection and implementation...Peo-

ple carrying out these difficult cognitive activities…do not proceed through these various activities in an orderly fashion. But they generally do all of these activities at some point during their problem-solving." [Olson and Olson 1991]

A long time ago, before multimedia became a billion-dollar software industry, marketing managers wrote large thick documents which detailed how a product should be designed. Sometimes they would ask potential customers what they thought of an idea— more frequently, they did not. Once a document was fully digested by the technical managers, systems engineers would write another document that specified how all those product features would be implemented in soft-

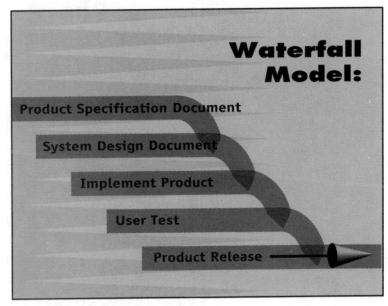

The *Waterfall Model* of software development.

ware. The programmers would then use this document to write their part of the product's software. They would then test and debug, sometimes even with real users, then send the product out into the world. Technologists have come to call this the *Waterfall Model* of software development [Mulligan, Alton, and Simkin 1991; Hix and Hartson 1993; Hourvitz 1994].

This process of development has fizzled out in its popularity. It was once regarded as "the right way" to design software: methodical, well-documented, and carefully planned design. On the other hand, with this method no visual prototyping or mock-ups are done, little user input or feedback is received, and almost no team design work is done. Opportunities for miscommunication are plentiful. Written documents are passed from group to group and reinterpreted with additional text as they are passed along. For typical users, these documents are complex and abstract at best, making it difficult to comment on any suggested designs until the product is well along in the development cycle. If any changes are to be made after the final specification documents are agreed upon, the changes can be time-consuming and costly.

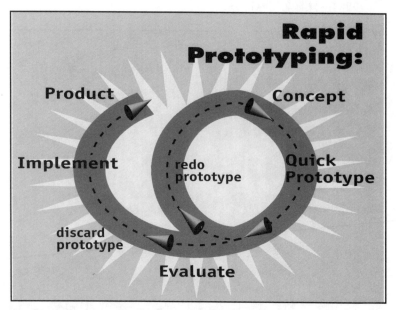

The *Rapid Prototyping* model of software development.

In the last 10 years, the *Rapid Prototyping* method of development has become quite popular [Hix and Hartson 1993; Hourvitz 1994; Preece, Rogers, Sharp, Benyon, Holland, and Carey 1994]. Instead of relying only on the words of complex documents to represent a product concept, a prototype, mock-up, and/or storyboard is created. These visual designs using paper, 35mm slides, three-dimensional models, or the computer screen can give an idea to the development team of what the product will eventually be. These visual sketches can also be used to solicit feedback from users right at the start of the development process. They are also useful to present to company management for funding or other resource support (needless to say management would always prefer to see something visually interesting rather than have to wade through an enormous document). In fact, most of the commercial product examples described in this book first began their product lives as a prototype, mock-up, and/or storyboard.

Once management has given the green light to a development team to continue on with a project, the visual prototype is used to create a product planning document, which includes a development timeline and resources needed to finish a product. Depending on the needs of company management, some design teams may write a document in parallel as they are developing their ideas visually [Druin 1994]. Whatever the case is, the visual prototype is eventually put aside and product development is done using more complex computer technologies. At that point, the process is similar to the *Waterfall Model* for final product implementation [Hourvitz 1994].

Even though the *Rapid Prototyping* method is immensely popular with multimedia developers today, difficulties can still be found in this process. First and most importantly, large product changes after the prototyping stage can still seriously impact the product schedule or budget. While Rapid Prototyping offers a great deal of flexibility for change in the beginning stages of product development, it later suffers from the same problems as the Waterfall Model. The other drawback to Rapid Prototyping, is that the work put into the creation of a prototype (especially a computer prototype) is put aside. It is not used for the programming of the final product. It is only used as a product specification [Hourvitz 1994; Druin 1994].

Today, as computer prototyping tools become more sophisticated, they seem to cross the line into product development tools (e.g., *Macromedia Director, Visual Basic, Apple Media Tool Kit*). Thanks to this, a new development model emerges: *the Iterative Process*. This model suggests that since our prototyping can be done with actual development tools, design feedback can be given and listened to, throughout the whole development process. There is always something inter-

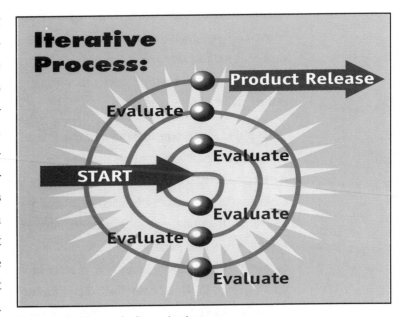

The *Iteractive Process* of software development.

active to see and discuss. Changes to the software product are less costly to make, no matter where the product is in the development process [Hix and Hartson 1993; Hourvitz 1994].

While this method of development is quite flexible, it may also lead to difficulty in the product scheduling and budget. If company management and user feedback can affect the product throughout the development process, it may be difficult to decide when a product is ready for commercial release. In general, this may also lengthen the process, which can add lots of development dollars to an already costly process. What I have found is that industry and academic researchers who are not concerned with deadlines, but focused on finding innovation can best take advantage of this process. For commercial developers with budgets to keep and timelines to follow, the *Iterative Process* is not made for them; *Rapid Prototyping* is a better solution [Druin 1994].

THE PROTOTYPING PROCESS

Automobile makers, architects, and sculptors make models; circuit designers use 'breadboards'; aircraft developers test 'mockups'; artists experiment with working sketches. In each case, the goal is to provide an early ability to observe something about the nature of the final product, evaluating ideas and weighing alternatives before committing to one of them. [Hix and Hartson 1993]

What *Rapid Prototyping* and the *Iterative Process* have in common is the importance of visual prototyping: capturing an idea quickly for management to understand; for a development team to use; and for users to give feedback. What is difficult, is finding a medium or tool that can be used by an entire team of interdisciplinary professionals, rather than one person. Most computer prototyping tools lend themselves to being used by one, perhaps two people. When design teams use them, the work falls to a few team members to quickly capture ideas and visually present them to the entire group. In which case, the brainstorming process becomes more of a show-and-tell experience, rather than a creative give-and-take of ideas.

An approach to prototyping that has become increasingly popular, and quite widely used, is a *Participatory Design Approach* [Blomberg and Henderson 1990; Druin and Withey 1990; Muller 1991; Tudor, Muller, Dayton, and Root 1993; Druin and Solomon 1995]. First pioneered by Scandinavian researchers, [Bjerknes, Ehn, and Kyng 1987; Bødker, Ehn, Knudsen, Kyng, and Madsen 1988], this technique emphasizes the importance of enabling an entire team of people to have input into a design project. In general, low-tech or noncomputer prototyping tools are used at the very beginning of the brainstorming process to explore various design possibilities. After they are captured by the team on paper, in models, or on video, computer prototyping tools can then take over. Keep in mind that, for the most part, Participatory Design does not lend itself to those people who feel most comfortable at a large conference table with a yellow note pad and a serious expression. Participatory Design asks a design team to be creative while having a social, messy exchange of ideas. There are a number of different approaches to prototyping and Participatory Design. I will discuss a few of these approaches that either colleagues of mine or I have used quite successfully.

The "Deal Me A Card" Approach to Design

Researchers at USWEST, AT&T Bell Labs, Pacific Bell, Bellcore, Apple Computer, and New York University have popularized what I have come to call the *Deal Me A Card approach* to design [Muller, Wildman, and White 1994; Druin and Perlin 1994; Cypher and Smith 1995; Muller 1995]. Essentially, this prototyping method uses paper index cards to represent a number of different pieces of a potential design. Index cards have been used to represent screen images (e.g., icon, menus), work objects (e.g., diskettes, printouts), tasks (e.g., searching information, sending email), and/or system input and output (physical multimedia environments' video, lights, sensors). Tuder *et al*, have used the word *CARD* to represent this process as "Collaborative Analysis of Requirements and Design" [Tuder, Muller, Dayton, and Root 1993].

It should be understood that the presence of simple index cards does not mean that people can suddenly be creative. It is what is done with them that seems to promote exciting design sessions. There are a number of ways that design teams seem to use index cards to spur on fruitful brainstorming sessions. One such approach uses index cards in a way that is similar to the popular board game *Pictionary* [Muller, Wildman, and White 1994]. To begin, one or more team members write the tasks on cards which verbally describe what they want a particular technology to do. Then the task cards are put in a hat to be selected by a *sketcher.* Each team member takes turns being the sketcher who tries to visually represent a word to the group in a given amount of time. (This can also be done with two groups playing against each other.)

Ideally, the sketches are done either on acetate sheets on an overhead projector or on large pieces of paper on a flip-chart. In this way, the sketches can be kept and later used when refining the look and feel of a software or hardware project. It is also quite useful to have a few people observe the process so that sketching strategies, miscommunications, and/or key visual cues can be noted. After the task cards have been sketched, the team can then review what they've done, and add to the team's sketches. This process has been demonstrated quite success-fully by researchers from USWEST, AT&T Bell Labs, and Bellcore [Muller, Wild-man, and White 1994].

Another card design approach was used at New York University to help develop physical multimedia environments (see Chapter 6). The cards were used as a basis to *act out* what input and output would happen in a physical multimedia environment (e.g., a user triggers a switch and a spotlight is turned on). A similar approach was used at Apple Computer by researchers in the Advanced Research Group to act out *KidSim*, a simulation authoring tool for children. When trying to establish if the authoring language was understandable to children, software designers at Apple asked fifth grade students to use the authoring language to program their bodies around the room. Instead of index cards, the children used *3M Post-It Notes*, so that they could stick each programming instruction on their clothing. It was in this way, that children tried authoring a simulation character. Not only did the children enjoy their activity, but they also learned in a concrete way how to program. The researchers from Apple discovered that their programming language was on the right track [Cypher and Smith 1995]. This is also an excellent example of how to involve children in the design process in a meaningful way. So often we forget that if children are to be our design partners, we need to find concrete ways to spark their design creativity (not just adults').

"A Day In The Life" Approach to Design

Another way of brainstorming with a large group of people is to act out ideas and videotape them for later design use [Muller, Wildman, and White 1994]. I call this *A Day in the Life* approach to design. Essentially, design team members are asked to represent parts of a computer system or the uses of it. I have found this method extremely useful in combination with the *Deal Me A Card* approach or in combination with the *Bag of Tricks* approach (I will describe that in the next section). Basically, by using people to improvise what a system should do, designers can work out the kinks before ever drawing, building, or developing. It is one thing to *talk through* a system with storyboards, but it is another thing entirely to pretend to use the system in real-time. You can see where your logic fails, and what additional features need to be added. The drawback to this approach is that it is not for the shy of heart. Many reserved researchers find this a difficult design process to master. Some would say that they did not enter the research or development fields so that they could stand on a stage one day and act like a *cursor.* Therefore, this type of activity can be uncomfortable for some members of a design team.

The "Bag Of Tricks" Approach to Design

Another approach I and others have used quite successfully is what I call the *Bag of Tricks* approach to design [Druin and Withey 1990; Druin and Solomon 1993-1995]. Dr. Muller, a researcher of Participatory Design at USWEST, has come to call it "PICTIVE: A Plastic Interface for Collaborative Technology Initiatives through Video Exploration" [Muller 1991; Muller 1995]. Essentially, it is *paper-bag dramatics* for designers. What you do is give a design team a bag of low-tech prototyping tools (e.g., paper, scissors, colored markers) and ask them to use these materials to prototype or mock-up their design ideas. What we have found is that the low-tech tools are an effective way to loosen people up and give equal footing to adults and children, visual and nonvisual designers, technical and nontechnical professionals. Most everyone knows how to use scissors, paper, and markers. Ideally, the process is videotaped and/or photographed to be used later for computer prototyping and design implementation. Interestingly enough, when design teams are asked to present their *Bag of Tricks* prototype, they generally use *A Day in the Life* approach.

AN EXAMPLE DESIGN SESSION

For the past five years I have been using many of these prototyping techniques at various conferences to give design professionals an idea of how to bring children into the design process. What comes out of these experiences for prototyping participants and for me, is a better understanding of team dynamics and the process of design. To give you a first-hand flavor of this experience, I will spend the next section describing one example of a recent tutorial I gave with Dr. Cynthia Solomon at CHI'95 (a leading computer conference on computer-human interface design).

THE INTRODUCTION

Imagine that you have just spent the morning listening to the equivalent of the first six chapters of this book. You've seen demos, had people analyze products, heard product design warstories, and considered the various styles of teaching and learning that each product promotes. Now your instructor, me, explains that in the afternoon we'll be putting to work what you have just learned. You'll be designing multimedia environments for the future that teach children about a part or parts of their body. I then pull out a bag of low-tech prototyping supplies and show you what we'll be using. To a chorus of nervous giggles, I pull out balloons, pipecleaners, clay, markers, colored paper, scissors, yarn, glue, and even toilet paper. I point out that by giving you these tools, your imagination won't be limited to, or influenced by, what is possible today. I promise that you won't be designing environments with windows, icons, and menus.

I go on to explain that in the afternoon we will be bringing in a group of fourth and fifth grade students from a local Denver elementary school. I explain that we won't be pretending that we know about children; we will be collaborating with them as design partners. I then ask you to consider a few questions when designing in the afternoon: Where will your multimedia environment be located? What is it that you want to teach? What is the scope of information you want to share? How is your approach the same or different as compared to the multimedia examples you have just seen?

I also remind you of a few team design trends (so you are not too shocked by the experience):

1. Your team will contain different people with different experiences.

2. You will disagree.

3. Some teams will work faster than others.

4. Focus on short term and long term goals.

5. Split up the work; different people are better at different tasks.

By this time, you have no appetite, but I send you off for lunch anyway.

When you come back in the afternoon, I ask that you and the 40 other professionals in the tutorial, categorize yourselves. I ask whether you're a technologist, a visual designer, a content expert/teacher, or miscellaneous. I then ask you to go to one corner in the room, depending on how you categorize yourself. Once everyone has grouped themselves, you find yourself in a corner with technologists from Microsoft, Apple Computers, MIT, USWEST, Tmaker, Compuserve, and more. I then disperse you evenly among the seven work tables. The same is done for the other groups.

Once you are all seated at a round table, you begin introducing yourselves. Your group consists of six professionals, two from universities and four from industry companies. Just as you are beginning to feel comfortable with your compatriots, three 10-year-old children are added to your group. Two are girls and one is a boy. All are shy when they meet you for the first time. It is then announced you have two hours to come up with your prototype.

THE DESIGN PROCESS
Your team decides that the best way to start is by dumping out the bag of prototyping tools. As the materials come pouring out of the bag, the children on your team seem to come alive. Instantly, two children begin to fiddle with the pipecleaners and one

starts to blow up a balloon. Two of the adults sitting next to the children start to play with the clay. The group seems to warm up as they begin to poke at the art supplies.

The adults in the group begin asking the children what their favorite body parts are. They receive answers such as a nose, hands, brain, and feet. When the adults ask the children to decide on just one body part for their system, the children cannot agree on which is best. One woman in the group abandons this tactic and tries a different approach. She asks the children what their favorite activities are. She receives answers such as dancing, playing baseball, watching TV, climbing trees. Then a man in the group asks the children if they know what body parts they use for each of these activities. The children begin to shout out body parts for each activity, while an adult writes down their suggestions. The group's harmony ends when they reach the activity of TV. The adults in the group cannot convince the three children that they need a brain to watch TV. The children say that they need a hand for the remote control, eyes to watch TV, but no brain. Eventually, a man in the group suggests that maybe this activity might be fun for their multimedia environment. Others in the group agree, including two of the children now building body parts out of clay.

TEAM DYNAMICS

If you were to walk around the room, you would see a similar design process taking shape in other groups. What you would also see are various team dynamics coming to the surface as each group begins to work. The most common team dynamic that you would see is the *Leader Takes Over* team. With this dynamic, you would see a team that has one adult leader that has naturally begun poking and prodding the group to find solutions. This person would ask questions, suggest possible solutions, and perhaps even parcel out the tasks that need to be done. In some groups, this would lead to happy followers and a team design solution. In other groups, this would lead to an unhappy team (the *Non-Group Group*) and people would withdraw from the design task at hand. This group might end up needing a facilitator from outside the team. This third party might prod the group along by asking questions about what they are doing, why they are doing it, and how they intend to make it

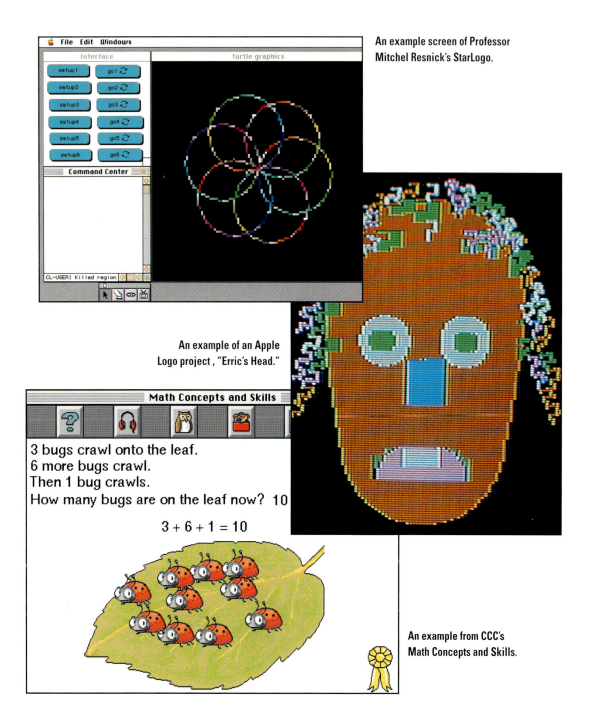

An example screen of Professor Mitchel Resnick's StarLogo.

An example of an Apple Logo project , "Erric's Head."

3 bugs crawl onto the leaf.
6 more bugs crawl.
Then 1 bug crawls.
How many bugs are on the leaf now? 10

$$3 + 6 + 1 = 10$$

An example from CCC's Math Concepts and Skills.

MULTIMEDIA ENV

RONM

Sample screen from Dorling Kindersley's *The Way Things Work.*

Sample screen from Brøderbund's
Where In Space is Carmen Sandiego?

Videodisc image from Bank
Street College of Education's
Voyage of the MIMI .

Designing Multimedia Environments for Children

Sample screen of a second grade
student's project using
Brøderbund's *Kid Pix* slide show.

Image from *The Great Solar System Rescue.*
Courtesy of Tom Snyder Productions.

The Great Solar System Rescue videodisc package.
Courtesy of Tom Snyder Productions.

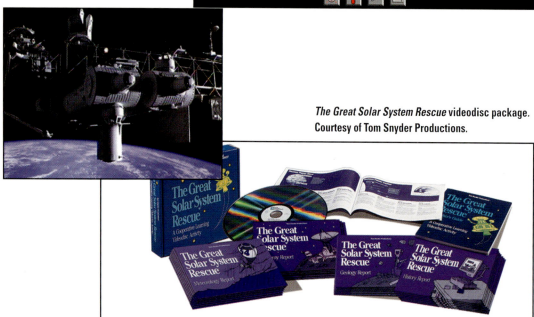

MULTIMEDIA

Designing Multimedia Environments for Children

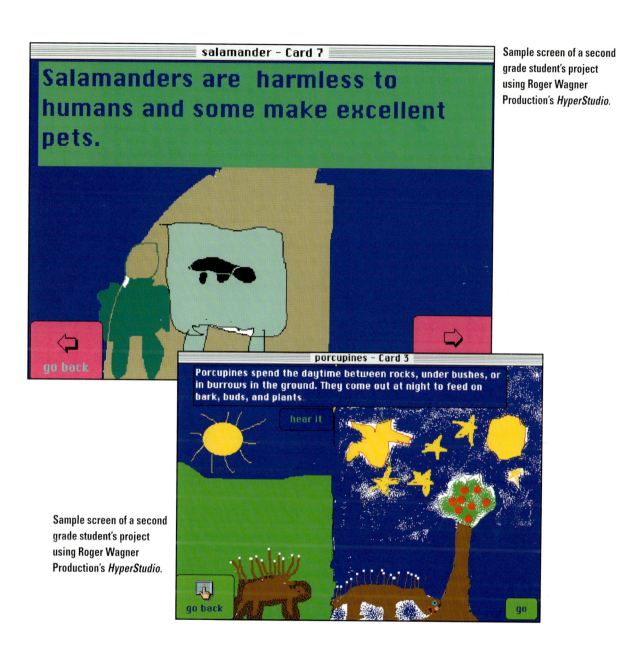

Sample screen of a second grade student's project using Roger Wagner Production's *HyperStudio*.

Sample screen of a second grade student's project using Roger Wagner Production's *HyperStudio*.

salamander – Card 7

Salamanders are harmless to humans and some make excellent pets.

go back

porcupines – Card 3

Porcupines spend the daytime between rocks, under bushes, or in burrows in the ground. They come out at night to feed on bark, buds, and plants.

hear it

go back

go

ENVIRONMENTS

Designing Multimedia Environments for Children

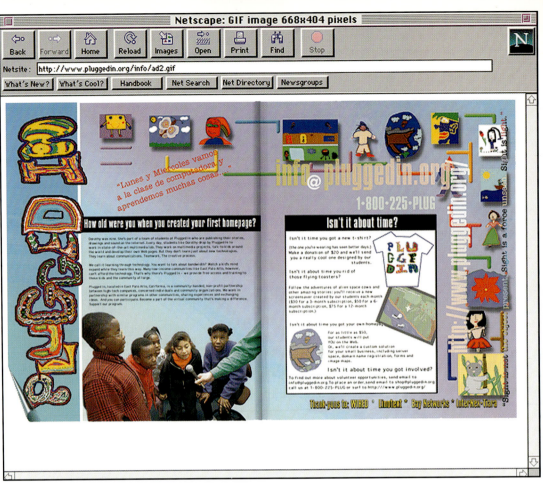

An image from *Plugged-In* from the World Wide Web.

An example screen from *Scholastic Network*.

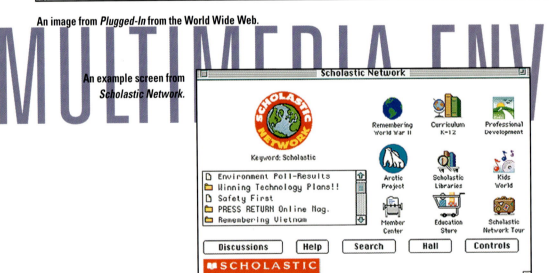

Image of MIT's Media Room.
Copyright MIT Media Laboratory,
used with permission.
Photo by Christian Lischewski.

Image of an Immersive Environment created and presented at
New York University.

ONMENTS

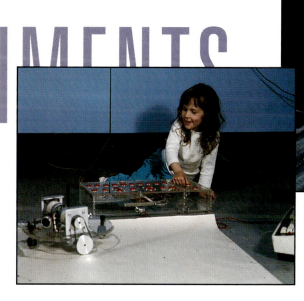

A child using a Logo
Floor Turtle.

Designing Multimedia Environments for Children

The start of a prototyping/design
session at a CHI '95 tutorial led by
Allison Druin and Cynthia Solomon.

Adult CHI professionals
partner with fourth grade
students to prototype a
multimedia environment.

A presentation of one
group's prototype.

happen. Many times this facilitator might also have to calm the tempers of the team members in the group.

If you were to walk over to another part of the room, you would see what I call the *Democratic* team. This team would seem to function as if they were born to work together. Each team member would contribute ideas, the group would reach a consensus, and they would focus on prototyping a design solution that suits the entire group.

If you were to continue to wander the room, you would also notice that some team dynamics are the result of what the children in the room are asked to do. In the *Children as Partners* team, you would see adults asking children for design suggestions: asking them what they like, why they like it, and why it is better than something else. On the other hand, you might also see the *Children as Observer* team. Unfortunately, there would be one team out of seven that ignores the children in the group. The adults in the group would talk among themselves and occasionally acknowledge the children. In most cases, this would be the group of adults who have never spent much time with children, let alone worked with them. They would not be sure how to communicate with children, so they wouldn't.

If you were to return back to your group, you would see that within 45 minutes your group would have discovered its prototype idea. You would also see that within an hour from starting the design exercise, your group would have split up the tasks at hand and begun work on building the prototype. Your group would work on the floor, would stand by the table, or would work somewhere in another corner. Within another half hour, your group would decide how to present your prototype to the rest of the tutorial audience.

PROJECT EXAMPLES

It's showtime. You learn that your group doesn't have to go first. Your team members join together for a collective sigh of relief. Instead, you sit back and watch other groups present their prototypes.

How A Baby's Brain Works

The first group begins by presenting a system that shows how a baby's brain works when he or she is trying to drink from a bottle. The group presents two parts to the system. One device is a display panel (in cardboard, cottonballs, colored paper, and markers) which shows the different parts of a person's brain. The other part of the system is a pair of robotic baby friends. These are represented by one adult and one child in the group. They are lying across a few chairs with cardboard bottles in their hands. Another child (the system's user) calls out brain commands and the robotic pair react to what is being said: "...grab bottle with right hand... swing right shoulder up... stop... bend right elbow down... twist right elbow...." While this is being said, the display panel is updating (thanks to a child connecting different parts of the brain with string to different body parts on the picture). It is quite comical to see what the robots do when the child calls out directions from the brain that aren't quite right. The cardboard bottles land in the robots' ears, shoulders, or noses. It is fascinating to see a prototype that clearly shows how difficult it is for the brain to learn even simple tasks.

A Trip Through The Body

This group begins their presentation by placing a girl, with balloons taped to her clothing, in the center of the group. An adult in the group explains that each balloon on their special robot is an internal body part: the kidney, the liver, the intestines. The adult user of the system comes forth wearing pipecleaner glasses that they call "special VR glasses." She touches the balloon on the robot child labeled "heart" and another adult in the group makes sound effects for the heart. The user with VR glasses continues touching different balloon parts and hearing very funny gurgling noises from the group. Eventually, another adult in the group explains that they can also use their robot to see what happens if it smoked cigarettes or gained too much weight. The robot shows what happens to the lungs and what the fat looks like (in the form of lots of toilet paper).

An Exploration of Chris

This group begins by presenting a picture of "Chris." An adult in the group puts on "magic glasses" (pipecleaner glasses) and the picture of Chris is then replaced with the internal body parts of Chris. Specifically, the brain, heart, stomach, and lungs are highlighted (with clay, markers, and colored paper). Another man in the group uses the "magic ear" (a pipecleaner stethoscope) to hear the body parts, while another man makes sound effects for each. The "special sensor gloves" are then used by one of the children in the group. They can touch Chris's body parts without hurting them. Finally, they pull out the "magic nose" (which looks more like a pig snout made out of pipecleaners). One man puts on the snout and sniffs Chris's body parts. Apparently, the smell of the stomach is a little much for the user and he is knocked out. Their presentation ends when the group's three children say a special public thanks to the adults in their group. Everyone is misty-eyed.

Now it is time for your group to present, except… wait… the order of presentations has been switched. Another group insists on presenting, at this very moment. They say that their prototype won't otherwise work. You breathe another sigh of relief, and sit back to watch the presentation:

The Brainiac

This group begins by presenting the "Brainiac," a detailed picture of a person's brain (with cottonballs, markers, colored paper, and a few balloons). The children of the group are holding up the picture. Then one of the boys in the group says, "This is your brain. This is your brain on pizza." The children then show what the Brainiac does when ordering out for pizza. One of the boys is the Brainiac's voice. He tells the hands to dial the phone number. He tells the mouth to ask for pizza and drool. The simulated pizza man (one of the adults in the group) sends over a pizza made out of clay. The Brainiac says that the pizza tastes like plastic. He calls the simulated pizza man again and asks that he send over a "hot one" this time. Just then, to the surprise of all, another adult in the group leads into the room a *real* Domino's Pizza

Delivery man. The entire audience breaks out in laughter and clapping. The children in the group seem to have had no idea this surprise was in the making by their adult collaborators. They, however, seem to appreciate it, judging by the way the children are jumping up and down and grabbing for some real pizza.

What Parts Do I Need?

Now it's time for your presentation. One of the men in your group begins by explaining the design process the group went through to reach the prototype that's now here. He explains that eventually the group was listing body parts for different activities. Then the man shows a simple written word on colored paper. The children in the group then take robotic body parts (made out of clay) and place them on the written word. The man calls out "watching TV" and the children each put in a body part. The man asks, "Where is the brain?" And the children all say in unison, "You don't need *that* to watch TV!" The audience gets a good laugh out of your disagreement with the children. Your presentation is complete.

Skeleton Assembly Kit

This group begins by presenting a large chart with lists and pictures. One woman in the group is the speaker for the team. She methodically walks the audience through their chart which reads: "Methods, Premises: (1) Constructivism, Learn by Doing, (2) Creating a being to achieve a goal, make comparisons, (3) Cooperation and Challenge, Exploration in content: gravity, obstacles, elements…." Eventually she explains that the "curriculum" is to construct a skeleton and then use the character to traverse an obstacle course. It seems obvious from her presentation that the children in the group have had little to do with the ideas or the eventual storyboard presentation. They are standing in the back fidgeting.

The Digestive System

The final presentation is by a group who wanted to know how the digestive system works. A model of a robotic digestive system (a picture with cottonballs, pipecleaners, plastic bags, and socks) is held up by children and adults in the group. One of the women explains that their prototype simulates what happens when we eat food.

The children put different foods in the robotic model's mouth and the group takes it through the system. At one point, they send the food down the small intestines and someone in the audience suggests that this may be factually incorrect. In response, one woman in the group explains they were lacking a content expert in this knowledge area.

AFTER THE PERFORMANCE

The experiences that I just described actually happened at a recent tutorial in Denver, Colorado, in May of 1995 [Druin and Solomon 1995]. For the past five years, I have taught similar seminars with either Cynthia Solomon or Kate Withey. Each time during this constructivist experience, we have seen similar results from our teams of adults and children. Tutorial participants would like the future to include robotic friends, holographic representations, and multisensory experiences. For the most part the teams' design simulation experiences (*Interactive Textbook*) rather than constructivist experiences (*Expressive Medium*). It seems that in the heat of designing with unusual visualization tools, the adults forget that we have talked extensively about the power of *Expressive Medium*. Another similarity that we find is that these prototypes are generally presented in *A Day in the Life* approach. At no time do we ever specifically say how design teams must present their prototype, but for the most part we see very creative performances. As for team dynamics, we generally see that four to five adults and two children are an ideal size group to get the job done. We also see that the better a team works together, the more exciting the final prototype project usually is.

After each team design experience is finished, we say good-bye to our new-found children friends and the adults in the group settle in for a discussion on what just happened. For the most part, these professionals start by discussing their impressions of their child collaborators. At CHI'95, we heard comments such as these:

I underestimated the kids…

Kids really know what they like…

The children seem to be catalysts and spark ideas I wouldn't have thought of...

The adults in the group refined the ideas the kids thought of...

I actually found it hard to get direct information out of kids...

The kid's interest seemed to fluctuate during the afternoon...

I think the children definitely changed the group dynamics...

They forced us adults to focus!

Eventually, the conversation moves on to a more general discussion of the hands-on design experience. At CHI'95, we heard these comments:

There were an impressive variety of projects!

We all had the same materials, but not the same ideas...

I was frustrated by my group, I think we could have done better...

It's amazing how much of the theory you forget when you're too busy designing...

Almost all of us created multimedia simulations even though constructivism is in!

I think this project should require that each group uses audience participation, as opposed to having someone in the group use the system. You'd probably see more interactivity...

STRENGTHS AND WEAKNESSES OF THE DESIGN PROCESS

What you have just been a party to is one approach to one type of prototyping experience. As I have pointed out, there are numerous ways to generate and capture ideas. You don't always need clay, markers, socks, or toilet paper to spark innovation. What you do need, are creative individuals with varying expertise that are willing to work hard. The strength of their initial design and brainstorming sessions can set the course for a project's rapid success or its eventual failure. People so often forget that the activity of innovation begins at the time of product conception. Sometimes a single person conceives of a direction to take or an idea to follow. Other times, it is the interaction of a group that finds a starting point. Once an idea has been conceived, it needs to be visualized. This could mean starting with a mock-up using toilet paper and cottonballs or some sketches on index cards. This could also mean starting with an interactive computer prototype. Whatever the initial path a design team takes, it is only the beginning of the innovation process. Prototypes and ideas must be translated into a working product or research project. The creative energies that are brought together in the prototyping experience must continue throughout the entire development process.

TEAM DYNAMICS

The strength or weakness of any design experience hinges on the quality of the team dynamics. The results of any team work are dependent on each team member contributing everything he or she has to offer. If the prototyping tools or the work practices of other team members keep this from happening, then the outcome can only be a modest success at best. We must keep in mind, that many design and technical professionals have never collaborated before. Still many more have never worked with children. If we are looking to assemble a productive team, capable of producing outstanding multimedia experiences for children, then we must consider a professional's *people skills*, as well as his/her design and development skills. Unfortunately, the best team on paper may not end up being the best team in practice. Many times you will not be able to tell that you have hired one professional that excessively interrupts people when they speak and another professional that has a phobia of speaking in front of more than three people. Only when a team begins to work together can you tell if the dynamics are constructive. If they are not, something must be done immediately to change the situation. If careful group facilitation

- Design teams are used in almost all major multimedia development projects
- Thousands of companies have hired design professionals with varying expertise
- The best success stories come from teams that worked well together

influences today

does not work, then I have found that quickly replacing team members with new ones, does much to help the situation. In my experience, it is rare that a design team does not have at least one person who was a replacement for another.

A technique that seems to foster constructive team design is a group debriefing after a frantic design session. I have found it very useful if design participants are asked by a third party (e.g., company management, an outside consultant) simply, "…how's it going?" What is key, is that all the team members be present at the time. If they are not, then the debriefing becomes nothing more than a time to complain about others who are not present. If, however, all are present, it becomes a useful time to evaluate what's been done, how it's getting done, and why it's important. It's amazing how quickly it can come to light that something's wrong with the design process. When a third party can see this, then something can be done to change the situation.

FROM COTTONBALLS TO COMPUTERS

I am often asked at tutorials that I teach, how do you actually get from cottonballs to a commercial product? In other words, many people find it difficult to understand how to translate a crazy low-tech prototype into an exciting new commercial product or a profound new research direction. For the moment, let me explain by using the project example of *An Exploration of Chris*, the multisensory tour of a body. Imagine if the design team who created this initial low-tech design prototype, decided that it was something they wanted to pursue. The design team would then take steps to *test-drive* this concept with more users (children outside the design team). Perhaps a few members of the design team would travel to an elementary school or they would invite a few local children to the design team's testing lab. To evaluate this prototype concept, the design team might use *A Day in the Life* approach to act out what the system would be like for users. As opposed to demonstrating the prototype with team members, this time, they might invite other children outside the team to use the *Magic Glasses* or *Magic Gloves*. The team might decide to record this process with videotape or take notes of what the children's general enthusiasm for the system was, the length of their attention span, and the ease of use of the system.

Once the design team has tested the product concept and found it to be a viable possibility, the team would then continue to refine their low-tech prototype. (At the same time, marketing professionals might do product research to understand what competition they could be up against. These professionals might also create a business plan to test the commercial profitability of the ideas.) In the meantime, the product design team would be fleshing out the product content (e.g., what different parts of the body do children want to explore?). The team would also refine the visual look and feel of their low-tech prototype (e.g., a more realistic product model).

In the case of *An Exploration of Chris*, the team might decide that Chris shouldn't be a multimedia CD–ROM, but a doll that takes advantage of new robotic technologies. The team might then create a doll with special gloves for users that enables them to feel the bone or muscle structures using force-feedback technologies. Perhaps, the team as it's refining its ideas, would come to the conclusion that the snout or special smelling device is just too technologically difficult and expensive to develop, so they would opt to simplify the design. Eventually, instead of a prototype made from pipecleaners, clay, and paper, the team would create an actual doll named Chris. At this point, the team would again test their prototype on users outside the group. What they might find this time from their tests is that users don't like the doll being a boy or users are more interested in looking for Chris's *private parts* rather than thinking about the bones or muscles. In general, the design team might discover that sample users seem to like the product concept, but the design details need more work.

After this testing session, the team would continue to refine their product concept. At this point, they might also receive valuable feedback from marketing professionals who explain that this could be a profitable venture if they were to sell the rights to other companies for them to use the character in animated television or movie projects. Therefore, the team might decide to create a fictional character which would be part bear, part dinosaur. Not only would this be a more marketable character to license, but it would wipe away users' gender and *private parts* problems. Again they would test out their new design on children. This time the design team might find out that their sample users love the product prototype. At this point, the technical people on the team would take over and begin to create the technologies that would allow Chris to become a fully interactive multisensory experience. As the development process continues, the design team might be faced with some difficult design trade-offs. Perhaps, they might realize that it would be too technologically expensive (in time and money) to give users force-feedback gloves. Instead, the design team might suggest a compromise solution: animating some of the body parts within the doll itself.

Finally, when some of the interactive features begin to work, the design team would again go through a round of user testing. When the product seems close to finished, a few sample products would be distributed to users to get their final feedback. At that point, the design team might suddenly discover that the fabric used for Chris is flammable and needs to be replaced. The team might also find out that the noises from Chris are too loud and need to be softened. Eventually, these product problems would be ironed out and Chris would be sent out in the world.

What I have just described to you is a simplified example of a product development process. The product is a fictional one, based on the initial work done by my tutorial participants at CHI'95. However, the development process is a real one. It is based on the *Rapid Prototyping* model described at the start of this chapter.

In one way or another, all of the multimedia examples in this book have benefited from a similar team-design experience. No, they did not all use socks, clay, and string to begin their prototyping experience, but they did all find tools and methods that fostered creative innovation. It is my hope that you, too, will find those tools and methods that can spark your creation of future multimedia environments for children.

- The majority of today's CD–ROM Edutainment, multimedia authoring tools, and on-line multimedia environments, all are designed and developed in teams.

- Many different people bring to the team many different perspectives and offer a wealth of resources to get the job done.

- In the design process there must be a way to offer a common language, where different points of view can be understood and concrete compromises can lead to creative decision-making.

- The *Waterfall Model*, the *Rapid Prototyping Model*, and the *Iterative Process* all are different approaches to the development process.

- The *Rapid Prototyping Model* is the approach most often used by commercial multimedia developers today, while the *Iterative Process* is well-suited for the research process.

- What is difficult, is finding a medium or prototyping tool that can be used by an entire team of interdisciplinary professionals, rather than by one person. Most computer prototyping tools lend themselves to being used by one, perhaps two people.

- There are different prototyping methods where professionals make use of low-tech prototyping tools and activities:
  - *The Deal Me A Card* approach
  - *The Day In The Life* approach
  - *The Bag of Tricks* approach

- There are various different team dynamics that surface as design teams begin their work:
  - *The Leader Takes Over Team*
  - *The Non-Group Group*
  - *The Democratic Team*
  - *The Children as Partners Team*
  - *The Children as Observers Team*

- The strength of your initial design and brainstorming sessions can set the course for a project's rapid success or its eventual failure.

Information SuperHighway

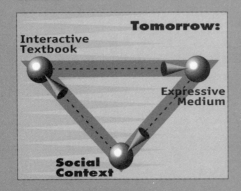

Today:

Interactive Textbook

Expressive Medium

Tomorrow:

Interactive Textbook

Expressive Medium

Social Context

THOUGHTS
About Tommorrow

INVENTING THE FUTURE

We live in a world where so many of us are fascinated with what will happen in the future. As more and more of our lives become increasingly dependent upon today and tomorrow's multimedia technologies, our obsession with the future continues to grow. We want to know if the technologies we are devoted to today will be important tomorrow. We want to know how our lives will change and why they will change. We want crystal-ball accuracy, yet we know the only thing certain about the future is that it is uncertain.

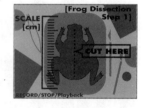

It used to be that we imagined the future at a World's Fair or from reading or seeing science fiction in books, movies, or television shows with lots of space-ships. Now, instead, we can visit places like Disney's Epcot Center or MIT's Media Lab. We can read magazines like *Wired* or *Mondo 2000*. We can read books like Danny Goodman's *Living at Light Speed*, Clifford Stoll's *Silicon Snake Oil*, or Nicholas Negroponte's *Being Digital*. We can even surf the Inter-net. It seems that everybody's got a crystal-ball for rent. Therefore, cutting through the hype and finding some clear thoughts on what the future may hold is not easy. Media gurus, technology visionaries, and a multitude of industry consultants all paint different pictures of what will be.

The one thing that people do seem to agree upon (to some extent) is that some version of the *Information Superhighway* will be an important part of our future. With the promise of vast amounts of information just a mouse-click away, I thought what better way to explore the future than by using this infamous tool. Therefore, when I began considering my thoughts for this chapter, I spent some time wandering the World Wide Web (WWW) searching for the future. Thanks to various search engines I found such Web pages as: "Future Atomic Releases," "Sterling on the Future of War," "Shock Wave (Anti) Warrior," "Ag—Commodities Markets—Experimental Orange Juice—Nearest Futures," and "Welcome to Future Net."

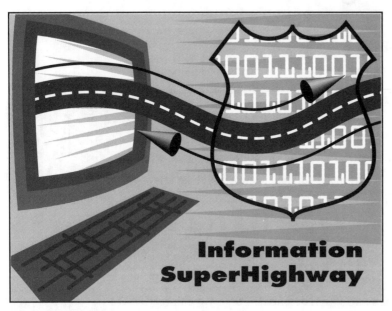

The Information Superhighway.

Unfortunately, the entries that offered me any true insights into the future were few and far between. For example, the "Future Atomic Releases" home page was a description of war games produced by Avalon-Hill. The home page for "Ag—Commodities Markets—Experimental Orange Juice—Nearest Futures" gave me the last closing price of orange juice, along with the highs, lows, and stock volumes that changed hands for that day. Even "Future Net," which had numerous topics from business to education to sports, had little insight into the future. It was an excellent resource for what was happening today, but not for tomorrow.

I did find a few interesting discussions of the future in on-line articles via *HotWired* (the on-line version of *Wired*). "Sterling on the Future of War," described Bruce Sterling's trip to the research labs at the Institute of Defense Analyses in Virginia. "Sterling discovers that the future of war is surgical, virtual, and replicable. Defense cutbacks, hi-tech weaponry, and the end of the Cold War have redefined warfare in an age of increasingly 'intelligent' machines..." (http://www.hotwired.com/club/95/45/sterling.html).

"Shock Wave (Anti) Warrior," I found to be a fascinating interview with futurist author Alvin Toffler. At one point in the interview Toffler explained,

I once had a class of 15-year-old high school kids and I gave them index cards, and I said, "Write down seven things that will happen in the future." They said there would be revolutions and presidents would be assassinated, and we would all drown in ecological sludge. A very dramatic series of events. But I noticed that of the 198 items that they handed in, only six used the word "I." So I gave them another set of cards, and I said, "Now I want you to write down seven things that are going to happen to you." Back came, "I will be married when I'm 21," "I will live in the same neighborhood, I will have a dog." And the disjuncture between the world that they were seeing out there and their own presuppositions was amazing. We thought about this, and concluded on the basis of just guesswork that the image of reality that they're getting from the media is one of high-speed rapid change, and the image that they're getting in their classrooms is one of no change at all. (http://vie.hotwired.com/Wired/1.5/features/toffler.html)

I spent days wandering the WWW and for some reason, the information I found most interesting was, for the most part, previously published papers or magazine articles that I could have found off-line. I'm not sure I got any closer to understanding the future than when I started, but it was interesting to compare the amount of truly useful information I found, to the amount of just plain noise. As I was fighting my way through today's commercial interruptions, professional chatting, and screens of listings to other screens, I found myself thinking back to a time when I was a graduate student at the MIT Media Lab. We used to think about the future, mostly by trying to make it happen. Dr. Alan Kay, a Senior Apple Fellow at Apple Computer and one of my advisors at MIT, used to say, "The best way to predict the future, is to invent it" [Kay 1990].

Unfortunately, few of us have the resources of a Media Lab, and most of us must be content with the words or inventions of others. However, when I look around at the swarm of developers furiously creating our future's *newest, neatest,* and *never-to-be-forgotten* technology, I am concerned. They seem to be reinventing the wheel, not because we need new wheels in our future, but because they say, "…it's the thing to do…" (translation: it makes money). That's why in this book we've taken so much time to discuss examples of what we think are exciting multimedia environments created yesterday and today. It's my hope that when you design your future multimedia environments you will invent a piece of tomorrow that thoughtfully builds on what has been, rather than blindly follows what can be heard the loudest.

At the beginning of this book I described a framework for how you might think about what others have created. This framework can also be a used to ponder the future:

1. What will our future approaches to teaching and learning be?

2. What will our future technologies be?

3. Where will our future technologies be used?

4. Where will our future technologies be created?

With this framework's group of questions, I also find myself asking one more:

5. What will not change in the future?

In the sections that follow I will give you my thoughts on each of these questions, based on what I know about today. I cannot promise crystal-ball accuracy, but I can promise more relevance than orange juice futures.

WHAT WILL OUR FUTURE APPROACHES TO TEACHING AND LEARNING BE?

Throughout this book, we've discussed examples of multimedia environments as falling on a continuum between *Interactive Textbook* and *Expressive Medium*. Some examples are one step away from traditional printed books, while others offer a tool for children to construct their own paths to learning. Then there are those examples that are somewhere in between. Tomorrow's educational multimedia environments will have an added ingredient: *Social Context*. Our future technology environments will offer greater opportunities to bring people together. Some environments will offer more than others, but I believe it will become an important factor in future development, much more so than what we see today.

As our communication technologies become more powerful and more common in our homes and schools, children will increasingly learn in a social context thanks to technology. In the past, computer critics have seen technology as offering an isolated learning experience for children. They have suggested that if technology plays an important role in our future, we will cut off people from people, and learn only to interact with machines. I believe in a very different future: a future where children, teachers, and parents will all have the opportunity to learn, work, and play together, *because* of technology.

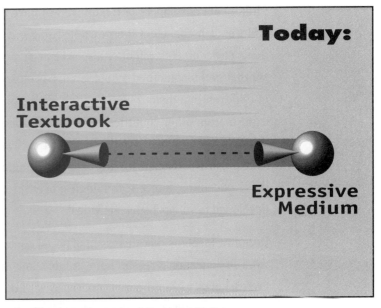

Today's *Interactive Textbook* and *Expressive Medium*.

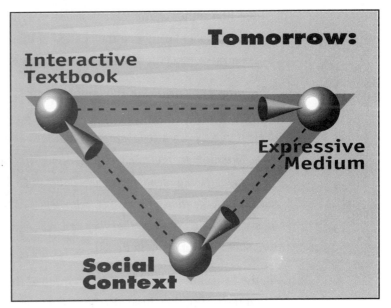

Tomorrow's *Interactive Textbook* and *Expressive Medium* with *Social Context*.

Multimedia developers of the future will have to consider not only to what degree children can construct their own learning environments, but also to what degree those environments can offer a social learning experience. Will one child work with another child in another school? Will a group of children work with another group of children in a distant community? Will a group of children work with content experts from other countries? Will children need to do research in their activities? Will this research necessitate accessing the New York Public Library and the Smithsonian Space and Science Museum in Washington, DC? If the answer is yes to any of these questions, future technologies, user interfaces, and content design must be developed to support such activities.

Recently, it seems that this issue of social context, has become more central to the work of educational researchers and developers. Only a few years ago, these same professionals were primarily concerned with the creation and/or evaluation of multimedia simulations or authoring tools. Now they have begun focusing on what they call *learning communities*. At Vanderbilt University, the Cognition and Technology Group (the author of *The Jasper Woodbury Series*), has begun to wrestle with what a social component can be in the context of their own development work. They see five central design criteria for future educational multimedia environments:

The nature of …learning communities can be summarized as providing students opportunities to: 1) plan, organize, monitor, and revise one's own research and problem-solving 2) work collaboratively and take advantage of distributed expertise from the community to allow diversity, creativity, and flexibility in learning 3) learn self-selected topics and identify one's own issues… 4) use various technologies to build one's own knowledge rather than using technologies as "knowledge tellers;" and 5) make students' thinking visible so that they can revise their own thoughts, assumptions, and arguments….[Lin et al. In Press]

In the Learning and Epistemology Group at the MIT Media Lab (home of today's Logo research), they have also begun to integrate learning communities into their work. They describe their on-going research on their World Wide Web page (http://el.www.media.mit.edu/groups/el/themes.html):

Much of our research focuses on the social nature of thinking, recognizing that how people think and learn is deeply influenced by the communities and cultures with which they interact. Our research projects explore how new technologies and new media can change relationships within existing communities (such as urban neighborhoods), while also encouraging the development of new types of "virtual" communities over computer networks.

How can we interpret these ambitious statements for the future? You need only to look at the numerous research projects with a social context coming out of Vanderbilt University and MIT. Today this research includes studying the ways in which children communicate on-line while authoring their own software environments [Evard 1994]. Their work also includes developing new technologies or tools needed for children to participate in on-line dramatic adventures (MUDs) [Bruckman 1994]. Another focus of research is in the use of video conferencing to enhance the assessment of new learning technologies [Cognition and Technology Group 1994]. Along with this, researchers have also begun to consider what types of on-line communities can support classroom teachers in the use of new technologies [Barron et al. 1993].

These thought-provoking research paths can be seen in contrast to today's commercial multimedia environments, where only a handful have considered the social context of what is possible with technology. Many times the social aspect of today's multimedia software has been used as a bandage for the lack of computers. Tomorrow, children may work in teams or collaborate on projects, not because there is only one computer in a classroom, but because it is an important component designed into the software for a more enriching learning experience. Cultural exchanges, team building, collaborative research, and vast informational resources are among the many opportunities that a social context can bring to an educational environment.

WHAT WILL OUR FUTURE TECHNOLOGIES BE?

It is generally agreed upon by most researchers that on-line multimedia technologies will be an important part of our future. Professor Marvin Minsky once wrote, "…we ought to recognize that we're still in an early era of machines with virtually no idea of what they may become. What if some visitor from Mars had come a billion years ago to judge the fate of early life from watching clumps of cells? In the same way, we cannot grasp the range of what machines may do in the future, from seeing what is on view right now..." [Minsky 1987].

I believe we are still in the *clumps-of-cells stage* with today's on-line technologies. It is impossible to imagine all that could change or be enhanced with technologies that offer a social context. The impact of these technologies could be as profound as what Gutenberg's first printing press did for society hundreds of years ago. Then, very few people had access to printed information. Even fewer people had the capability to create this information. All of this changed with the printing press: Millions of people had access to information. The importance of the printed word changed our political systems, our leisure activities, and certainly our education. Still, however, the creation of published information lay in the hands of a few. With the emergence of our on-line environments, millions of people now have the ability to instantly publish to an enormous worldwide audience. Stephen Gilliard, a *HotWired* user recently explained what he thought the impact of on-line technologies were: "Every time you sit in a movie theater or watch TV, you digest someone else's vision.... Simple technology has given many people a voice they wouldn't have otherwise... its... about promoting democracy in a very scary way, with no filters, no politicians..." (http://www.hotwired.com/).

TO BE OR NOT TO BE ON THE INFORMATION SUPERHIGHWAY

While the social context of technology will come to play a crucial role in our future technologies and our future lives, I also believe that there will still be a place for our more local software environments for one computer and one child. Certain learning activities are more personal and more solitary in nature. Many times writing and drawing need to be done without anyone looking over our shoulder. In many instances, we need time to understand our own vision and not be influenced by others. In fact, I'll take a somewhat controversial stand and say that I do not believe that all of our local technologies will disappear thanks to the proliferation of on-line environments.

There have always been people enamored with new technologies that predict the demise of the old. When television became a popular form of entertainment in the 1950s, people predicted the demise of radio and film. When home videos became popular to rent in the 1980s, people predicted the demise of movie theaters. Just the opposite has happened. Instead of killing one media with another, we have redefined the role of each. For example, radios are no longer the center of nightly home entertainment as they once were in the 1930s and 1940s. Instead, radio has become, among other things, a technology for the car and its content has become music, news, and talk shows.

We may see the same history played out with CD–ROMs or local storage technologies. As the floppy disk of the future, local storage technologies will be capable of storing an enormous number of digitized movies, sound, or images. We may find that future Edutainment software is best accessed from the Internet, while using multimedia authoring tools and creating our own projects are best left to run on local storage devices. I believe there will be a place for many

The demise of the old and the rise of new technologies.

different technologies, with many different distribution possibilities in our future. For developers, it may become a matter of understanding the important qualities each has to offer.

OUR VIRTUAL AND PHYSICAL WORLDS

As I pointed out in Chapter 6, I expect physical multimedia environments to play a part in our future as well. This will happen not only because our future technologies will become smaller, faster, and cheaper, but also because of the social needs we have as people. Professor Ben Bederson, from the University of New Mexico, and I explained this in a recent publication on physical multimedia: "It is our belief that people still want and will continue to need face-to-face interaction in shared social spaces. For example, people choose to attend music concerts, even though listening to a compact disc at home can be more convenient and the sound quality is perhaps better. People also still choose to discuss business in social settings such as restaurants, instead of taking advantage of less expensive methods of communication, such as meeting in a conference room or even email ..." [Bederson and Druin 1995].

Our future computer environments will not be confined to our desktops, but will be a part of each and every environment in which we live, learn, work, and play. Many people have asked me if I believe *Virtual Reality* as we know it today, with its special goggles and gloves, will be a part of our future as well. To this I answer, perhaps in some ways. Simulating a virtual world wearing goggles and gloves takes people away from their physical environment. For some who need to visualize architecture that has not yet been built or chemical compounds that have not yet been created, Virtual Reality may become a very useful tool. For others, especially in education, I do not believe this is what is wanted or needed. Children need to learn about their world with other children and with teachers and mentors. Putting them behind goggles that block out the rest of the world may not be our best path to learning. Children need the opportunity to collaborate, to see what others are doing and how they are doing it. Even sitting behind today's plastic glowing boxes still offers a chance for the rest of the world to creep in.

However, with technologies similar to Virtual Reality, we will begin to see more and more information *superimposed* on our physical surroundings. One example of this is a research project led by Professor Steve Feiner at Columbia University. This work has been to develop special goggles which visually superimpose information on a physical environment to help technicians better service a laser printer. Users can still see their physical surroundings while receiving help generated by a computer application [Feiner, MacIntyre, and Seligmann 1993].

Imagine in the future if children could use this type of system to learn how to dissect a frog in a biology class, or fix a car, or even learn how to swing a baseball bat. Physical multimedia environments would have the ability to augment children's everyday activities without taking them away from their physical surroundings or social context.

Another change that we can expect in the future of physical multimedia environments, will be the way in which we interact with them. Today, for the most part, we either touch an object or move in space, and a sensor embedded in the environment is activated. In the future, children will be able to use hand gestures or their voices to trigger an activity. Today we have rudimentary forms of this. Simple gestures can be recognized with special gloves embedded

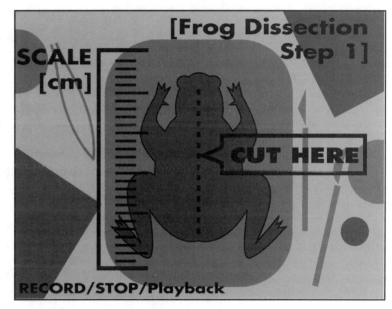

Superimposing information on a physical space.

with sensors and simple voice commands can be understood with speech-recognition software. In the future, though, you won't need to wear sensor-ridden gloves or memorize specific keywords that a computer can recognize. In the future, you will be able to communicate to a computer as you normally would to a person. In research labs around the country in companies such as Xerox, PARC, and Interval Research Corporation, and in universities such as MIT and New York University, the future of physical multimedia environments is being invented.

INFORMATION VISUALIZATION

When pondering tomorrow people often wonder what will become of our familiar computer screens filled with beloved trash cans, folders, and windows. Today we spend so much of our time *double-clicking* our way through folders that it seems hard to believe that anything will ever change. But as more and more of our information becomes digital, we will need better ways of organizing the huge quantities of text, graphics, and sound in our future. Mountains of folders inside other folders may not be the answer. Researchers throughout the world are considering new ways to visualize information.

At the University of New Mexico, New York University, and Bellcore researchers have begun to develop a software environment called *Pad++*. It offers users the ability to *zoom* through enormous information spaces, rather than double-clicking into a black hole. Documents become places to wander and explore in a new visual way. Pad++ also offers users the ability to interact with multiple representations of the same information. For example, by placing a *lens* over a document, a picture may replace where a written word or mathematical symbol once was [Bederson, Hollan et al 1995].

These types of tools offer exciting possibilities for multimedia environments in the future. Imagine using the *zooming* and *lensing* technologies of Pad++ with children who cannot read. Imagine if they could place different lenses over a word. One lens might *say* the word. Another lens might *sound out the word*. And yet another lens might show a simple picture icon that represents the meaning visually. Imagine further if children could create their own lenses. With the zooming capabilities, there would be no limit to the amount of information they could wander through or create. This, for me, offers exciting possibilities for our future multimedia environments for children.

INFORMATION MADE TO ORDER

Another trend I have begun to see in the development of various technologies is the ability to personalize information. From the news we read to the controls and options we use when authoring multimedia, we are able to customize what we use. This trend will not only continue, but become an expected and needed part of all of our technologies in the future. With the glut of information that can bombard us each day electronically, we need a way to tune out the noise, a way to personalize what we see and how we see it. Some researchers suggest this will come in the form of a software agent. Professor Pattie Maes from the MIT Media Lab, has been among the many researchers developing these new technologies. With a team of researchers, Professor Maes has found that, "We need technology to help us weed through all the information to find the items we really need, and to rid us of the things we do not want to be bothered with… Techniques employed by (technology) could potentially be used to recommend books, movies, news, articles, products and more…" [Maes and Schardanand 1995].

One way that researchers have recently begun to explore personalizing information has been by using the opinions of others. For example, in the physical world, it is easy to pick up a paperback book that a friend has read and see her or his favorite parts. Pages have been folded over or the spine has been bent in certain areas. In the electronic world, imagine if the computer automatically kept track of your friend's history of interaction. Obviously there are significant

Word-of-mouth systems.

privacy issues, but it would enable the computer to recommend places you might want to look based on the similar taste of your friend. Now, imagine if the computer could make recommendations based on people with similar tastes that you don't know.

This type of *word-of-mouth* system is being explored at Bellcore for recommending videos [Hill and Hollan 1992] and at the MIT Media Lab for recommending music [Maes and Schardanand 1995]. To see examples of these systems you can send an email message to videos@bellcore.com or access the MIT Media Lab WWW page: http://www.agents-inc.com/.

Critics of these systems do point out the dangers of this type of help. Danny Goodman has explained this in his book *Living at Light Speed*: "…software agents can potentially close our minds to new ideas. If our entire information flow comes from the Information Superhighway, and we establish filters and agents to grab only what we tell them to, we define limits for ourselves that may never be broken…" [Goodman 1994].

Some schools, parents, and legislators would suggest that an important way to personalize information for our children is to weed out the *inappropriate* information that is at their on-line fingertips. Some would suggest it is unsafe for our children to roam in an on-line world that offers *alt.sex* discussion groups. We must find a way to strike a balance. I do not believe we should use our technologies to personalize information to sanitize our children's world. There are important places on-line for gay teens to discuss issues that are relevant to their lives. There are important places on-line for teenage girls to discuss issues important to them. But some would say these are as *unhealthy* for children to explore as *alt.sex*.

The question is, *who* is to decide what is unhealthy and what is not? Some organizations are developing rating systems and some filters, but ultimately that will not stop children from getting at the stuff *they shouldn't*. Children will go home or over to another child's house whose computer doesn't have a filter. Eventually children will need to understand how to make critical decisions. They will need to learn that there are information and people in this world that are upsetting and not useful in the growth of their knowledge. They will need to understand how to weigh what their needs are and use any information resource with a careful eye. This is not just an issue that affects us only in our on-line world. It is an issue that impacts us in the world of print publications and broadcast television as well. We will continue to struggle with this not only in our homes and schools, not only with our children, but also among ourselves as adults, technology users, and developers.

Another future technology that may offer us a way to personalize information is Interactive Television (ITV). In recent years there has been a flurry of activity surrounding the development of ITV at such companies as Bell Atlantic, Microsoft, TCI, Time Warner, USWEST, AT&T, and GTE. While there are currently few commercial services available, it is expected there will be a flood of choices in the next few years. With these systems, users will be able to choose among such options as movies, interactive games, and home shopping. At this point, there are more questions than answers about this emerging technology: "…the 500-channel, all digital, high fiber, world of the future. Will it be a happy time bursting with 'choice, control, and convenience,' the mantra of every company getting into the business? Or will we take one look at it, snort and go back to watching reruns of *Baywatch*? For that matter will it even happen?" [Schwartz 1995].

Critics of ITV suggest that home consumers are content with their passive consumption of information from the television, and that they may be more interested in interactivity from their computers. According to some, we relax in front of the television and we work in front of the computer. Critics and supporters alike continue to ask such questions as: What will the content of ITV be? Are home shopping and games enough? How much will people be willing to pay for such a ser-

Interactive TV.

vice? Will it be technology that is cable-based? Will it use the phone lines? Will it use a PC?

In the future we will see a merging of entertainment and information technologies. It will not matter if we use a television or a computer. From my point of view, we can expect to find interactive entertainment on whatever technologies are available in the future. However, the success of this new activity will rest heavily on the shoulders of content. If interactive entertainment can offer people exciting fiction, virtual town hall meetings, or personalized news and information, it may be well worth having. However, if it just serves to clutter our brains with shoot'em up games or more ways to shop, it may not be worth the technology it runs on. Users must be given a compelling reason to try something new. The shiny new black box on the top of a television may just not be enough.

WHERE WILL OUR FUTURE TECHNOLOGIES BE USED?

As we consider grand visions of future technologies, we must also consider where these technologies will be used and how they will affect the larger educational landscape. I am not naive enough to believe that overcrowded classrooms, gang violence, or decrepit school facilities will suddenly disappear because of the emergence of new technologies. In the future, new and better multimedia environments may offer more exciting learning opportunities for some. For others, though, new technologies may be something as common as the opportunity to fly to the moon.

Yes, as much as I don't want to believe it, I've come to see that future technologies may serve to polarize our children into two groups: *the information have's* and *the have not's*. The opportunities technology can give us may only be enjoyed by a small portion of our school children in the future. Today, the contrasts are startling from school to school throughout the world. In some schools there are new technologies everywhere you turn, but in others, there are antiquated computers collecting dust in an unused part of a classroom. The U.S. government is concerned about these inequalities and announced recently that, "…a new program will be established that will target low-income households, minorities, and Americans living in rural areas, giving them access to computers and training on how to use them… If we do not act, the next generation of American workers may divide between those who have used

computers—at home and at school—for their entire lives and those for whom merely logging on is an arcane and intimidating ritual…" [*Investor's Business Daily* 1995].

On the other hand, some would say that our schools are best off being *have not's*. According to Clifford Stoll in his book *Silicon Snake Oil*, "Elementary and high schools are being sold down the networked river. To keep up with this educational fad, school boards spend way too much on technical gimmicks that teachers don't want, and students don't need" [Stoll 1995].

Computer flower pot stands.

Needless to say, I do not agree with this author. I believe that technologies can provide chil-
dren with important learning experiences. That is what the last eight chapters have been all about. But, on the other hand, only some will come to enjoy these techno-
logical opportunities. I wish I could say I knew how to solve this problem, but then that would be as if I was sure I knew how to fight crime, poverty, or drugs in our children's lives. What I can be sure about is that tomorrow's technologies will become cheaper and easier to provide to schools. However, what our educational systems choose to do with these technologies is no sure thing. I have seen all the technology in the world stifle creativity as much as enhance it. I have seen computers used to hold flower pots, and I have seen computers at the center of engaging learning. Unfortunately, this will not change in the future. It will just become ever more obvious that we have a growing number of flower pot stands.

Today, on average, there are one to two desktop computers in a classroom and/or 15 to 20 computers in a school's computer lab. In the future we will see school computer labs disappear and larger numbers of computers integrated directly into classroom environments. Computer labs have long been a symptom of the lack of money available for purchasing technology and the lack of computer expertise available among classroom teachers. In the future, both will change. Buying technology will become as crucial as buying today's textbooks, because they will be tomorrow's textbooks. As for classroom teachers in the future, they will have grown up using technology; therefore, they will be much more aware of what to do with these tools than our classroom teachers are today.

The *computer teacher* or *computer lab resource specialist* will become our librarians of tomorrow. Libraries with dusty books and a desktop computer in the corner will become a place of the past. Libraries will be a place where information consultants (librarians of the future) can help children traverse the Internet to the Library of Congress or to the Louvre in Paris. They may still offer books to enjoy, but libraries will not be limited by what one school or school district can afford. Huge amounts of information will become free and accessible.

Finally, I believe that the educational landscape will change thanks to the proliferation of home computers. We will see a decentralization in our educational systems similar to what we have seen in the work place. Today, it is common for many people to work from their homes or telecommute. Children will also be afforded greater opportunities for independence thanks to more technologies at home. Home schooling will become a far more common form of education as technologies offer opportunities for distant learning communities. Parents will not need to be the all-knowing knowledge providers in home schooling. Instead they can depend on the vast online resources of content experts and information libraries and archives. This may lead in the future to a decentralization of school systems, but I do not believe it will lead to their demise (as many radical school reformers suggest). Schools in the future will still be an important social context to explore learning; however, they may be smaller, more specialized places to learn. What exactly will be the educational landscape of the future is hard to say. What I am certain of is that things will change and they will change thanks to new and better technologies in our future.

WHERE WILL OUR FUTURE TECHNOLOGIES BE CREATED?

Designing multimedia environments in the future will take place much in the same way as they have been created today, but just more so. Today we see interdisciplinary teams of people collaborating between research labs in universities, industry companies, and government agencies. Partnerships, industry mergers, and royalty arrangements have all become the norm. Television, film, telecommunications, cable, software and hardware industries have become wary collaborators in this emerging world of multimedia. Thanks to these intimate new relationships, It will soon be hard to tell the difference between a telecommunications company and a software company.

In the future, you can expect that interdisciplinary design teams will work together, perhaps from different companies, perhaps in different time zones, perhaps meeting only via the Internet or video conferencing. We can expect to see the rise of *virtual companies*, with only email addresses, WWW sites, and voice mail. The world will become a more global place in a more intimate way.

As multimedia technologies become easier and easier to use and develop with, the pool of developers will expand. Parents, teachers, lawyers, doctors, children, and anyone with something to say and content to offer, will be given the opportunity to create it. We can already see the first signs of this today with the proliferation of WWW sites and Web pages. Schools in particular may become the biggest source of new developers in the future. Just as teachers have developed their own curriculum materials for years, so too may they develop multimedia materials.

Out of these new opportunities will emerge new questions concerning intellectual property. Who owns what and how? The definitions are liable to be redefined and refined more times than not in the coming years. Commerce over the Internet will become commonplace and our forms of payment for other's ideas will become standard. As for how this may happen, I am not sure. These are complex issues which offer no clear-cut answers anytime soon. What I can be sure is that lawyers, content providers, and multimedia developers will continue to struggle with these issues for a long time to come.

WHAT WILL NOT CHANGE?

So many times we equate the future with change and upheaval, and for that reason the future frightens many people. As for me, I look forward to the future. Change can be exciting and scary all at the same time. I also believe that there are certain things that don't change. In particular, how we design and what we design will not change. There are certain design principles that seem to stand the test of time. That is why we began this book with a look at the past, then moved to the present. Much of what we know about design has been around for a long time, though maybe not always in the software industry. This knowledge has long been a part of the worlds of education, visual design, television, and film production.

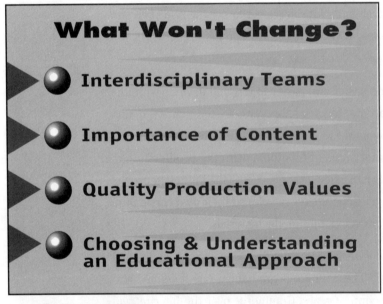

What Won't Change?

● **Interdisciplinary Teams**

● **Importance of Content**

● **Quality Production Values**

● **Choosing & Understanding an Educational Approach**

In the Future What Won't Change.

The power of an interdisciplinary design team has for years been understood as one of the most important tools television and film producers can use when developing complex productions. The importance of content design has been well understood by educators and curriculum designers for years. Quality production values have long been the focus of visual designers in creating print, video, and physical installations. Finally, the importance of choosing an educational approach (and understanding why you've chosen it) has been a concern of educators throughout time. Together, I believe these design principles will serve multimedia developers today and well into the future. In the sections that follow, I will summarize the importance that each may have in the years to come.

INTERDISCIPLINARY TEAMS

In the future, I expect that technologies will merge the activities of entertainment, communication, education, and work. As this merging of disciplines occurs, the more interdisciplinary our design teams will need to be. Throughout this book, we have discussed numerous multimedia examples that have benefited from the diverse talents of a team. The future will be no different. It is impossible for one person to do everything that needs to be done in developing a multimedia project. One person may have the initial vision or project concept, but you need many different professionals to actually make an idea a reality. It may become easier in the future as more people acquire multi-disciplinary skills through experience or education. Graphic designers of tomorrow may also be our user interface designers and programmers as well. Educators of tomorrow may also be our technical writers, quality assurance experts, and content designers. As we develop multitalented professionals in the future, our design teams will become smaller and more intimate in size. I do not believe, however, that we should ever promote the *one-man-band*. It is important to have different perspectives on the same project. It would be as if we decided that writers could be their own editors. Imagine all the things we would miss! Therefore, I believe that interdisciplinary design teams are here to stay.

THE IMPORTANCE OF CONTENT DESIGN

No matter what the multimedia technologies we create in the future, the importance of content design will continue to be paramount. Without a compelling reason to use the latest, greatest gadgets, users just won't. If those users are children, they won't be polite in telling you why they're bored or why they don't care about what they're supposed to be learning. Today's multimedia developers pay great lip-service to the importance of content, but then that doesn't explain why we have tens of thousands of lukewarm Edutainment CD–ROMs out there for children. The pictures seem to be getting prettier, but in comparison, the content quality does not seem to be taking any great strides. Tomorrow's multimedia developers will *have* to consider the quality of the content they offer. It will be a crucial way to distinguish their product from the next. It will also be a crucial way for children to learn. Without content, there can be no learning; that's what it's all about in designing educational multimedia environments for children.

QUALITY PRODUCTION VALUES

As technology becomes commonplace in our future, people will become less forgiving of the bugs, ugliness, and confusing interfaces. People will come to expect higher quality experiences. In the past, it was okay for people to sit behind green-glowing screens of unreadable text. In the past, it was okay for people to be confused every time they used a new technology. In the future, with tens of thousands of new competing multimedia products, users will not settle for shoddy craftsmanship. They will expect easy-to-use, consistent interfaces. They will expect well-designed visuals. They will expect something that makes sense. I can't tell you how often I wander about a commercial multimedia product and find myself with no way to go back to a previous screen or no way to quit. Overlooking such simple but important interface issues drives me crazy! It will drive users even crazier in the future. Quality product values from developers will be crucial to the commercial success of multimedia environments in the future.

THE IMPORTANCE OF CHOOSING (AND UNDERSTANDING) AN EDUCATIONAL APPROACH

Finally, if we are to create environments for children, we must know why we are choosing the paths we do for teaching and learning. If you believe in an *Interactive Textbook* approach, then say it with your product design, and say it well. If you believe in an *Expressive Medium* approach, then do not hide it in a simulation; say it loudly in a creative tool for children. If you are not sure what your approach is, then your users are likely to be unsure as well. And, since your users are perhaps the least forgiving users on the planet (and kids will tell you so), then you must do your homework. You must understand the design choices you make and stand by them throughout the development of your product. The importance of understanding why you're doing what you're doing will never change. It is our hope that this book will serve you in that understanding.

In the future you can expect greater challenges. Given the proliferation of new technologies and new, more demanding users, your choices as a designer must be carefully thought out. You have a chance to leave a fingerprint in the future, some steps in the sands for tomorrow. And you have the chance to make a child's life a little better. I cannot think of any greater challenge for you as a multimedia developer in the future.

- We live in a world where so many of us are fascinated with what will happen in the future.

- "The best way to predict the future, is to invent it" [Kay 1990].

- Some questions we can ponder about our future:
  - What will our future approaches to teaching and learning be?
  - What will our future technologies be?
  - Where will our future technologies be used?
  - Where will our future technologies be created?.
  - What will not change in the future?

- Tomorrow's educational multimedia environments will have an added ingredient: *Social Context*.

- As our communication technologies become more powerful and more common in our homes and schools, children will increasingly learn in a social context thanks to technology.

- While the social context of technology will come to play a crucial role in our future technologies and our future lives, there will still be a place for our more local software environments for one computer and one child.

• With technologies similar to Virtual Reality, we will begin to see more and more information *superimposed* on our physical surroundings.

• As more and more of our information becomes digital, we will need better ways of organizing the huge quantities of text, graphics, and sound in our future.

• Another trend that has begun, is the ability to personalize information from the news we read to the controls and options we use when authoring multimedia.

• In the future, interdisciplinary design teams will work together—perhaps from different companies, perhaps in different time zones, perhaps meeting only via the Internet or video conferencing.

• As we consider grand visions of future technologies, I am not naive enough to believe that overcrowded classrooms, gang violence, or decrepit school facilities will suddenly disappear because of the emergence of new technologies.

• As we look towards the future, there are certain design principles that will not change:
  • Interdisciplinary team design
  • The importance of content design
  • Quality production values
  • The importance of choosing an educational approach
    (and understanding why you've chosen it)

BIBLIOGRAPHY

CHAPTER 1

Abelson, H., and A. diSessa. 1981. *Turtle Geometry*. Cambridge, MA: MIT Press.

Computer Curriculum Corporation. 1993. *SuccessMaker*, Release 16 Preview: New and Enhanced Courses. Computer Curriculum Corporation, A Paramount Communications Company.

Computer Curriculum Corporation. 1994. *Reference Manual for Math Investigations*. Sunnyvale, CA: Computer Curriculum Corporation.

Computer Curriculum Corporation. 1994. *Reference Manual for Math Concepts and Skills*. Sunnyvale, CA: Computer Curriculum Corporation.

Davis, R.B. 1967. *A Modern Mathematics Program as It Pertains to the Interrelationship of Mathematical Content, Teaching Methods, and Classroom Atmosphere*. The Madison Project. 2 vols. Submitted to the Office of Education, U.S. Department of Health, Education and Welfare.

Davis, R.B. 1977. "Elementary School Mathematics." Demonstration of the PLATO IV Computer-based Education System, Final Report. Edited by G. Slottow. Computer-based Education Research Laboratory. Urbana, IL: University of Illinois.

Davis, R.B. 1979. "One View of Studying Mathematics Education Research and Development in the Soviet Union." *An Analysis of Mathematics Education in the Union of Soviet Socialist Republics*, by R.B. Davis, T.A. Romberg, S. Rachlin, and M.G. Kantowiski. 47–86 Columbus, OH: Ohio State University, ERIC, Clearinghouse for Science, Mathematics and Environmental Education.

Davis, R.B. 1984. *Learning Mathematics: The Cognitive Science Approach to Mathematics Education*. Norwood, NJ: Ablex Publishing Corporation.

Davis, R.B. 1992. "A Theory of Teaching Mathematics." *Journal of Mathematical Behavior* 11: 337–360.

Davis, R.B. 1993. "Theoretical Foundations of Writing in Mathematics Classes." *Journal of Mathematical Behavior* 12: 295–300.

Davis, R.B. and C. McKnight. 1979. "Modeling the Processes of Mathematical Thinking." *Journal of Mathematical Behavior* 2(no. 1): 91–113.

Hooper, P. 1994. "... They Have Their Own Thoughts: A story of constructionist learning in an alternative African-centered community school." *Constructionism in Practice: Rethinking the roles of technology in learning.* Edited by Y. Kafai and M. Resnick. Presented at the National Educational Computing Conference, Boston, MA, June 1994. Cambridge, MA: The Media Laboratory 89–99.

Minsky, M. 1986. *The Society of Mind.* New York: Simon and Schuster.

Minsky, M. 1986b. "Preface". *LogoWorks.* Edited by Solomon, Minsky, and Harvey. New York: McGraw-Hill vii–xii.

Minsky, M. 1987. "Form and Content in Computer Science." ACM Turing Award Lectures: The First Twenty Years 1966-1985. New York: ACM Press. (Minsky won the Turing Award in 1969).

Minsky, M., and S. Papert. 1969. *Perceptrons.* Cambridge, MIT: Press.

National Council of Teachers of Mathematics, Curriculum and Evaluation 1989. *Standards for School Mathematics.* Reston, VA: The National Council of Teachers of Mathematics, Inc.

Papert, S. 1970. Teaching Children Thinking. April 11, unpublished talk.

Papert, S. 1980. *Mindstorms: Children, Computers and Powerful Ideas.* New York: Basic Books.

Papert, S. 1990. "Introduction." *Constructionist Learning.* Edited by I. Harel. Cambridge, MA: The Media Lab, MIT, April 17, 1–8.

Papert, S. 1993. *The Children's Machine.* New York: Basic Books.

Papert, S., and C. Solomon. 1976. "NIM: A Game-Playing Program" (1970). Solomon, Problem-Solving in An Anthropomorphic Computer Culture. Master's thesis, Boston University.

Resnick, M. 1994. *Turtles, Termites, and Traffic Jams: Explorations in Massively Parallel Microworlds.* Cambridge, MA: MIT Press.

Seiler, B. 1993. *How the West Was One + Three x Four.* Sunburst Communications, Inc., Macintosh version.

Solomon, C. 1976b. *Problem-Solving in an Anthropomorphic Computer Culture.* Master's thesis, Boston University.

Solomon, C. 1986a. "Davis: Socratic Interactions and Discovery Learning." *Computer Environments for Children.* Cambridge, MA: MIT Press. 31–68.

Solomon, C. 1986b. "Papert: Constructivism and Piagetian Learning." *Computer Environments for Children.* Cambridge, MA: MIT Press. 103–133.

Solomon, C. 1986c. "Suppes: Drill-and-Practice and Rote Learning." *Computer Environments for Children.* Cambridge, MA: MIT Press. 16–30.

Solomon, C. 1986d. *Computer Environments for Children.* Cambridge, MA: MIT Press.

Solomon, C., M. Minsky, and B. Harvey, eds. 1986. *LogoWorks: Challenging Programs in Logo.* New York: McGraw-Hill.

Suppes, P. 1964. *The Development of Mathematical Concepts in Children.* Cooperative Research Project no. OE 727, Final Report. Stanford, CA Stanford University.

Suppes, P. 1969. "Computer Technology and the Future of Education." *Computer-Assisted Instruction: A book of readings.* Edited by R. Atkinson and H.A. Wilson. New York: Academic Press. 41–47.

Suppes, P. 1978. "A Philosopher as Psychologist." *The Psychologists: Autobiographies of Distinguished Living Psychologists.* Edited by T.S. Krawiec. Brandon, VT: Clinical Psychology Publishing.

Suppes, P. 1980. "Impact of Computers on Curriculum in Schools and Universities." (1975) *The Computer in the School: Tutor, Tool, Tutee.* Edited by R. Taylor. New York: Teachers College Press. 236–247.

Taylor, R.P., ed. 1980. *The Computer in the School: Tutor, Tool, Tutee.* New York: Teachers College Press.

CHAPTER 2

Armstrong, L. 1995. "Knowledge Adventure's Trickiest Game: Success." *Business Week* (11 April): 32.

Deutschman, A. 1994. "Putting Zip in Educational Software." *Fortune Magazine.* (28 November): 200.

"Education Software Market Booming." 1995. *Investors Business Daily* (19 April): A6.

Gardner, H. 1982. *Developmental Psychology.* Boston: Little, Brown and Co.

Goldstein, K. 1995. Telephone interview with Allison Druin, 18 April.

Holzberg, R. 1995. Telephone interview with Allison Druin, 5 April.

Knowledge Adventure. 1995. "Corporate Backgrounder." La Crescenta, CA: Knowledge Adventure.

"Knowledge Adventure: From Science to Multimedia." 1995. *CD–ROM Today* 3, no. 5 (May).

Macaulay, D. 1988. *David Macaulay The Way Things Work.* Boston: Houghton Mifflin.

Macaulay, D. 1995. Telephone interview with Allison Druin, 2 April.

"Market Triples for CD–ROMs." *New York Times,* 22 March. 1995. A15.

Minsky, M. 1986. Position Paper about AMT's Future, unpublished. Boston: MIT.

"Of Special Interest." 1995. *Indelible News* 1, no. 4 (April).

Orban, L. 1994. *Press Releases*: "Random House and Knowledge Adventure Form Alliance to Develop Multimedia Titles"; "Steven Spielberg to Collaborate with Knowledge Adventure on Education Software"; Knowledge Adventure Appoints Ruth L. Otte as President." La Crescenta, CA: Knowledge Adventure.

Ray, L., ed. 1994. *The Living Books Framework*. Novato, CA: Living Books Co.

Ray, L. 1995. Telephone interview with Allison Druin, 18 April.

Schlichtig, M. 1995a. Telephone interview with Allison Druin, 28 April.

Schlichtig, M. 1995b. Telephone interview with Allison Druin, 1 May.

Sterngold, J. 1995. "CD–ROMs Hitch a Ride on a Man on a Spider." *New York Times*, 2 April. B4.

Vygotsky, L.S. 1978. *Mind in Society: The Development of Higher Psychological Processes*. Cambridge, MA: Harvard University Press.

CHAPTER 3

Bank Street College of Education. 1985. "What is Voyage of the MIMI?" Video. Pleasantville, NY: Sunburst Communications.

Barron, B., and R.J. Kantor. 1993. "Tools to Enhance Math Education: The Jasper Series." *Communications of the ACM* 36(no. 5): 52–54.

Barron, B. 1994. Email correspondance with Allison Druin, 20 January.

Cognition and Technology Group. 1994a. "The Jasper Series: History, Theory, Lessons and Next Steps." Collection of Papers. Nashville, TN: Vanderbilt University.

Cognition and Technology Group. 1994b. "CD–ROM Japser and Japser Toolkits: A New Format Plus New Tools." Proposal to National Science Foundation. Nashville, TN: Vanderbilt University.

Decisions, Decisions, Teachers Guide. 1991. Cambridge, MA: Tom Snyder Productions.

Dockterman, D. 1991. *Great Teaching in the One Computer Classroom*. Cambridge, MA: Tom Snyder Productions.

Dockterman, D. 1994. *Coopertive Learning and Technology*. Cambridge, MA: Tom Snyder Productions.

Dublin, P., H. Pressman, E. Barnett, D. Corcoran, and E.J. Woldman. 1994. *Integrating Computers in Your Classroom: Elementary Education*. New York: HarperCollins College Publishers.

Eisner, E. 1994. *Cognition and Curriculum Reconsidered*. 2d ed. New York: Teacher's College Press.

Fox, R. 1995. "NewsTrack." *Communications of the ACM* 38 (no. 2):11.

La Follette, J. 1993. "Interactivity and Multimedia Instruction Crucial Attributes for Design and Instruction." *Proceedings of Selected Research and Development Presentations at the Convention of the Association for Educational Communications and Technology* (ERIC Document Reproduction Services no. ED 362-179).

Marston, P. 1995. Telephone interview with Allison Druin, 11 July.

McGilly, K., ed. 1995. "From Visual Word Problems to Learning Communities: Changing Concepts of Cognitive Research." *Classroom Lessons: Integrating Cognitive Theory and Classroom Practice.* Cambridge, MA: MIT Press/ Bradford Books.

Pellegrino, J.W., D Hickey, A. Heath, K. Rewey, N.J. Vye and the Cognition and Techology Group. 1991. "Assessing the Outcomes of an Innovative Instructional Program: The 1990-1991 Implementation of the Adventures of Jasper Woodbury." *Technical Report* no. 90-1. Nashville, TN: Vanderbilt University, Learning Technology Center.

Snyder, T. 1994. "Blinded by Science." *The Executive Editor.* (March Reprint) distributed by Tom Snyder Productions, Cambridge, MA.

The Great Solar System Rescue, Teachers Guide. 1992. Cambridge, MA: Tom Snyder Productions.

CHAPTER 4

Apple Computer. 1991. *A Design Perspective on the Visual Almanac Video.* Cupertino, CA: Apple Multimedia Lab.

Carver, S.M. 1987. "Transfer of LOGO Debugging Skill: Analysis, Instruction, and Assessment." Ph. D. diss., Canegie-Mellon University.

Collins, A. 1991. "The Role of Computer Technology in Restructuring Schools." *Phi Delta Kappan* 73(no. 1): 28–36.

Cushing, B. 1995a. Classroom discussions and observations with Allison Druin, 13 March. Los Almos, NM: Barranca Mesa Elementary School.

Cushing, B. 1995b. Discussions with Allison Druin, 13 April. Santa Fe: University of New Mexico.

Cushing, B. 1995c. Unpublished paper. Spring Project ITS Program. Santa Fe: University of New Mexico.

David, J.L. 1990. "Restructuring and Technology: Partners in Change." In *Restructuring for Learning with Technology*, eds. K. Sheingold and M. Tucker. Center for Technology in Education, Bank Street College of Education and National Center on Education and the Economy.

David, J.L. 1992. "Partnerships for Change." *ACOT Technical Report, no.* 12. Cupertino, CA: Apple Classrooms of Tomorrow.

Druin, A. 1995. Email Correspondence with 37 classroom teachers in the Albuquerque and Santa Fe Public Schools.

Harel, I. 1991. *Children Designers: Interdisciplinary Constructions for Learning and Knowing Mathematics in a Computer-Rich School*. Norwood, NJ: Ablex.

Hickman, C. 1995. Telephone interview with Allison Druin, 10 April.

Hooper, K. 1988. "Interactive Multimedia Design." *Apple Technical Report, no.* 13. Cupertino, CA: Apple Multimedia Lab.

Papert, S. 1980. *Mindstorms: Children, Computers and Powerful Ideas*. New York: Basic Books.

Papert, S. 1985. "Computer Criticism vs. Technocratic Thinking." *Proceedings of LOGO'85, Theoretical Papers*.

Ringstaff, C., M. Sterns, S. Hanson, and S. Schneider. 1993. *The Cupertino-Freemont Model of Technology in Schools Project: Final Report*. Cupertino, CA: SRI International.

Sandholtz, J.H., C. Ringstaff, D.C. Dwyer, and Apple Computer. 1990. "Teaching in High-Tech Environments: Classroom Management Revisited First Fourth-Year Findings." *ACOT Technical Report, no.* 10. Cupertino, CA: Apple Classrooms of Tomorrow.

Sheingold, K. 1991. "Restructuring for Learning with Technology." *Phi Delta Kappan*, 73(no. 1): 17–27.

The Multimedia Lab. 1991. "The Visual Almanac." *Technical Report #L0178LL/A*. Cupertino, CA: Apple Computers.

Wagner, R. 1995a. Email sent to Allison Druin, 6 February.

Wagner, R. 1995b. Telephone interview with Allison Druin, 7 April.

Wilson, L. 1995. Telephone interview with Allison Druin, 7 April.

CHAPTER 5

Adamson, E. 1995. Telephone interview with Allison Druin, 26 June.

Feldman, A.H., and H. Nyland. 1994. "Collaboartive Inquiry in Networked Communities: Lessons Learned from the Alice Testbed." *Proceedings from the Annual Meeting of the American Educational Research Association*. New Orleans AERA.

Gibson, W. 1984. *Neuromancer*. New York: Ace Books.

Goodman, D. 1994. *Living at Light Speed: Your Survival Guide to Life on the Information Superhighway*. New York: Random House.

Julyan, C.L. 1993a. "Mapping a Journey to Understanding." *Hands On!* 16(no. 2).

Julyan, C.L. 1993b. "A Developer's Perspective on Telecomputing." *TERC Technical Report*. Cambridge, MA: TERC.

Julyan, C.L. 1995. "Getting Connected to Science." *Hands On!* 18(no. 1).

Lewis, P. 1995. "Ill Children to get 3-D Playground out in Cyberspace." *New York Times*. (June): C3.

Long, M. 1994. "We are the World." *Netguide*. New York: CMP Media.

Meyer, M. 1995. "The Haves and the Have-Nots." *Newsweek* (February): 50–51.

Rheingold, H. 1995. "The Virtual Community." *Utne Reader* no. 68(March/April): 62.

Tinker, R.F. 1993. "Telecomputing as a Progressive Force in Education." *TERC Technical Report*. Cambridge, MA: TERC.

Utne, E. 1995. "Networks are *Not* Communities." *Utne Reader* no. 68(March/April): 3.

CHAPTER 6

Adamson, E. 1993. "Lego, Logo, and Art: Use of Artistic Imagination in the Technological Classroom." *ICTE'93 Conference Proceedings*. Boston: ICTE.

Association for Computing Machinery. 1993. "ComputerAugmented Environments: Back to the Real World." *Communications of the ACM* 36(no. 7) Special Issue.

Bederson, B.B., and A. Druin. 1995. "Computer-Augmented Environments: New Places to Learn, Work, and Play." In ed. J. Neilson, *Advances in Human-Computer Interaction*. Norwood, NJ: Ablex.

Bolt, R.A. 1994. *The Human Interface: Where Computers and People Meet*. Belmont, CA: Wadsworth.

Druin, A. 1988. "NOOBIE: The Animal Design Playstation." *ACM SIGCHI Bulletin*. 20(no. 1): 45–53.

Druin, A. 1993. "The Immersive Experience: The Babysitter." Unpublished paper, New York University Media Research Laboratory. New York: New York University.

Druin, A., and P. Perlin. 1994. "Immersive Environments: A Physical Approach to the Computer Interface." *Proceedings of CHI'94 Conference Companion*. New York: Association for Computing Machinery. 325–326.

Eisner, E. 1994. *Cognition and Curriculum Reconsidered*. 2d ed. New York: Teacher's College Press.

Hutchinson, E.J., and M.T. Whalen. 1995. "Female Students and LEGO TC Logo." *The Computing Teacher* (December/January): 22–25.

Lippert, K. 1995. "Should Your Toddler Be a Techie?" *New York Times*. (1 June): B1.

Papert, S. 1980. *Mindstorms Children, Computers, and Powerful Ideas*. New York: Basic Books.

Perlin, K., and A. Druin. 1993. "NYU Educator-in-Residence Program: A Model for Interdisciplinary Collaboration." NSF Proposal to the Advanced Technological Education Program.

Resnick, M. 1993. "Behavior Construction Kits." *Communications of the ACM* 36(no. 7): 64–71.

Schramn, W. 1977. *Big Media, Little Media*. Beverly Hills, CA: Sage.

CHAPTER 7

Cypher, A., and D.C. Smith. 1995. "KidSim: End User Programming of Simulations." *CHI'95 Conference Proceedings*. Denver: ACM 27–34.

Bjerknes, G., P. Ehn, and M. Kyng, eds. 1987. *Computers and Democracy: A Scandinavian Challenge*. Aldershot, UK: Avebury.

Blomberg, J.L., and A. Henderson. 1990. "Reflections on Participatory Design: Lessons from the Trillium Experience." *CHI'90 Conference Proceedings*. Seattle: ACM 353–359.

Bødker, S., P. Ehn, J. Knudsen, M. Kyng, and K. Madsen. 1988. "Computer Support for Cooperative Design." *CSCW88: Conference Proceedings of Computer-Supported Cooperative Work*. Portland, OR: ACM 377–393.

Druin, A. 1994. "Multimedia Product Design and Marketing." *New York University Center for Digital Multimedia Industry Seminar*. New York: New York University.

Druin, A., and K. Withey. 1990. "Designing User Interfaces for Children." *CHI'90 Tutorial*. Seattle: ACM.

Druin, A., and S. Solomon. 1993. "Designing Multimedia Environments for Children." *SIGGRAPH/Multimedia'93 Tutorial*. Anaheim, CA: ACM.

Druin, A., and P. Perlin. 1994. "Immersive Environments: A Physical Approach to the Computer Interface." *CHI'94 Conference Companion*. Boston: ACM 325–326.

Druin, A., and S. Solomon. 1994. "Designing Educational Computer Environments for Children." *CHI'94 Tutorial*. Boston: ACM.

Druin, A., and S. Solomon. 1995. "Designing Educational Computer Environments for Children." *CHI'95 Tutorial*. Denver: ACM.

Hix, D., and H.R. Hartson. 1993. *Developing User Interfaces: Ensuring Usability Through Product and Process*. New York: John Wiley and Sons.

Hourvitz, L. 1994. "Introduction to Multimedia: The Software Development Process." *New York University Center for Digital Multimedia Industry Seminar*. 4, April New York: New York University.

Kim, S. 1990. "Interdisciplinary Cooperation." In ed. B.Laurel, *The Art of Human Computer Interface Design*. Reading, MA: Addison-Wesley. 31–44.

Muller, M.J. 1991. "PICTIVE—An Exploration Participatory Design." *CHI'91 Conference Proceedings*. New Orleans: ACM 225–231.

Muller, M.J., D.M. Wildman, and E.A. White. 1994. "Participatory Design through Games and Other Techniques." *CHI'94 Tutorial*. Boston: ACM.

Muller, M.J. 1995. "Diversity and Depth in Participatory Design: Working with a Mosaic of Users and Other Stakeholders in the Software Development Lifecycle." *CHI'95 Tutorial*. Denver: ACM.

Mulligan, R.M., M.W. Alton, and D.K. Simkin. 1991. "User Interface Design in the Trenches: Some Tips on Shooting from the Hip." *CHI'91 Conference Proceedings*. New Orleans: ACM 232–236.

Olson, G.M., and J.S. Olson. 1991. "User Centered Design of Collaboration Technology." *Journal of Organizational Computing* 1: 61–83.

Preece, J., Y. Rogers, H. Sharp, D. Benyon, S. Holland, and T. Carey. 1994. *Human-Computer Interaction*. Reading, MA: Addison-Wesley.

Tuder, L.G., M.J. Muller, T. Dayton, and R. Root. 1993. "A Participatory Design Technique for High-Level Task Analysis and Redesign: the CARD Method." *InterCHI'93 Tutorial*. Amsterdam, Netherlands: ACM.

CHAPTER 8

Barron, B., N.J. Vye, L. Zech, D. Schwartz, J.D. Bransford, S.R. Goldman, J. Pellegrino, J. Mossirs, S. Garrison, and R. Kantor. "Creating Contexts for Community-Based Problem-Solving: The Jasper Challange Series." Forthcoming in eds. C. Hedley, P. Antonacci, and M. Rabinowitz, *Thinking and Literacy: The Mind at Work*. Hillsdale, NJ: Earlbaum.

Bederson, B.B., and A. Druin. 1995. "Computer Augmented Environments: New Places to Learn, Work, and Play." In ed. J. Neilson, *Advances in Human-Computer Interaction*. New York: Ablex.

Bederson, B.B., J.D. Hollan, K. Perloh, J. Meyer, D Bacon, and G. Furnas. 1995. "Pad++: A Zoomable Graphical Sketchpad for Exploring Alternate Interface Physics." *Journal of Visual Language and Computing*. In press.

Bruckman, A.S. 1994. "MOOSE Crossing: Creating a Learning Culture." *Ph.d. Thesis Proposal*. Cambridge, MA: MIT Media Lab.

Cognition and Technology Group. 1994. "From Visual Word Problems to Learning Communities: Changing Conceptions of Cognative Research." *Tech Report*. Nashville, TN: Vanderbilt University.

Evard, M. 1994. "Articulation of Design Issues: Learning through Exchanging Questions and Answers." In eds.Y. Kafai and M. Resnick, *Constructionism in Practice: Rethinking the Roles of Technology.* Cambridge, MIT: Media Lab.

Feiner, S., B. MacIntyre, and D. Seligmann. 1993. "Knowledge-Based Augmented Reality." *Communications of the ACM* 36(no. 7): 52–62.

Frankel, M. 1995. "Horseless in Cyberspace." *New York Times Magazine,* 28 May.

Goodman, D. 1994. *Living at Light Speed: Your Survival Guide to Life on the Information Superhighway.* New York: Random House.

Hill, W.C., and J.D. Hollan. 1992. "Edit Wear and Read Wear." *CHI'95 Conference Proceeding.* Monterey, CA: ACM 3–9.

Kay, A. 1990. "User Interface: A Personal View." In ed. B. Laurel, *The Art of Human-Computer Interface Design.* Reading, MA: Addison-Wesley.

Keegan, P. 1995. "The Digerati!." *New York Times Magazine,* 21 May. 38–88.

Lin, X.D., J.D. Bransford, C. Hmelo, R. Kantor, D. Hickley, T. Secules, A. Petrosino, and S.R. Goldman. "Instructional Design and the Development of Learning Communities: An Invitation to a Dialogue." *Educational Technology.* In press.

Maes, P., and U. Schardanand. 1995. "Social Information Filtering: Algorithms for Automating 'Word of Mouth'." *CHI'95 Conference Proceeding.* Denver: ACM 210–217.

Minsky, M. 1987. *The Society of Mind.* New York: Simon and Schuster.

Negroponte, N. 1995. *Being Digital.* New York: Alfred A. Knopf.

"Program Targets Information Have-Nots." 1995. *Investor's Business Daily.* (10 March): A15.

Schwartz, E. 1995. "People Are Supposed to Pay for This Stuff?" *Wired* 3(no. 7): 147.

Stoll, Clifford. 1995. *Silicon Snake Oil: Second Thoughts on the Information Highway.* New York: Doubleday.

INDEX

SOFTWARE LICENSE FOR QUICKTIME

Please read this license carefully before using the software. By using the software, you are agreeing to be bound by the terms of this license. If you do not agree to the terms of this license, promptly return the unused software to the place where you obtained it and your money will be refunded.

1. License. The application, demonstration, system, and other software accompanying this License, whether on disk, in read-only memory, or on any other media (the "Software") the related documentation and fonts are licensed to you by John Wiley & Sons. You own the disk on which the Software and fonts are recorded but John Wiley & Sons and/or John Wiley & Sons's Licensor(s) retain title to the Software, related documentation and fonts. This License allows you to use the Software and fonts on a single Apple computer and make one copy of the Software and fonts in machine-readable form for backup purposes only. You must reproduce on such copy the John Wiley & Sons copyright notice and any other proprietary legends that were on the original copy of the Software and fonts. You may also transfer all your license rights in the Software and fonts, the backup copy of the Software and fonts, the related documentation and a copy of this License to another party, provided the other party reads and agrees to accept the terms and conditions of this License.

2. Restrictions. The Software contains copyrighted material, trade secrets and other proprietary material. In order to protect them, and except as permitted by applicable legislation, you may not decompile, reverse engineer, disassemble or otherwise reduce the Software to a human-perceivable form. You may not modify, network, rent, lease, loan, distribute, or create derivative works based upon the Software in whole or in part. You may not electronically transmit the Software from one computer to another or over a network.

3. Termination. This License is effective until terminated. You may terminate this License at any time by destroying the Software, related documentation and fonts, and all copies thereof. This License will terminate immediately without notice from John Wiley & Sons if you fail to comply with any provision of this License. Upon termination you must destroy the Software, related documentation and fonts, and all copies thereof.

4. Export Law Assurances. You agree and certify that neither the Software nor any other technical data received from John Wiley & Sons, nor the direct product thereof, will be exported outside the United States except as authorized and as permitted by the laws and regulations of the United States. If the Software has been rightfully obtained by you outside of the United States, you agree that you will not re-export the Software nor any other technical data received from John Wiley & Sons, nor the direct product thereof, except as permitted by the laws and regulations of the United States and the laws and regulations of the jurisdiction in which you obtained the Software.

5. Government End Users. If you are acquiring the Software and fonts on behalf of any unit or agency of the United States Government, the following provisions apply. The Government agrees: (i) if the Software and fonts are supplied to the Department of Defense (DoD), the Software and fonts are classified as "Commercial Computer Software" and the Government is acquiring only "restricted rights" in the Software, its documentation and fonts as that term is defined in Clause 252.227-7013(c)(1) of the DFARS; and (ii) if the Software and fonts are supplied to any unit or agency of the United States Government other than DoD, the Government's rights in the Software, its documentation and fonts will be as defined in Clause 52.227-19(c)(2) of the FAR or, in the case of NASA, in Clause 18-52.227-86(d) of the NASA Supplement to the FAR.

6. Limited Warranty on Media. John Wiley & Sons warrants the diskettes and/or compact disc on which the Software and fonts are recorded to be free from defects in materials and workmanship under normal use for a period of ninety (90) days from the date of purchase as evidenced by a copy of the receipt. John Wiley & Sons's entire liability and your exclusive remedy will be replacement of the diskettes and/or compact disc not meeting John Wiley & Sons's limited warranty and which is returned to John Wiley & Sons or a John Wiley &

Sons authorized representative with a copy of the receipt. John Wiley & Sons will have no responsibility to replace a disk/disc damaged by accident, abuse, or misapplication. Any implied warranties on the Diskettes and/or compact disc, including the implied warranties of merchantability and fitness for a particular purpose, are limited in duration to ninety (90) days from the date of delivery. This warranty gives you specific legal rights, and you may also have other rights which vary by jurisdiction.

7. Disclaimer of Warranty on Apple Software. You expressly acknowledge and agree that use of the Software and fonts is at your sole risk. The Software, related documentation and fonts are provided "AS IS" and without warranty of any kind and John Wiley & Sons and John Wiley & Sons's Licensor(s) (for the purposes of provisions 7 and 8, John Wiley & Sons and John Wiley & Sons's Licensor(s) shall be collectively referred to as "John Wiley & Sons") expressly disclaim all warranties, express or implied, including, but not limited to, the implied warranties of merchantability and fitness for a particular purpose. John Wiley & Sons does not warrant that the functions contained in the software will meet your requirements, or that the operation of the software will be uninterrupted or error-free, or that defects in the software and the fonts will be corrected. Furthermore, John Wiley & Sons does not warrant or make any representations regarding the use or the results of the use of the software and fonts or related documentation in terms of their correctness, accuracy, reliability, or otherwise. No oral or written information or advice given by John Wiley & Sons or a John Wiley & Sons authorized representative shall create a warranty or in any way increase the scope of this warranty. Should the software prove defective, you (and not John Wiley & Sons or a John Wiley & Sons authorized representative) assume the entire cost of all necessary servicing, repair or correction. Some jurisdictions do not allow the exclusion of implied warranties, so the above exclusion may not apply to you.

8. Limitation of Liability. Under no circumstances including negligence, shall John Wiley & Sons be liable for any incidental, special or consequential damages that result from the use or inability to use the software or related documentation, even if John Wiley & Sons or a John Wiley & Sons authorized representative has been advised of the possibility of such damages. Some jurisdictions do not allow the limitation or exclusion of liability for incidental or consequential damages so the above limitation or exclusion may not apply to you. In no event shall John Wiley & Sons's total liability to you for all damages, losses, and causes of action (whether in contract, tort [including negligence] or otherwise) exceed the amount paid by you for the Software and fonts.

9. Controlling Law and Severability. This License shall be governed by and construed in accordance with the laws of the United States and the State of California, as applied to agreements entered into and to be performed entirely within California between California residents. If for any reason a court of competent jurisdiction finds any provision of this License, or portion thereof, to be unenforceable, that provision of the License shall be enforced to the maximum extent permissible so as to effect the intent of the parties, and the remainder of this License shall continue in full force and effect.

10. Complete Agreement. This License constitutes the entire agreement between the parties with respect to the use of the Software, the related documentation and fonts, and supersedes all prior or contemporaneous understandings or agreements, written or oral, regarding such subject matter. No amendment to or modification of this License will be binding unless in writing and signed by a duly authorized representative of John Wiley & Sons.